AFFEERCE

Volume II - The Plan

4.1.5

Jeff Graubart

Beneath the governmental machinery, in the shadow of political institutions, out of the sight of statesmen and priests, society is producing its own organism, slowly and silently; and constructing a new order, the expression of its vitality and autonomy, and the denial of the old politics, as well as of the old religion. – Pierre Joseph Proudhon

ACKNOWLEDGMENTS

I thank the following individuals and organizations for helping in some way, big or small, in helping to shape the vision and the plan. Inclusion in this list does not imply endorsement of AFFEERCE or any of the ideas presented. All errors are my responsibility, alone.

Nate Blair, Kevin Carson, Mike Curtis, Ed Dodson, Fred Foldvary, Henry George School of Chicago, Todd Kemnitz, Lorraine Lee, Peter Loudon, Helen Marsh, Edward Miller, Will Schnack, Jami Steinberg

Contents

Introduction

Some plans for a better world assume that armed conflict will usher in the new age. Yet more often than not, hate begets only hate, and predicting the outcome of revolution is like predicting the location of debris after an explosion. Revolution is the purview of the hopeless for whom even tyranny is better than the status quo.

Wishing to avoid this miasma, others simply describe a better world, believing a new society will follow from rational discussion and education. However, against fundamental economic interests, "rational" and "facts" are subjective. The world is awash in a sea of conflicting ideology According to Thomas Kuhn[FTN.1] – and common sense – it must all be rejected. Like a band of third-world beggars surrounding us, the most successful is the most aggressive. The most aggressive is the most desperate. Smiling and nodding, we seek a quick exit. Rational discussion and education can serve notice on economic interests that concession is better than revolution, but they are incapable of fundamentally changing society.

All is not futile. There is a solution, and it is only available to those who cherish both free enterprise and a safety net through which none can fall; who know that the fruits of our labor belong to us alone, and the fruits of the Earth belong to each of us and all of us. Such talk will send most of our beggars scurrying, cursing at us for deviating from their left-wing or right-wing ideas. But we proudly proclaim that there is only one way to create a just society – through a business plan. Yes, a business plan! A plan designed to attract individuals at every stage because it is both economically advantageous and morally satisfying. A plan that relies on human nature and never fights it. A plan to nurture an embryo that will grow up to save the world.

We are going to buy land – ultimately all the land in a single state! Impossible you say? No, sound! And the magic formula is based on long-standing economic truths, although the technology to pull it off is recent. I hope you will become part owner of this land; a pioneer in our new world. The plan begins with a city, a city called Prosperity. It doesn't end until peace and prosperity prevail everywhere.

Here is that plan.

Time Line

Step 1 – The Waiting List

You are being called upon to serve time in a venture that has the potential to wipeout hunger and homelessness from the planet. You will have dormitory living, plenty of nutritious food and warm shelter, but only $25 a week in cash. The work will be brutal. The hours will be long. One day you will be working in an office, the next day in the sewers, the following day teaching a course. This is not the Peace Corps, for unlike the Peace Corps you will not be serving the downtrodden of the Earth, the poverty stricken or illiterate. You will be serving their masters!

It is no small irony that a solution to all the injustices that beset mankind involves service not to the weakest but to the strongest. How counterintuitive it is that world peace and prosperity can come from serfdom and slavery redux. But there will be one crucial difference between your toils and the miserable servitude of workers past and present. For it shall be the case that every cocktail you serve, toilet you clean, factory you work, road you pave, or class you teach, will take place on land that is literally owned by you.

In 1879, the economist Henry George took the well-known law of rent of David Ricardo and Adam Smith one step further, demonstrating that ALL wages above the wages of those who toil on remote free land, and ALL return on capital above the risk-based rate of return would sooner or later be eaten up by rents. Every innovation, efficiency and economy of scale, boons for humanity at the start, ultimately is rendered worthless by higher land values. In his main work, *Progress and Poverty*, George showed that progress itself was the cause of poverty.

The common reaction to George's assessment is "major bummer" and then quickly forgotten. To show how quickly, consider that *Progress and Poverty* was once the number one best-selling book in economics, outselling Marx's *Capital*. And now, who ever heard of Henry George? Some attribute this to the influence of wealthy land owners, but I consider it more a failure to complete the vision, or present a workable plan to create a Georgist economy.

In *Volume I – The Vision*, I presented the AFFEERCE vision of society where the land was owned in common by the people. It covered the theories of collection and distribution of the rent, cellular democracy, natural rights and justice. In this work, *Volume II – The Plan*, the business plan to reach that vision is rigorously defined. It is well-known to the followers of Henry George that all wages and return on capital above that which can be obtained on free land, find their way to land values. To these Georgists, this is the problem. I'm here to tell you that these wages and profits finding their way to land value is also the solution!

I like to say that Georgism, an economy based on George's ideas and a key part of the AFFEERCE vision, contains the seeds of its own creation. In this book you will not only learn how to plant those seeds but sow them as well. This book can serve as your personal answer to financial success. In fact, hunger and homelessness will not be eradicated unless those who participate in this great plan build a substantial nest egg for their own future. The wealthier the participants get, the more likely poverty will be eradicated.

You are being asked to serve in this collective for a peaceful and prosperous future, not only for all of humanity, but for your own legacy as well. This collective I so desperately want you to join is named the Affeercianado Guild. I want you to become an affeercianado!

Go to the website, Affeercianado.org, create an account and say, "Yes, I will serve," by checking the appropriate box on the Affeercianado tab. Then request membership in the AFFEERCE Benefit Company so that you can earn scrip and land credits. With a proper email address on the Profile tab, you will receive regular update information.

Does this obligate you to serve? Not legally. There is no contract here. Nor is the Guild obligated to accept you. I know it sounds like a cult, but if we can sign up even half the people in crazy cults today, world peace and prosperity will ultimately follow. And unlike a cult, as a participant, you will have an equal democratic voice with other participants, in shaping the ongoing business plan, and redefining the vision.

It costs nothing to sign up, obligates you to nothing, and if you sign up early, there is a good chance you will be admitted into the Guild. I can promise you this. If we are successful, ten years into the new city of Prosperity, being in the Affeercianado Guild will be one of the most coveted positions in the entire world.

It is counter-intuitive that affeercianados provide service to the wealthy. You might ask, "Why would I ever want to be on call to give Mrs. Fussbudget a pedicure, even if I do own the land on which she sits?" The principle is clearer if you consider building a skyscraper, for no pay, on land that you own. It all goes back to Ricardo's law of rent and Henry George's demonstration that sooner or later, all wages, interest, convenience, innovation, and services find their way to increased land value.

It breaks my heart to see disillusioned young people joining foreign terrorist groups because they lost all hope in our Western values. I say to you, here is hope, comradeship and mission. Being an affeercianado offers personal spiritual and financial wealth and brings it also to the world.

What exactly does being in the Affeercianado Guild entail? The numbers used below come from the spreadsheets that can be found on the website, with snapshots throughout this volume. The applicable spreadsheet shares the same version 4.1.5 as the book. The spreadsheets were prepared using conservative estimates, so numbers are likely to be higher, but could be lower. So why become an affeercianado?

- 60 hours a week of potentially grueling work, but less strenuous work for higher skilled workers, and students in good standing at Jane Jacobs University.
- Free education in the building trades, architecture, construction, engineering, urban planning, and other disciplines at Jane Jacobs University, accredited and soon to become prestigious
- $25 a week in spending cash.
- Dormitory living. 3 per room in motel style dorms for first two years, 2 per room in luxury dorm, thereafter.
- To meet new friends and live in a collective environment with plenty of camaraderie, good food, entertainment and athletic options, division of labor and economies of scale.
- To get the kind of discipline found in the military, serving the people instead of serving war.
- 24 hour all-you-can-eat dining hall.
- Free medical care. No premium, no copay. Affeercianado owned hospital in city from first year going forward.
- $20,000, per year in the Guild, death and disability benefit.
- $600 per month in the Guild, "take the money and run" severance option, to leave the Guild and forego all future Guild obligations.
- Luxury dorms will contain game rooms, computer rooms, library, meeting rooms, swimming pool, steam room, sauna, gym, and bowling alley.
- Receive regularly issued citizens' dividends after Year 5.
- Once accepted into the Guild, you can only be terminated by a 2/3 majority vote of the Guild.
- Opportunity to run for political office on the AFFEERCE party ticket once approved in a Guild primary. We will likely control the local city council, county board, some state, and possibly one or more federal legislative positions.
- Dropping out or flunking out of Jane Jacobs will not adversely affect Guild membership or benefits, but will lead to significantly increased field work where needed, with emphasis on acquired skills.
- If the work is too much for you, resigning only suspends Guild membership. Unless you use the "take the money and run" severance option, all future benefits for months served in the Guild will still be yours.
- In 21 years from the start of this time line, based on 2015 dollars, you will receive $68,591 for every year in the Guild or more exactly, $27.44 for every hour worked (based on average 50 hours/week, 50 weeks/year, even more for 60 hours/week). If you survived the full 21 years in the Guild, you will receive a lump sum payment of $1,440,406. This event is called, "the end of Phase-I." The money comes from the monetization of land you owned and helped develop. Once you are paid off, the land is owned by the commons and administered for the following 40 years as outlined in this plan.
- Every year thereafter, for about 40 years, you will receive a minimum of $3,565 for every year in the Guild. An affeercianado who spent 21 years in the Guild and then retires will therefore receive an annual payment of $74,871. Annual payments end with death and heirs receive the $20,000 per year in the Guild death benefit.

The money comes from the monetization of land purchased by the affeercianados in Phase-I and newly developed in Phase-II. Payments should rise with inflation and increased productivity.

- For those affeercianados who continue on (many will have recently come on board) after the end of Phase-I, in addition to all of the money described above, they receive dividends from affeercianado businesses, in particular, the hospital which will be netting close to $1 billion. If all affeercianados continued on, these dividends would be $2,867 annually for each year in the Guild. However, if most of the long-timers retire at the end of Phase-I, which is expected, the dividend could easily be 10 times higher, with a historic growth rate of well over 10%.

- To build a world where your children are guaranteed nutritious meals, warm and safe shelter, basic medical care and unlimited free education, direct democracy, no taxes on productivity and free enterprise. (See, *AFFEERCE Volume I – The Vision*.)

So there you have it. Put in 21 years of service, get a completely free education at a prestigious school, and retire with $1,440,406 and a pension of $78,579/year thereafter. Put in 3 months of service over a youthful summer, and at the end of Phase-I, get a one-time check for $17,148 and $891/year for the rest of your life. And all of it keeps up with inflation, almost by definition. And your actions will have already lowered medical costs around the country. But the real benefits to humanity will start in Phase-II, and it would not have been possible without your years of service. So, consider that money well-earned.

I beg you to put down the book, go to the website and put yourself on the waiting list. Now that you have, it is time to move on to the next step.

Step 2 – Formation of the AFFEERCE Benefit Corporation

As the waiting list to become a member of the Affeercianado Guild grows larger, I your lone author and first affeercianado (I formally began my service on January 1, 2016) will seek out a Georgist organization, or land collective willing to forego peace, love and poverty today for peace, love, and prosperity tomorrow.

Many of the Georgist organizations were once huge. Remember, Henry George was the most popular economist of his time. But alas, over the ensuing decades they have become mere shells of their former incarnations, supported by the legacies of Georgists, long gone. They believed, and still do, that once the public learned about the power of the collection of ground rents (or more dubiously, taxing privately held land) to right wrongs and create a more efficient and humane economy, the collection of ground rents (or taxing privately held land) would be quickly adopted. For various reasons, that was not the case.

Others have tried to take what they felt were the principles of Henry George to the land itself. Though they try to feed, clothe and house each other, George held that all such benefits come from the value of the land. Typically these beard and sandal collectives are on land so marginal that there is no value at all. Nor do these communards understand how to increase their own land's value so they might increase the funding for their programs. Instead, funding usually comes from the pocketbook of a wealthy idealist.

So the plan is to find one of these organizations willing to forego the failed methods of the past and embrace not only the AFFEERCE vision of what Georgism might be, but more importantly, the only path to real Georgism. That path is the plan you are reading right now.

I come to the table with a vision, a plan, and an affeercianado waiting list (which I hope you are on). Joining forces with an existing organization can jumpstart the corporate infrastructure, although how this step plays out will likely be driven by chance meetings of the mind. If you like what you are reading, particularly the section on viral community theory that follows these opening 7 steps and if while reading viral community theory, you leap to your feet, pump your fist in the air and shout "Yes", don't be shy. You too can be a founder, sit on the Consensus Board, or be elected to the Board of Directors.

The corporation is named the AFFEERCE Benefit Corporation, or the ABC for short. A benefit corporation is legally and financially in the grey realm between a profit and not-for-profit corporation. Ahead of profits, we will create a benefit. The benefit is our promise that 60% of all proceeds from ground rent, and 99% of all funds raised through investment or donation go into the land trust where it is ultimately used to purchase more land to be leased.

To certify that we are meeting the conditions of our benefit, an independent audit is done annually.

I hope the ABC will be known for its impeccable honesty and transparency. From the earliest donation forward, every single financial transaction of the ABC, the Affeercianado Guild, and the City of Prosperity will be visible to the public. The political objective of every economic maneuver will be available for public inspection and discussion, and described in detail in the corporate charter. There will be no backroom deals, coups, or surprises, nor anything clandestine. If, as a last resort, an existing law must be broken, it will be done as open and proud civil disobedience. If the current government of the United States is too repressive for this kind of openness, then AFFEERCE will fail, and whatever barbarism is waiting in the wings will take its place.

The ABC headquarters will likely locate in the new city of Prosperity once it is established. Departments will grow to include media and marketing, fund-raising, early municipal planning, development inducement, municipal benefits, VIP development, online land system development, affeercianado training, import analysis and accounting. These will be discussed later in the book.

All employees are affeercianados receiving the same pay, although highly skilled individuals will be required to work less hours (at the expense of fewer land credits). Fund-raisers receive a 1% commission on donations or investments.

The first ABC Board will consist of three affeercianados, called the Consensus Board because decisions must be attained by consensus of all three members. I intend to be a member. This Board might already be in existence by the time you are reading this. We, the Consensus Board will be responsible for:

1. Articles of incorporation and corporate charter
2. Incorporation of the AFFEERCE Benefit Corporation
3. Create the first draft of a future constitution based on *Volume I – The Vision*
4. Revise and produce a new updated business plan based on this book, *Volume II – The Plan*

The lifespan of the Consensus Board is of unknown duration. Upon completing our tasks, I will issue a new version of *The Vision* and *The Plan* to account for the changes. If you are reading these words and this is the latest available version then that has not yet occurred.

The final act of the Consensus Board will be to select a fourth board member, after which time all future decisions of the Board will be by majority rule. The description of the Board of Directors that will form is now taken from a preliminary corporate charter, as the actual corporate charter does not yet exist.

The ABC Board will grow to consist of 14 members. Ten will be affeercianados and four will be open to the largest four investors, investor/donors, or donors, in that order. An ideal board might consist of those with business, software, political, economic, legal, land, education, medical, and urban planning experience.

The Board will finalize the prospectus for investors and donors.

During the Consensus Board, and the first year or so of the regular board there is no money, so even the meager affeercianado pay is distributed as scrip. When the donate button on the website is used, 1% of that donation can be used to redeem scrip equally. The rest goes into a land trust account. Subsidiaries of the ABC, such as GEOScrip.com will pay 50% of EBITDA before affeercianado pay for scrip redemption and 50% to the land trust. However, once rent is actually collected, 4% of the proceeds go to the ABC, first for scrip redemption, and then to finance our projects.

Donation carries with it a benefit that can be quite valuable. Rather than a tee-shirt or mug, a cumulative donation of at least $1,000 buys the donor entry into the Phase-II distribution auctions. Granted 21 years is a long time, but when the time comes, you will consider it the best investment ever. Furthermore, the amount of the cumulative donation is an automatic free opening bid in the auction. Donations are not tax free, but the opening bid, years later, is simply a return of capital and not subject to U.S. income tax. (This will be clearly explained later. For now, just accept that it is a valuable benefit of donation.)

As another benefit, should there be less than four investors open to serving on the Board, the top donors, in order of donation amount, will be invited.

When a donation is made, you will receive a donor ID. All subsequent donations are made with this ID to add to previous donations. Because of our promise of transparency, the donor has the option of being listed as anonymous on the public financial statements. However, the donor ID will always be listed.

All donations, payment and redemption of scrip, and land ownership accounting will be done in GEOScrip. The software will be available to other organizations and small businesses as a means of generating revenue.

Step 3 – Seeking a Host State

The ABC Board will use its collective expertise to refine the business plan. In particular, we will narrow the list of potential states for the city of Prosperity, and make a revised version of this plan for each of those states.

There are many things to consider, not the least of which is being welcome. Furthermore, not every state gives its counties the latitude to substitute 30% of the rental proceeds for a county, city, and school district property tax. Prior to incorporation, the majority of the 30% tranche will go to the county, however, the evolution of the distribution based on future population and services will be the subject of intense negotiation. Rules for state, county, and even federal revenue sharing must be well-understood and incorporated into the models. If we can excite them, some states and counties will be open to negotiation and special legislation.

If the state has union-only rules for the construction of municipal buildings and schools, as well as union-only rules for municipal and educational employees, we need certification that the Affeercianado Guild is an acceptable union. They are a democratic organization, take orders from no one, and can go on strike any time they please. Not that they ever would, since going on strike would be tantamount to throwing billions of dollars off a tall building. In fact, the Guild will demand harder work and longer hours at lower pay. The old-school unions will simply scratch their heads. Either certification of the Guild as a union, or locating in a right-to-work state is essential.

We must also look at land prices 1.5 hours distant by automobile from a major city in a finalist state. Optimally we want land, approved for development by state and federal law, for around $5,000 an acre. Water, sewer, electric, cable/fiber, and possibly gas should be available somewhere on the property. The external grid must be sufficient to support a city of 300,000.

The major city 1.5 hours distant from the site of our future Prosperity will be called Old Metropolis until an actual city is known.

When the list of potential locations has been narrowed down, we need to visit the counties, meet with the county boards, share our spreadsheets, and talk about Prosperity. Since there is no money, ABC board members will self-finance the travel and turn in their expenses for scrp.

States have nothing to lose and should be receptive. Even failed experiments add to state coffers, and successful ones excite the state's business community. In this case, where we ultimately "threaten" to buy up all the land in the state, legislatures should be actively competing to be the host. If things work out as they expect, they will get rich from our folly. If things work out as we expect, they will get rich from our success.

Step 4- Finalize the Virtual Map

Even before the land is purchased we want a map of our projected landmarks and regions and their relationship to one another. We talk of north, south, east, and west, but they are all virtual directions. We do not know how these directions will map to a physical space, or how they will relate to natural elements and boundaries. The map will be updated from virtual to real once the actual land is purchased. Here is the virtual map used in the business plan, showing 1,500 of the initial 5,000 acres.

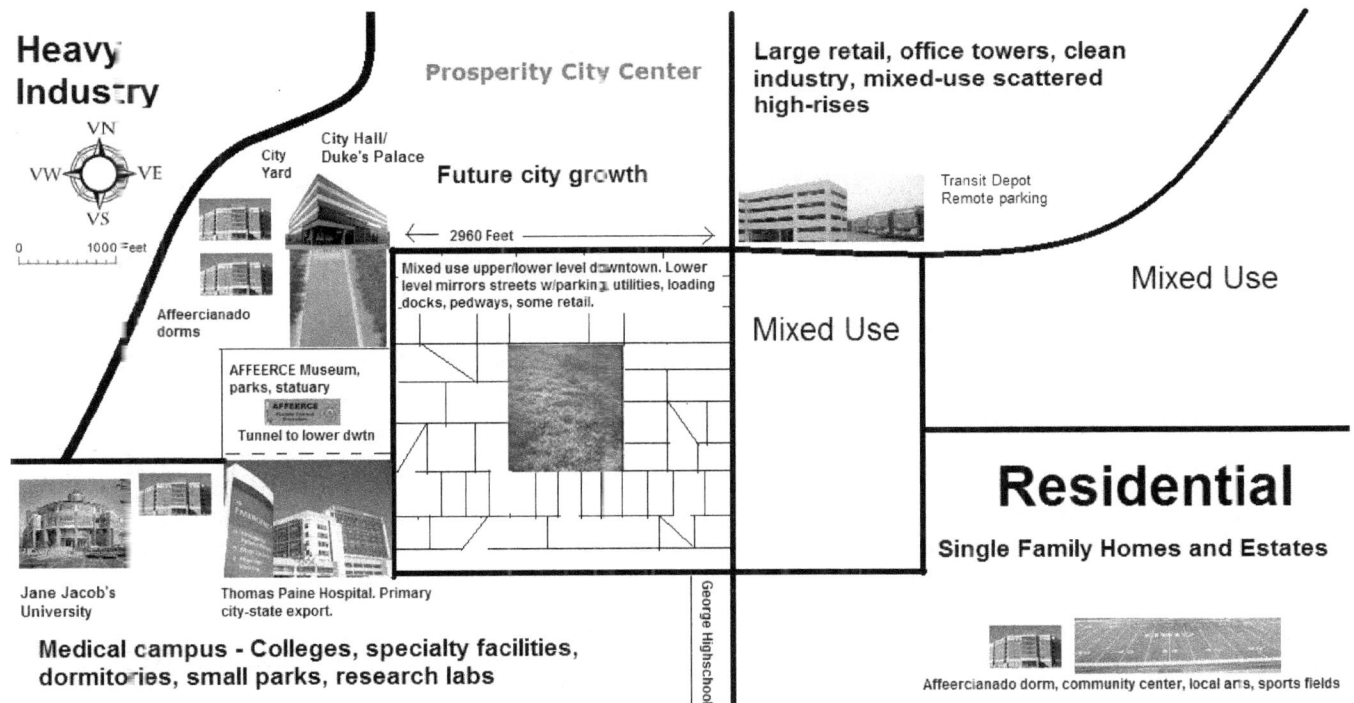

Urban planners on the ABC Board will modify this map to match the final vision going into land purchase, and after the purchase to integrate features of the natural landscape. Modifications will follow each land auction, primarily with the first. Subsequent auctions will have diminishing impact on the city center.

In software design, city design, as well as design in other engineering disciplines, strategies usually involve some combination of both a top-down and bottom-up approach. In a future AFFEERCE economy, I expect the top-down approach will be used primarily by private communities, cities or counties. Otherwise, levels of federation will form from the bottom-up. These towns and counties will change their form, fuse, divide, or die, like cells in a living organism.

In the beginning, our intention is a business plan to achieve AFFEERCE in the first place. Top-down design is a necessity. Phase-I is planned to maximize land value, while in Phase-II bottom-up experimentation begins, Phase-III is bottom-up, and Phase-IV extends top-down planning to the nation as a whole, as residents of the host-state will thrive in an organic, fluid economy. Following Phase-IV, there is the capitulation, where bottom-up collective communities and top-down planned communities throughout the nation will challenge existing cities for dominance.

Whether design is from the top down or bottom up, when done in the public domain, rapid iteration, testing of new ideas and continuous feedback from the affeercianados, investors, and other residents is essential. We must never be so committed to an idea that we fail to see and account for problems when they arise.

Step 5 – Hunting for a Whale

Once we have over 5,000 affeercianados on the waiting list, and the ABC board has narrowed the list of potential host states and counties to two or three finalists, all with well-researched and rigorously defined business plans, it is time to hunt for a whale, that is, an investor who will finance the operation.

While an informal whale hunt will have begun much earlier, once Step 5 is reached without an investor, finding one becomes the primary focus of the Board. Keep in mind that this implies a large affeercianado waiting list, a short list of candidate counties and sites, several modifications of the business plan, and specific plans for each candidate site.

Inv Div
$233,500
$397,550
$674,763
$1,185,575
$1,128,333
$1,648,954
$2,187,745
$2,778,637
$1,654,621
$1,973,391
$2,344,266
$2,625,439
$2,932,071
$3,398,546
$3,426,939
$3,758,093
$4,274,618
$4,578,230
$5,314,870
$8,274,261

If the ABC board has conducted itself professionally to this point, and there is a long waiting list of affeercianados, venture capitalists, idealist members of the .1%, or simply businessmen who know a good deal when they see it, will jump at the chance. Here's why.

The plan calls for starting capital of $65 million. This money is supplied by the investors. Ownership of land trust funds is divided equally between the investors and affeercianados. That is, the land trust is stipulated to be 50% owned by the investors and 50% owned by the affeercianados. In return for this free land, 5% of all subsequent investments in the land trust by the affeercianados will be owned by the investors. Using time weightings on predicted donations to the trust, investors will benefit from affeercianado purchases, receiving a return equivalent to an initial investment of $139,404,762. Given this breakdown, investors own $32,500,000 and affeercianados $32,500,000 of the land trust at the start, although the affeercianado percentage could be higher as donations are invested as affeercianado contributions. Over the course of 21 years, the predicted annual dividends for investors (from the ground rents) can be seen in the column to the left.

The decrease in the dividend in several of the years corresponds with large purchases of undeveloped land by the affeercianados, vastly increasing the affeercianado share of developed land as it increases the investor share of undeveloped land. The ratio of affeercianado land to investor land is the same for both developed and undeveloped land and is the sum of 95% of affeercianado contributions and half the original investment divided by affeercianado contributions and the full investment. If you are so inclined, the explanation is easier to follow mathematically. Complexity aside, it is just a common-sense way to determine the percentage of land owned by the affeercianados versus the investors.

$$\frac{\sum_i 95\% \times \text{Contribution}_i \times \text{Years since contribution}_i / 21 + \text{Original investment}/2}{\sum_i \text{Contribution}_i \times \text{Years since contribution}_i / 21 + \text{Original investment}}$$

This is the Affeercianado Land Ratio (ALR) and it is used to compute both the investor dividend, as well as the distribution of proceeds from monetized land following Phase-I.

Throughout Phase-I, the total holdings of developed and undeveloped investor land continue to grow. After 21 years, the model predicts a lump sum payment to the $65 million investor of $2.06 billion. The investor will go on to receive $107 million/year every year for about the next 40. These figures are automatically inflation adjusted by the nature of land value. Unlike affeercianados whose payments cease with death and the death benefit, the investor pension continues until all undeveloped land, purchased during Phase-I, is developed, or capitulation occurs, whichever comes first.

Should capitulation occur before all Phase-I undeveloped land is auctioned off, both the living affeercianados and investors or their heirs, will receive a second windfall. If 100,000 acres of undeveloped Phase-I land remains at capitulation, the geographically closest rent on developed land will be used to compute the land value. With a rent of $32,262/acre, the investors would receive a final payment of about $3.2 billion, and the affeercianados would split by years of service a final payment of $61.3 billion.

An investment of $65 million produces a variable dividend averaging over 3% for 20 years, with no dividend in the first year, called the Setup Year. At the end of the 21st year, the investment is expected to pay out over $2 billion, with a pension of $107 million for each of the next 40 years. If the spreadsheet is verified, and no legal or political showstoppers are uncovered, investors will beat a proverbial path to our door and many will be turned away.

In the table below, the Phase-I distribution of the rent payments is shown. These are the ground rents from tenants on land purchased by the land trust. Note that the investor dividend is equal to:
5% x (1 – ALR), while income for the Affeercianado Guild is: 5% x ALR. Outstanding scrip will be paid from the 4% ABC administration allocation.

5%	Dividend to investors and affeercianados
4%	ABC administration, training, and marketing
1%	Fee to the land broker who closed the deal (to $8 million) and repayment of closing costs
30%	Property tax substitute for municipal and county services
60%	Reinvestment in the land trust

Phase-I Rent Allocations   Table-I1

Step 6 – Purchasing the Land

With $65 million in the land trust, the time has come to purchase 5,000+ acres for $25 million. For this task, an experienced land broker is needed. The broker will have extensive knowledge of toxic wasteland, federal and state restrictions, easements, liens, regional zoning, taxes, fees, utility capacity, access and charges, timber, minerals, water rights, flooding, local weather, septic and sewage, neighboring sales history and so forth. The broker will be paid handsomely with 1% of the rent up to a maximum commission of $8 million on this land going forward.

It is expected that several brokers in finalist states will submit their resume to the ABC board. The quality of the broker might influence a final decision on location. That decision is based on achieving maximum value toward realization of the business plan.

Before an offer is made, the virtual map is optimally positioned on the actual land and modified for natural elements and boundaries. From this it can be determined the rent to charge any existing tenants on the land at closing. Optimization of available buildings is a consideration for bootstrapping the community and will cause modifications to the plan. In any case, the equivalent of at least one large farmhouse must be vacant and strategically located near the proposed downtown area for the initial headquarters and domicile of the affeercianados.

Before the land can be purchased, it is important for our ambassadors to wine and dine the county board, and enter into final negotiations on path to incorporation, assessment, revenue sharing and home rule.

Step 7 – After Closing

Although purchasing, accounting, and architecture will be done by affeercianados out of ABC headquarters still earning scrip, the affeercianados on site will receive real pay, except for weekly cash.

Monthly Affeercianado Cost Table-I2	
Food	$220
Housing	$370
Salary @$25/week (scrip pay, prior to hospital)	$110
Medical and liability	$110
15% Social Security and Medicare on paid wage	$136
Total	**$946**

At this time, a full time CEO of the Prosperity project will be hired by the ABC Board in conjunction with an executive search firm, to oversee Phase-I itself. The requirements include extensive experience as a CEO of a company with 50,000+ employees. Although the CEO will not be an affeercianado or have a vote in the Guild, they will receive, in addition to their $200,000 compensation, 37.5 land-credits per week, so they can partake in the windfall at the end of Phase-I. The CEO must share our passion.

The CEO will be hired contingent on a business plan that is approved by the board, including approval by at least 3 out of 4 of the investors/donor seats. The CEO will modify the business plan and submit it to the board for approval. If the CEO and ABC board cannot come to terms, a new CEO will be found.

Once approved, the modified business plan will be made available at the on-demand publication site, and a free copy sent to all potential affeercianados on the waiting list (Another reason to get on the waiting list!)

A new edition of *Volume II – The Plan* will be released. The remainder of this volume is my current best guess for this business plan. Regardless of details, important principles of a viral community are demonstrated.

The CEO will hire a prefabricated construction manager and a roads and infrastructure manager for $100,000 each plus 37.5 land-credits/week.

These executives will build their initial teams from the affeercianado waiting list and other sources. All employees will be hired as affeercianados and become members of the Guild. Several additional paid positions will be added over the next several years; however, literally 99.9% of the team bringing Prosperity to life will be affeercianados.

The paid executives constitute a very thin layer between the ABC Board, all of whom are affeercianados, members of the Guild, and accountable to the Guild, and the average affeercianado who is part of a hierarchy under these paid executives. It is my strongly held belief that this arrangement produces an optimally efficient workforce; all the while the Affeercianado Guild retains ultimate power.

Although affeercianados will receive school credit for construction projects in the second year, experience in one or more of the building trades is a requirement for service in the first year, as there will be limited ad hoc instruction at best. Early affeercianados are likely to become Jane Jacobs' instructors.

Some might argue that the business plan should place Prosperity closer to urban areas where the buildings are already constructed. In the 2016 movie, *The Revenant*, fur traders in 1820's Dakota, create immense lifesaving value from simple labor at the margin. That isn't the point of the film, just a minor take-away. While turning $5,000/acre land into $10 million/acre land is far more difficult than changing $1 million/acre land into $10 million/acre land, the former generates 200 times the value of the latter. That value is the currency of our success.

Critical too, to the success of our venture, is a speculative ring of undeveloped land surrounding Prosperity. That ring serves several purposes in the business plan discussed later. Closer to an urban area, the cost of such speculation would be prohibitive.

With the hiring of a CEO, a new incarnation of the plan approved by both the Board and the CEO, and the hiring of two construction managers, the 21 year clock begins. It consists of a setup year followed by 20 years of Phase-I. The setup year is broken down by month, from January to December. Year 1, is the first year following the setup year, so Year 20 is the final year of Phase-I.

All setup activity can be found on a single spreadsheet. Beginning in Year 1, spreadsheets are distinct for separate businesses and departments. Balances are consolidated under the spreadsheets for affeercianados, municipal, and education. This is true even though Prosperity will not be incorporated until the start of Year 4. Spreadsheets can be found on the website with a version number matching the version of this book.

Before beginning the plan, it is useful to have a more detailed understanding of the theory on which the plan is based. This next section on viral community theory is essential to that understanding and will allow the plan to be viewed in a more critical light. If you have spent many years searching for the answer and feel only hopelessness as a result, viral community theory might very well change your life.

Viral Community Theory

Objectives

The viral community is an embryo; the seed of a new political economy gestating within the old order. Like a virus, it uses host mechanisms to grow. Ultimately, it will consume its host and become the new state.

Political strength is achieved through economic success and is accomplished within the law. It is beneficial to scions of the old order and young revolutionaries alike to join our movement. The process can best be compared to the rise of the bourgeoisie in feudal Europe.

The viral community is also a laboratory. New ideas are tested and new systems attempted while mistakes are still easy to correct.

The specific goal of this business plan is to bring AFFEERCE Georgism to one of the 50 U.S. states, then to the United States as a whole, and ultimately to the world. It succeeds initially by making it profitable to move land from private ownership into the commons. However, once established as a significant economy anywhere, it relies on the carrot of its great wealth, freedom, and absence of poverty, and the stick of a systemic balance of trade surplus to spread throughout the world.

Land Value

In self-defense, the objective is to use the enemy's strength against them. That too, is the essence of viral community theory. The strength of the enemy is the law of rent. It is what keeps wages and profits down and turns progress into poverty. The actual law as stated by Ricardo is obtuse, but the corollaries of the law are easy to understand. They tell us that the benefits of progress, efficiency, infrastructure, population, higher wages and profits, and countless other things of positive value, go to the owners of the land.

As Georgists, we are experts in the myriad ways the law of rent increases land value. If our goal is to increase land value, we have an inside track. Unfortunately, the primary goal of most intentional communities is to create a moral community, one that cares for the sick, feeds the hungry, and works the land to generate income. No matter how they try to differentiate themselves, the community motto comes down to some form of Marx's adage, "From each according to their ability, to each, according to their need."

Yet as Henry George showed, it is the ground rents, the just distribution of labor that feeds the hungry and provides healthcare for the sick. And ground rents come from land value. As counter-intuitive as it is to most Georgists, the primary objective of a viral community is to increase land value, increase it fast, and increase it ruthlessly.

Like self-defense to a pacifist, ruthlessly increasing land value leads to a moral dilemma for Georgists who's Georgism is more personal than political. We should recognize that the viral community is not for everyone. Yet those who eschew the viral community are the ones who most anxiously await its ultimate success, so there is no reason to cast aspersions. One thing practical Georgists should consider is that everything we do is perfectly legal. Using the law of rent to increase land value is as American as apple pie.

What we aim to do is place this valuable land in the commons. It follows, almost by definition, that if half the nation's land value were in the commons, then so too would rest half the nation's industry, wealth, and political power.

The virus spreads by converting privately owned land to commonly owned land. If the process is consistent with human nature, like the rise of the bourgeoisie in feudal times, it will spread to the entire world. Of course, there is a conundrum. How could the conversion of privately owned land to commonly owned land be consistent with human nature? The answer can be found in viral community theory.

Phase I

Phase I is the first 20 year period in the business plan, where the primary goal is to raise land value and the secondary goal is to increase land holdings.

Standard Land Trust

In most intentional communities, land is owned by a land trust. The same is true for a viral community. Investors invest in the trust, which then uses the proceeds to purchase land. The land is rented out to the highest bidder. The rents are used to pay a dividend to the investors and pay the property taxes. What remains, is reinvested in the land trust, which uses the new money to buy more land.

The land is not really in the commons, but owned by the investors. However, usually investor dividends are limited to a small percentage of the ground rents, such as 5%

In a standard land trust, there is very little dynamic toward increasing land value. The investors want it but community members usually don't. Remember that land value is a simple multiple of the ground rent bid on new land. Beyond dedication by those who set up the land trust, and the wishes of investors, there is no reason why ground rents should increase faster than rents in efficient and high-tech cites. Rather than the community having a greater and greater percentage of the nation's land value, it will have a smaller percentage over time.

Landlord-Working Class

The most important feature that differentiates a viral community from a standard land trust is the landlord-working class. In AFFEERCE, they are called the affeercianados. This is a pure play on the law of rent. It is a self-defense maneuver that takes all of mankind's desire for wealth and converts that desire into viral community land value. Rather than fighting the status quo to bring about Georgism, we allow the status quo to bring Georgism to us.

We begin by stipulating that 50% percent of any investment in the land trust is donated to the landlord workers, who will be called the affeercianados from this point on. In exchange, it is stipulated that 5% of all subsequent affeercianado land trust contributions will be donated to the investors. This works to the investor's advantage as it not only provides a strong catalyst for increasing land value, but increases investor share of total land owned over a time weighted 100% of their initial investment based on predicted affeercianado purchases.

The power of the affeercianado comes from their labor. There are three critical points on a graph of labor compensation. Lowest, is the subsistence cost of labor. Next, is the price paid for labor, and at the top, is the value of labor. Although anomalies occur where the three points fall in a different order, these anomalies are rare and quickly corrected by the market.

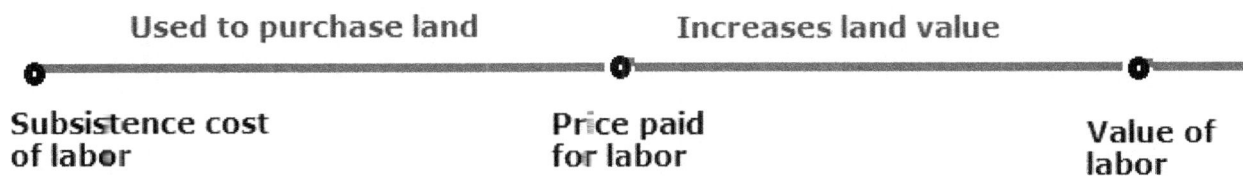

Used to purchase land	Increases land value	
●————————————————	●————————————————	●
Subsistence cost of labor	Price paid for labor	Value of labor

A market will tend to pull all three points close together. But that is unimportant because the viral community is not a market but collusion. It is the goal of the affeercianados to keep these three points as far apart as possible. Since they are the laborers, they can do that. That is why the price paid for labor at the margin does not appear on our graph. The subsistence cost to maintain an affeercianado should be as low as possible, the value of their labor as high as possible and the price paid for their labor somewhere right in the middle.

The difference between the price paid for labor and the subsistence cost of labor is all used to purchase more land in the name of the affeercianados. On the other hand, the difference between the value of labor and the price paid for labor increases the land value of both affeercianado and investor land by the law of rent.

With the affeercianados owning 50% of the land at the start, they share the investor goal of increasing land value, rather than rushing to purchase more land. It will be 5 years before the second land purchase. A rapid increase in land value is tinder for the early viral community. Accumulating a large buffer of undeveloped land is necessary, but can be done at a more relaxed pace, like the gathering of logs to feed a burning fire. By the end of Phase-I, the affeercianados will have purchased enough land to own over 94% of the trust, anyway. If the affeercianados own 94% of the trust, they own 94% of the developed land and 94% of the undeveloped land. Ownership is time weighted, but it is not associated with specific parcels.

How is land value rapidly increased? The business owner profits from the difference between the value of labor and the price paid for labor. Usually these profits are lost to an increase in rent. However, assume the bid rent by tenants on auctioned land is frozen until the last year of Phase-I. This imputed rent is then retained by the business owner as profit. Not only does this lead to a higher bid rent to begin with, but the actual retention of surplus labor profits by businesses will raise land value and produce even higher bids in subsequent auctions.

The affeercianados as a group profit from the difference between the price paid for labor and the subsistence cost of labor. Generally this money is turned over to the trust for more land purchases in the name of the affeercianados. But the best bang for the buck in early years comes from increasing land value. The money is used for infrastructure, and exceptional public services, driving up future bids at auction. In the business plan, the first affeercianado land purchase does not occur until Year 5.

It is in the interests of the affeercianados to attract industry to the viral community. This leads to a virtuous cycle that increases both the percentage of land owned by the affeercianados and the value of that land. In Phase-I, the price paid for labor is optimally centered between the subsistence cost of labor and the value of labor to maximize business profits, land value and land holdings.

To keep the price of labor at the optimal point, the supply of affeercianados on the market must vary based on demand. Unlike with ordinary workers, this is not a problem when idle affeercianados can increase land value through public service. In addition to being bid out on jobs, the affeercianados build their own housing, have their own businesses, and fill public service jobs in such areas as police, fire, streets, sanitation, and education.   There is always a long list of projects to increase land value during slow periods. Many of these projects are features of viral community theory, itself, and will be discussed later. When demand from business is great, new affeercianados are brought on board, even to the point of overcrowding dormitories and prefabricated housing. When demand slows, new dorms can be built. Demand is further controlled by limiting the amount of land auctioned.

Benefits of Being an Affeercianado

Free dormitory living   1 land credit per hour worked
24 hour buffet   Free medical coverage Camaraderie
Free education   Luxury dorm amenities Political power
Serve the people Save the world
Huge payout in 20 years based on land credits earned!

Minimizing Subsistence Costs

The affeercianados live collectively to maximize economies of scale. With dormitories that include a 24 hour buffet, a gym, swimming pool, steam, and sauna, the cost is less than $600 per month. Including free medical care, liability,

Social Security and Medicare payments, and $25/week in salary, the monthly cost of an affeercianado is $946. Bid out at $9/hour for 172 hours per month (40 hour week) brings net revenue of $1,548 or $602 per month profit for new land purchases. Affeercianados who are not enrolled in classes are expected to put in an additional 12 – 20 hours per week in overtime at an overtime average bid rate of $13/hour. At the low end, this is an additional $670, which is all profit. Thus the average affeercianado who spends their entire time bid out to business will bring in $1,272 for new land purchases every month. Two thousand affeercianados bid out to business will exceed the original $25 million land purchase in a year's time, greatly increasing affeercianado ownership of the trust.

Value of Labor

It is the goal of the viral community to recruit skilled affeercianados, who are medical professionals, educators, experts in the building trades, public safety, software, engineering, urban planning, and other skills demanded by businesses and residents. However, even good household cleaning help or nannie services has a value of $15 to $20/hour. And this bid is for "agency" help, where all tax related responsibility is assumed by the agency. Software and engineering temps can have a value of $50/hour. Of course such a high labor value will likely increase the engineer's bid rate above the minimum bid of $8/hour. We will attempt to keep the average bid rate for all labor at $9/hour and the average overtime rate at $13/hour to maximize profits for tenant industry. In the early years, money for land purchases is redirected to increasing land value. In the table below, the average value of labor is conservatively assumed to be $20/hour.

Desired Labor Parameters	Parameter/Hour	Land purchased	Increased Land Value
Subsistence cost of labor (40 hour week)	$5.50/hour		
Average value of labor	$20.00/hour		
Average price paid for labor	$9.00/hour	$3.50/hour	$11.00/hour
Overtime price paid for labor	$13.00/hour	$13.00/hour	$7.00/hour

Although the subsistence salary is the same for all affeercianados, 1 land credit is received for every hour worked. An affeercianado who puts in 60 hours work in a week will earn 60 land credits, while an affeercianado bedridden with an illness will receive no land credits at all during their illness.

If there are an insufficient number of affeercianados available for bid to keep average price paid for labor at or below $9/hour, other projects must be halted and the amount of land put up for bid at the land auctions must be reduced until equilibrium is reached.

The success of the viral community in Phase-I is directly correlated with the number of affeercianados which is a function of the rate of building affeercianado housing, the success of the land auctions, and the recruiting effort. It is expected that success will depend on achieving sufficient numbers of affeercianados.

While saving the world might appeal to some young idealists, this will typically be insufficient motivation to dedicate up to 20 years of one's life to unremunerated potentially harsh working conditions, 24 hour buffet notwithstanding. The primary tool of recruitment is the payoff after 20 years based on land credits earned. These payoffs will be huge. Where the money comes from is critical to viral community theory and will be discussed in detail later.

The Affeercianado Hospital

It might seem wrong that one particular business, a hospital, would be critical to viral community success. But the hospital plays a role in so many different ways that it is clearly an integrated part of the solution.

The hospital today is a protected monopoly with huge profits going to shareholders. However, a hospital where doctors, nurses, surgeons, technicians, aides, maintenance, and administrators each have a cost of $946 a month is hyper-competitive. Even if the top surgeons and chief administrator had to be paid a normal salary, due to a lack of affeercianado talent, profits would still be phenomenal.

Although there are no savings on drugs and medical equipment, assume an average labor cost at a standard hospital of $30/hour including Social Security, Medicare, and overtime. For a 250 hour month, the standard cost per employee would be $7,500/month versus $946/month at an affeercianado hospital. The cost of labor is 8 times less expensive at the affeercianado hospital. Assuming just over 2/3 of the cost of hospitalization is for labor (this is consistent with spreadsheets in the business plan), the total cost of hospitalization is reduced by a factor of 3.

Affeercianados are provided with free medical care. The amount allocated for insurance is $100/month. Ignoring any tax benefits or credits, this is far too low for comprehensive health coverage, even for a group policy on mostly young people. However, when increased by a factor of 3 for affeercianado labor, $300/month easily pays an HMO policy to a self-insured hospital. That includes medevac and travel PPO coverage.

With such inexpensive coverage, why stop at affeercianados? A great play on the law of rent is to provide free medical coverage for all residents. Residents with Medicare will receive a free supplemental policy. Those already enrolled in a PPO that the affeercianado hospital is a member (see below), receive a $25/month rebate. Because medical savings to resident tenants are greater than our costs, the money spent in this program increases land value with greater than 100% efficiency!

When combined with a $35 copay for doctor visits, testing, ambulance, and hospitalization, a $100 premium leads to large profits. As a self-insured HMO hospital, profits come from the insurance arm as well. There is no reason to restrict coverage to affeercianados and tenants, when residents of nearby counties will gladly pay $100/month for a no deductible, $35 copay policy. In this way, medical care becomes the chief export of the viral community. A balance of trade surplus is essential to achieving financial and political domination in later phases.

The greatest profits do not come from the very reasonable premium. Because the cost of services is so low, the affeercianado hospital becomes a member of every PPO in the nation. Remember that PPO payments are designed to be profitable for standard hospitals. For our hospital, they are hyper-profitable. The same is true for Medicare payments. Though they bring very little profit to standard hospitals, Medicare payments are very profitable for the affeercianado hospital. Many tenants will be covered by Medicare or a PPO at work. In the latter case, the city will save $75 on premiums per month ($25 will be rebated). Premiums will be paid for Medicare supplemental policies, but a rebate might be possible there as well. In both cases, payments to the hospital from a PPO or Medicare will be very profitable.

The final benefit of an affeercianado hospital does not occur until Phase-II when allocated basic income and benefits packages are auctioned off (discussed below). At that point free health coverage will be part of the package and no longer automatically free for tenants and affeercianados.

In the business plan, the hospital is named the Thomas Paine Hospital after the great revolutionary who was among the first to conceive of the collection and distribution of ground rents by the people.

The Affeercianado University
Profits from a university will not be as high as profits from the hospital. Nevertheless, the $946 monthly cost of teachers, administrators, and maintenance workers will provide a significant advantage.

Although the affeercianados are a for-profit syndicate, they have chartered obligations that place them in a quasi-governmental role. As such, they compete with private enterprise, only when necessary to fulfill those obligations.

While not strictly necessary, there are several very good reasons why a viral community needs an affeercianado university.

First, continuous training is a good way to increase the value of affeercianado labor. The greater the difference between the value of labor and the $946 monthly subsistence cost, the greater the increase in land purchases and land value.

For this reason, the university should emphasize the building trades, engineering, medicine, city government, public safety, urban planning, education and other roles affeercianados will take to assure business plan success.

When possible, classes will center on projects in the field. These infrastructure projects serve to increase land value at no labor cost. While most of the students will be affeercianados, paid the $946/month regardless, outside students will not only pay a small tuition, but will provide free labor in the building of infrastructure for course credit. The work will always be under the constant supervision of experienced instructors. It is likely that some of these instructors, in the early years, will be paid normal salaries until there are affeercianados with sufficient experience.

One of the best ways to attract intelligent affeercianados, in the current environment of outrageous student loans, is to provide an accredited university education as an affeercianado benefit. A free college education could even carry more weight than the large payout at the end.

Affeercianados who are full time students are still expected to earn 40 land credits per week. However, class work in the field will count toward land credits as well as course credits. To reach the 40 hour goal, student affeercianados can bid themselves out at $8/hour for house-sitting, baby-sitting, night watch, and other jobs that are conducive to studying. Student affeercianados have considerable leeway in how to meet land credit goals, such as 80 hour work weeks during school breaks, two semesters on, one semester off, or advanced courses that give course credit for work on affeercianado building teams with minimal classroom time.

Other features of a university that have a positive effect on land value include synergy with the hospital, attraction of big-name entertainment, world-class library, campus town, and college athletics. Like the hospital, the university is an export that increases the balance of trade surplus.

Critical to the business plan is that without an affeercianado university, we could not guarantee free and unlimited education in the basic income package introduced in Phase-II.

The university in the business plan is named Jane Jacobs University after the late urban pioneer.

Rent Freeze

Auctions are held every year, or as needed, for the limited land available to be developed. The amount of land auctioned off is a function of the number of full-time and student affeercianados, other buildings trade workers, the number of primary and secondary schools and other parameters designed to assure stable growth.

To facilitate a rapid rise in land value, the ground rent is frozen at the high bid for the duration of Phase-I. The imputed rent goes to the tenant, and increases bids in subsequent auctions. It should be pointed out that land value appreciation is far more important than ground rent revenue. During Phase-I, increases in land value should go toward business profits and homeowner equity. Ground rent revenue is dwarfed by profits from affeercianado labor. These too, are used to increase land value through public services and infrastructure during the early years. Nevertheless, with free medical care, the cheapest possible labor, high quality city services, and frozen rents for all but the final year of Phase-I, bidding on ground rents will be fast and furious.

The rent freeze should not be affected by land transfer. If the home or business improvements are sold before the rent freeze has expired, this will produce a windfall for the original homeowner who profits from the rising land value. The opportunity to make such a profit will add considerably to land value in the early years.

We want to create the psychology and reality that whenever one becomes part of the viral community, the opportunity for wealth is greater than those who will come later. This might be difficult in Year 20, the end of the rent freeze, when self-assessment with land seizure converts imputed rent into actual ground rent revenue. In Year 21, an infusion of cash from land monetization, subsidized annuities, and an untold number of new business opportunities will make that psychology a reality again.

Speculative Ring

The law of rent tells us that land speculation extends the margin and raises land value in the developed core. This is exactly what we want. The high land value in the developed core raises ground rent. At the end of Phase-I, total ground rent will determine the initial payout for investors and affeercianados.

There are many competing requirements. Maintaining a thick speculative ring of undeveloped land around a developed core will not be the highest priority. Prior to affeercianado land purchases in Year 5, the speculative ring will be tiny or non-existent. However, it does have the following benefits and should be employed before the land prices for expansion become excessive:

- Fosters density and efficiency within the community
- Growth rate under our control
- Land always available for growth
- Ring radius maintenance a consideration in direction of growth
- Cost to purchase new land is much cheaper at the margin than it is near the developed core
- Land brokers have more bargaining power
- Easier to work around those who refuse to sell
- Years of post-payout annuities is a function of undeveloped ring size

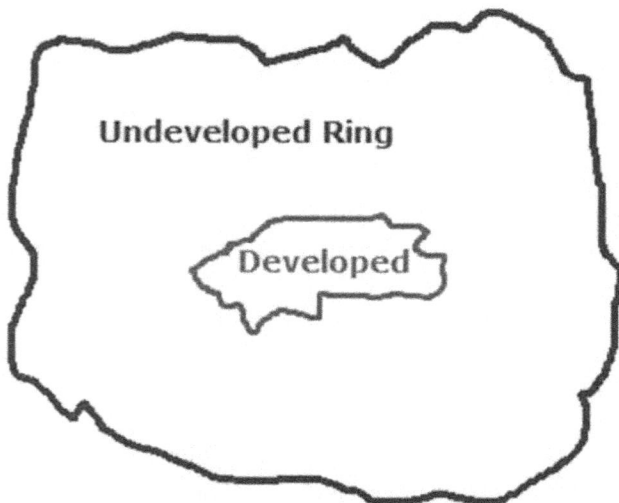

Viral community business planners in conjunction with the Affeercianado Guild must balance the need to increase land value, with the need to purchase land for the undeveloped ring. The size of the ring should be inversely proportional to the general availability of land at the host site.

Phase II

With the rent freeze lifted in the final year of Phase-I, ground rents reflect the true land value. There are no scheduled land purchases during Phase-II. With profits at affeercianado enterprises no longer used to purchase land, they are distributed instead to active affeercianados based on land credits. High profits from the hospital provide large salaries to long-time affeercianados. Annuities from newly developed land provide both active and retired affeercianados with a healthy payout based on land credits.

Easily afforded in Phase-II, affeercianados must pay for their own food, housing and medical coverage. Tuition at the university is no longer free. In Phase-II, the residents must also pay for their own medical coverage and pay a higher tuition at the university. It is hoped this will encourage participation in the distribution auctions for a lifetime of food and housing vouchers, free medical care and unlimited free education.

Because the affeercianados are concerned only with increasing land value and not purchasing more land, the minimum bid-rate in Phase-II drops to $5/hour or less. Such immense surplus labor increases land value in the undeveloped ring, but has less of an effect in the developed core where ground rents are already quite high. Annuities for affeercianados and investors are based on rents in the speculative ring.

Monetizing the Land

In one of the most important principles of viral community theory, currency is created when land is moved into the commons. There are several required features of the currency.

1. Pegged to the U.S. dollar at 2:1
2. Tied to land value in U.S. dollars, estimated at 20 times current ground rent
3. Issued at the Central Bank in exchange for U.S. dollars at the peg
4. Issued at the Central Bank and paid to the land owner at 20 times current ground rent in exchange for moving the land to the commons
5. Good for the payment of ground rent at the peg
6. Good for payment at all affeercianado enterprises (e.g. hospital, bid labor) at the peg
7. Good for distribution auctions (basic income annuities) at the peg (See, below)

In the business plan and vision, this currency is a biometric, virtual currency called the VIP$.

A large thriving metropolis is needed to support faith in the VIP$. For this reason it must not be introduced until the 21st year, and only if population milestones are achieved. Because the VIP$ is stipulated by the land-trust charter to be good for payment of ground rent; premiums, copays, and PPO medical bills at the HMO hospital; tuition, fees, room and board at the university; and bidding for affeercianado labor, the currency will be accepted everywhere.

At the end of Phase-I, all of the land is owned by the land-trust in the name of the investors and affeercianados. After monetization, the land is owned by the land-trust in the name of the commons. Investors and affeercianados receive gigantic payouts. Time weighted formulas (See *Step 5 – Hunting for a Whale*) use initial investment and subsequent affeercianado purchases to determine proportional ownership between the investors and affeercianados. Land credits determine proportional ownership for individual affeercianados.

Although land purchases by the affeercianados have ceased, undeveloped land in the speculative ring is monetized as it is developed. This land, too, belongs to the affeercianados and investors. The monetization pays annuities to investors and affeercianados for about 40 more years. Like the original payout, annuities for affeercianados are based on individual land credits. Although affeercianados must pay for food, housing, and medical care, they continue to earn land credits throughout Phase-II and Phase-III. They also divvy up profits from their enterprises based on total land credits.

Inflation or Deflation

Phase-II begins with a sudden infusion of new currency at 20 times ground rents. The affeercianados and investors who receive the VIP$ could use it to treble properties throughout the community and pay 150% objective depreciated value on the improvements. Other responses include selling the VIP$ at a discount. These would be inflationary in the short run.

The most common use will be to purchase distribution packages at auction (see below). This will be slightly deflationary to the extent that VIP$ are withdrawn from circulation.

But what is the true nature of the VIP$? It is backed by land value, but only land value at the moment the land is transferred to the commons. As the value of land in the commons continues to increase, there is no currency created to account for this increased value (until the capitulation.) This places deflationary pressure on the currency.

It is essential that the VIP$ become scarce. As you will see below, land values will be under constant upward pressure in Phase II. This will lead to deposits of U.S. dollars at the Central Bank and the creation of new VIP$. This is an important tool of financial domination.

Auctions for Selective Distribution

During Phase-II, the land trust has halted all land purchases. Ground rents that previously were used to purchase land, or used to pay dividends to investors and affeercianados, are available for other uses.

It is imperative that all of this money is used at auction to subsidize basic income annuities. These annuities pay a lifetime of distributions for food, housing, medical care, and unlimited free education. They also include other perks such as free parking, day care, access to small business loans, and the right to treble so many acres of undeveloped land a year. The annuities will also pay for public goods and services for the owner, freeing up more ground rents to be used in auction subsidies.

Medical and educational costs, as well as the cost of government services, are lower, due to affeercianado labor.

The present value of 40 years of distributions is $230,000. A 4% interest rate is assumed. If an interest rate this high is unrealistic, the present value will need to be raised. In 40 years' time, if capitulation has not yet occurred, distributions will be paid directly from ground rents.

The actuarial value of lifetime distributions for a person 65 or older is $125,000. If an average lifespan extends beyond 80, the actuarial value will need to be raised. The cost of distributions is not a linear function of age. The present value of the distributions for a 45 year old would be $178,000, and a 55 year old $158,000.

Annuities are generally poor investment choices. Purchasing these basic income packages at full price, particularly since they are used, in part, to pay for government services already covered by the ground rents, would be unwise. What make these investments irresistible are the subsidies. The only ones who will pay close to full price are individual affeercianados who have just received a large windfall and initially fear holding the currency. For others, particularly residents who gain additional auction credit for years of residency, a 40% subsidy turns these dogs into must-have investments. Sales of the new currency at a discount will also encourage bidding at the auctions.

This is a Dutch auction where all bidders receive the largest subsidy bid until funds for the particular auction are exhausted. Over the years, the subsidies will rise as wealthier residents are already covered. Residency credits and a one year residency requirement will provide some relief for the less affluent as new wealthy immigrants grab the annuities at lower subsidies than poorer residents can afford.

There are auctions for residents, family of previous auction winners, affeercianados, Phase-I and earlier donors, and those who score highly on skills testing.

These subsidized annuities will pick up where the rent freeze left off in raising land values. In fact, far more ground rents will be returned to the people through the auctions, than imputed due to the Phase-I rent freeze.

Only entitled citizens who have won a distribution package at auction will be eligible to treble undeveloped lands in the speculative ring (also called the AFFEERCE territories). As a result, land auctions for outsiders will be much smaller in Phase-II than Phase-I. This will force greater efficiency in the developed core to accommodate immigrants seeking the subsidized annuities, further putting upward pressure on land value.

When taken together with the low $5/hour minimum bid price for affeercianado labor and the housing distribution which will pay up to $370/month for ground rent, apartment rent, mortgage, utilities, repairs and renovations, Phase-II should detonate an explosion in land value that will easily reverse any inflationary pressure from affeercianado and investor payouts.

Phase-III

The goal of Phase-II is to extend selective distribution to 95% of the residents who lived in the community at the end of Phase-I. With that accomplished in 18 to 20 years, we are ready for Phase-III which will be marked by explosive growth in territory, ultimately expanding our borders to encompass virtually all of the host-state. Land monetization and subsidized selective distribution come together to form the most explosive stage of a viral community: deluxe land expansion. Political control of the state is likely to happen early on in Phase-III.

Deluxe Land Expansion

When Phase-III begins, the currency of the virtual community must be as respected as the U.S. dollar. This is likely, as the VIP$ is backed by land value in U.S. dollars and U.S. dollars directly. However, there should also be pressure on the peg as the overwhelming direction of transfer is from dollars to the VIP$ at the Central Bank.

After 40 years, the ground rents have grown considerably. At this point, 95% of public goods and services are funded by the distributions, not the ground rents. If 30% of the ground rents fund public goods and services generally, only 1.5% of the ground rents are still needed to fund public goods and services with 95% covered by the distributions.

Deluxe land expansion is both simple and elegant. We negotiate a reasonable price for the land at 20 times whatever ground rent the current owner would be willing to pay. For the most part the current owner calls the shots and sets the price. Too low, and the property might not qualify for deluxe land expansion. Even if it did, the current owner risks a treble. The dilemma of Sun Yat-Sen keeps the price from being set too low or too high.

> **From the very definition of our currency, we create the currency to purchase the land.**

Not only does the land purchase cost nothing, but the stability of our currency is fully maintained. But, of course, why should anyone sell, even if the price is fair?

This is where we create an offer that cannot be refused, or at least those who did would be foolish; an offer where the average landowner will be pleading with us to buy their land.

The lifetime distributions for food, housing, medical care, and unlimited education, grabbed at auction with a 50% subsidy will, in general, be given to every tenant on the land absolutely free, as a condition of sale.

Annual expansion is limited by density of population and the amount of ground rents available for distributions. The term of the annuity (lifetime of distributions) need only last 20 years, and decreases by one year, per year. If at the end of this time, the ground rents will be sufficient to pay all distributions, the amount of money placed in the active fund per distribution can drop every year until such time as all citizens in the state who were tenants on land sold to the commons, are covered.

The predicted outcome is computed on a spreadsheet. In a gross simplification, on average, $200,000 per distribution needs to be added to the active fund in the first year of Phase-III. At a density of 1 person per acre, an annual ground rent of $5 billion (conservatively expected at the start of Phase-III) will allow 25,000 acres to be purchased for the commons. 25,000 people will receive lifetime distributions. Increases in land value and land holdings could double ground rents every 10 years. In that same time period, the amount per distribution is halved. In 10 years, $10 billion in ground rents will be available annually to fund 100,000 distributions. In the next five years, the amount per distribution is halved again, while the ground rents are at least $15 billion. This funds 300,000 distributions. However, the process is constrained by the need for the ground rents plus interest on the active fund to ultimately equal the annual distribution. The spreadsheets show that by the 18th year, the entitled population would exceed 2.7 million. This exceeds the population of about 16 states.

The cost of 2,790,000 distributions is $32.3 billion. In the 60th year of the embryo, the spreadsheets predict this entitled population with ground rents of $30.3 billion with interest on the active fund of $2.5 billion, satisfying the distributions with a citizens' dividend and/or decrease in floating rents of $500 million.

The business plan uses conservative assumptions. Deluxe land expansion in the plan requires a minimum stipulated ground rent of $2,200 per distribution. This might require a charitable fund to aid in purchasing overcrowded slum dwellings. Stipulated ground rents in excess of 5% of land value, cropland surcharges, and new mortgages on improvements, are all used as techniques to keep deluxe land expansion a winning proposition for both the viral community and the seller.

Deluxe land expansion extends protectionism to the entire state. With real wages greater than nominal wages, ordinary citizens takeover the role of the affeercianados in making the state hyper-competitive. A balance of trade surplus will cause a deflation in the rest of the United States, a situation politically conducive to capitulation.

Summary of Viral Community Theory

Phase-I
1. A land trust funded by investors, reinvests a significant portion of the ground rent collected from tenants in new land.
2. A landlord-working class increases land value and acquires land holdings by the difference between the value of its labor and the subsistence cost of its labor.
3. A hospital staffed by landlord-workers, is highly profitable, handles medical care for the landlord-workers, provides free medical care to tenants on the land, is a chief export, and is instrumental to the distribution package.
4. A university staffed by landlord-workers, handles training for the landlord-workers, provides a university degree as incentive to become a landlord-worker, increases land value of campus town, classes provide free labor in building the town, and is instrumental to the distribution package.

5. A speculative ring extends the margin, allowing inexpensive land purchases at the border, provides a direction for growth, increases land value in the developed core, and provides up to 40 years of post-payout annuities.
6. A rent freeze raises bid rent at auction, increases land value, and aids local business in rapid growth.

Phase-II

1. Monetizing the land creates a currency backed by land that rewards landlord-workers and investors, is good for the payment of ground rents, medical care and education and will be widely accepted, is pegged to the dollar at 2:1, and is used for deluxe land expansion.
2. Auctioning off distribution packages, subsidized by the ground rent, provides a basic income, funds public goods and services, is a great investment, will ultimately become affordable to poorer residents.

Phase-III

1. Deluxe land expansion monetizes new land and uses ground rents to fully subsidize distributions for tenants on the land.

This is the viral community theory on which the business plan is based. Although there is a Phase-IV, it is not included in the theory. It is far more political than economic.

Viral community theory will become increasingly clear as you read through the plan. Feel free to return to this section as your understanding deepens.

We now return to the business plan, Phase-I, the start of the Setup Year

Phase 1

Setup Year

Much of this chapter is detailed as a proof of concept and of no interest to the casual reader. **Important concepts are displayed in purple coloring (this shade/font for readers of the black and white edition). First-time readers should read the purple text and refer to neighboring black and white text as a reference if interested.**

January

Employees: The farmhouse will be a crowded place It will have 24 residents, 22 affeercianados and the two construction managers. The affeercianados will be divided into two main teams. 8 workers will be on the prefab and pumping station team. 10 workers will be on the roads and infrastructure team. There will be three affeercianados responsible for cooking, cleaning, communications, and household purchasing. In addition, four affeercianados will sleep in their rigs, with housing money going toward truck stop amenities and food on the road.

In addition to basic team skills, affeercianados that also have the following skills will quickly move into team leadership positions.

1. Urban planner
2. Architect

3. General contractor
4. Surveyor
5. Electric grid and fiber infrastructure
6. Water and sewage infrastructure
7. Licensed physician or paramedic
8. Building engineer and material engineer
9. Road engineer and traffic infrastructure
10. Software engineer
11. Educator in the building trades, architecture or engineering
12. Public safety – police academy graduate
13. General construction
14. Human resources
15. Minimal culinary skills, house cleaning, laundry

Major Purchases: Key – (depreciation years) in parenthesis, [Inheriting department] in brackets, SOM-Start of month, EOM-End of month, AA-As approved

Asset Setup January	Life	Debit
Road infrastructure tools and equipment (5) [RoadsInfra] AA	5	$1,000,000
Utility infrastructure materials (16) [RoadsInfra] AA	16	$83,333
Road infrastructure materials (10) [RoadsInfra] AA	10	$83,333
2 Refrigerated Food Trucks (5) [Depot] SOM, EOM	5	$80,000
3 rigs (5) [Depot] SOM, EOM, EOM	5	$150,000
4 trailers (3) [Depot] SOM, AA	3	$40,000
4 flatbed trucks, boom/rollback (5) [Depot] SOM, SOM, EOM, EOM	5	$200,000
10 cargo containers (4) [Depot] AA	4	$30,000
Underground fuel tank and pumping station (16) [Garage] - SOM	16	$20,000
1 luxury buses (6) [Metrobus] AA	6	$400,000
Equipment for prefabricated construction (6) [ACC] - SOM	6	$500,000
Bulldozer/Dump truck (8) [ACC] - SOM	8	$50,000
Rooftop solar panels (25) [ACC] - SOM	25	$100,000
Garbage Truck - Roll off (8) SOM WasteMan	8	$130,000
Garbage Truck -Front load 98) SOM WasteMan	8	$225,000
Prefab dining hall/kitchen 20,000 Sq. Ft. EOM (not depreciated)		$200,000
Prefab bathhouse 36 private toilet/shower SOM (not depreciated)		$100,000

Discussion: **The roads and infrastructure crew begins the task of building the roads and extending the utilities.** Most importantly, infrastructure must be extended to the area just to the virtual east of the city hall building ground labeled "Future City Growth" on the virtual map (See *Step 4, above*). This area will house our prefabricated town, trailer park, and dining halls for affeercianados, as well as building crews brought in by the developers. It is sufficiently distant from the area proposed for prime residential.

The prefab and pumping station crew will install a gas pump and underground tank in the proposed municipal yard behind city hall. They will complete construction on a prefabricated bathhouse with 36 private shower/toilet stalls and semi-private sinks. Private toiletry areas allow comfortable use by both men and women.

The drivers will be busy bringing in supplies. The prefabricated materials are brought in on flatbeds from the nearest port or railroad. The equipment for building prefabricated units will be purchased in Old Metropolis (the nearest major city) and delivered by rig and trailer. Incidental supplies are brought in the same way. Food is purchased either much closer or from an Old Metropolis wholesaler and brought in by refrigerated food truck or rig and trailer.

Why are we purchasing a luxury bus? Consider what we need for a new city to rise up from the hills or prairie.

1. Inexpensive land/infrastructure
2. A ready supply of inexpensive labor
3. Inexpensive building materials
4. Easy access to a major city

How do we do it?

1. The land is free and the taxes are what the developer will pay at auction and frozen for up to 19 years.
2. Affeercianados can be leased for $8/hour. Other workers can access our inexpensive accommodations.
3. Our large fleet of trucks will supply import/export on demand to rail yards, ports and wholesalers for a fraction over cost. Our builder's supply depot will sell standard construction tools and materials at wholesale and transit cost plus a small profit.
4. A fleet of luxury buses will leave every morning for Old Metropolis one and a half hours away and return in the afternoon and evening. The service is free. Wi-Fi enabled to allow a productive commute or simply catch up on sleep. No gas expense. No downtown parking expense.

So the luxury bus is the first contribution to the fleet. It will be used in the setup year to transport affeercianados to Old Metropolis for shopping, appointments, and other errands, to transport ex-affeercianados to the airport, and pickup newbies, to support a messenger service, and to initiate a contract for daily mail transport with the U.S. Post Office and other shipping companies.

Although "January" is presumed to last only one month, weather difficulties, shipping delays, accidents, or problems with an inadequate electrical, water, or sewage infrastructure could extend this virtual month over several actual months. The labor cost per month for "January", including executive pay is $52,817.

February

Employees: The farmhouse gets more crowded as we bring two more affeercianados to the prefab team.

Major purchases:

Asset	Setup February	Life	Debit
Road infrastructure tools and equipment (5) [RoadsInfra] AA		5	$1,000,000
Utility infrastructure materials (16) [RoadsInfra] AA		16	$83,333
Road infrastructure materials (10) [RoadsInfra] AA		10	$83,333

For the roads and infrastructure crew it is another million dollars in tools and equipment, plus materials. The same will be true for the following month, March, so I won't bother showing it again.

Asset	Setup February	Life	Debit
1 Ambulance (5) [Fire] AA		5	$60,000
Prefab for 200 units EOM (not depreciated)			$700,000
Prefab laundry 20,000 Sq. Ft. EOM (not depreciated)			$200,000
Purchase 80 washers/dryers (6) [ACC] AA, EOM		6	$60,000
Dining hall folding chairs/tables EOM (not depreciated)			$12,000
400 dining hall cots/sleeping bags EOM (not depreciated)			$40,000
Rooftop solar panels (25) [ACC] - SOM		25	$100,000
Purchase kitchen equipment including walk-in freezer/refrigerator (8) [ACC] EOM		8	$55,000

Discussion: Purchase of an ambulance is essential. Construction accidents are likely and the nearest hospital is possibly an hour away. One of the farmhouse household affeercianados should have paramedic training and certification, so they can aid the patient during the trip. At least two others should be highly proficient in first aid.

The main event for this month is the building of the dining hall. At 20,000 square feet, it can easily seat 1,000-1,500 with room for a large kitchen and buffet area. During the setup year and beyond, this will be the affeercianado hangout. With food served 24 hours a day, including coffee, tea, milk and cookies, it will likely become the center of affeercianado social life.

The 10 member prefab team has the ambitious task of hoisting this building in 30 days. The cement floor might have been started in the previous month. The shell is the extent of the structure with the majority of materials being the 9 foot high roof and support columns. The kitchen stoves should supply sufficient warmth in the spring and fall with screened windows to control temperature in the warmer months. Electric heaters can be used in the winter. **A large solar rooftop could make the dining hall a net electric supplier.** Once construction is complete, folding chairs and tables for 1,500 will be purchased and 400 assembled, as will 400 cots and sleeping bags. With a working kitchen, the first real class of affeercianados can be hired.

Following completion of the dining hall, the prefab team builds a similar 20,000 sq. ft. prefabricated structure for washers and dryers. Although several dining halls will be built over the next two years, there will be only one laundry, ultimately with hundreds of washers and dryers.

The end of the month marks the arrival of prefabricated materials for 200 motel style housing units, with a bathroom and three beds per unit.

Readers should keep in mind that the actual numbers will be modified by the Prosperity CEO and prefabricated construction manager. Numbers used in this initial estimate that turn out to be, on average, far too low, will constitute a significant risk to the plan itself.

March

Employees: Three new paid non-affeercianado positions are added in March. They include a local director of human resources, a director of public safety, and doctor/medical administrator. All three report directly to the CEO. Beginning in March, the farmhouse is set aside for paid executives and the affeercianados who run that household.

Although the presence of executives gives the appearance of an elite group, appearances are deceiving. The executives, with their great body of knowledge, enable the affeercianados to work at their optimal efficiency. Each executive works at the pleasure of the CEO who works at the pleasure of the ABC board of directors. The CEO can fire an executive at will, and the ABC board can fire the CEO or recommend the termination of some executive. ABC board members are members of the Affeercianado Guild and they can be removed from the board by a 2/3 majority of the Guild. An executive, on the other hand, has no power to terminate an affeercianado, only the power to remove said affeercianado from the team under management. Ultimately, both the executives and the ABC board of directors work at the pleasure of the Affeercianado Guild.

Positions	Setup March	Workers	Debit	Credit
Roads and Infrastructure Project Manager (NA) - Farmhouse		1	$8,333	
Prefab Building Manger/Building Engineer (NA) - Farmhouse		1	$8,333	
Prosperity CEO/City manager (NA) - Farmhouse		1	$12,500	
HR Director of Affeercianado Hiring (NA) - Farmhouse		1	$8,333	
Director of Public Safety (NA) - Farmhouse		1	$8,333	
Doctor/Medical Administrator (NA) - Farmhouse		1	$8,333	
Affeercianado Cooking/Cleaning Farmhouse Maintenance		3	$2,838	
Affeercianado full time drivers/security/paramedics/misc.		8	$7,568	
Total Affeercianados/Managers in Farmhouse		17	$0	
Affeercianado Prefab Team - Dining hall, credit half utilities		300	$283,800	$99,000
Affeercianado Road and Infrastructure Team - Dining Hall		70	$66,220	$23,100
Affeercianado Cooking/Cleaning/Dining Hall Maintenance - Dining Hall		30	$28,380	$28,380
Total Affeercianados in Dining Hall		400	$0	

Expansion of the prefab and roads and infrastructure teams along with a new kitchen crew for the dining hall fills all 400 cots. During the course of the month, 4 other affeercianados, 2 paramedics and 2 security officers will be hired. In the table above, there is a third column of numbers for affeercianados living in the dining hall. This is money allocated to affeercianado housing cost that is saved on utilities.

Major purchases:

Asset	Setup March	Life	Debit
Prefab dining hall/kitchen 20,000 Sq. Ft. EOM (not depreciated)			$200,000
Prefab supply depot 20,000 Sq. Ft. EOM (not depreciated)			$200,000
600 mattresses, pillows, linen, dressers EOM (not depreciated)		600	$180,000
Purchase 100 washers/dryers (6) [ACC] AA, EOM		6	$75,000
Prefab for 300 units EOM (not depreciated)			$1,000,000
Rooftop solar panels (25) [ACC] - SOM		25	$100,000
Medical Supplies			$15,000
Fuel			$108,000
Supplies and bus cargo credits for mail/shipping services			$20,000

Discussion: **The business of March is to build the prefab units as quickly as possible**. One manufacturer suggested that 6 people could construct 1 unit in 6 days. Therefore, all 200 units could be completed by a team of 300 in 24 work days, or 1 work month. Units and hot water are heated electrically. Rooftop solar panels will make these bed + bath units energy neutral allowing further credits on affeercianado housing cost.

Units hold 3 affeercianados each, allowing all 400 to leave the dining hall for better quarters in three weeks' time. By the end of the month there will be 66 vacant units and 200 free beds for new affeercianados. Some of those units will be temporarily used for executive offices, an infirmary, and storage. **The specifics of the plan are very much control ed by the number and location of vacant buildings on the purchased land**.

Prefab materials for 2 other 20,000 sq. ft. warehouse style buildings and 300 more motel style units are ordered for the following month.

April

Employees: The number of affeercianados on the prefab team is expanded to 320. 20 more affeercianados have been hired for maintenance and linen service in the prefab units. A new paid building engineer/experienced contractor is hired to head the hospital annex building project. There are also more drivers and additional security.

> Although the environment is still a bit primitive, affeercianados enjoy services most people don't, such as prepared meals any time of the day or night and weekly linen service.

In April, the total number of affeercianados in service is 464, costing about $439,000 a month. By the end of the month of April, there is a deficit of $11,521,900.

Where does the money come from? One function of the land trust is to provide interest free loans to the affeercianados, the municipality of Prosperity, and the school district. As you'll see, these loans will be quickly repaid.

Major purchases:

Asset	Setup April	Life	Debit
Utility infrastructure materials (16) [RoadsInfra] AA		16	$83,333
Road infrastructure materials (10) [RoadsInfra] AA		10	$83,333
Road signs and signals (12) [RoadsInfra] AA		12	$83,333

The roads and infrastructure team has finished purchasing tools and equipment and has added signs and traffic signals to their monthly purchases. These purchases will continue every month throughout the setup year and won't be mentioned again.

Asset	Setup April	Life	Debit
Prefab dining hall/kitchen 20,000 Sq. Ft. EOM (not depreciated)			$200,000
Prefab for 300 units EOM (not depreciated)			$1,000,000
Rooftop solar panels (25) [ACC] - SOM		25	$100,000
Dining hall folding chairs/tables EOM (not depreciated)			$12,000
Purchase kitchen equipment including walk-in freezer/refrigerator (8) [ACC] EOM		8	$55,000
600 mattresses, pillows, linen, dressers EOM (not depreciated)		900	$270,000
Purchase 100 washers/dryers (6) [ACC] AA, EOM		6	$75,000
Medical Supplies			$5,000
Materials for 32 bed Hospital Annex (20) [Hospital]		20	$4,000,000
Construction tools and equipment (5) [ACC]		5	$2,000,000

Material for yet another dining hall, and another 300 motel style units is purchased, along with items to furnish and equip the dining hall and units just completed. Materials for a 32 bed hospital annex and the tools for its construction are procured.

Discussion: The hospital annex is the first permanent building project of the affeercianados. Architects at the ABC have purchased and modified the plans. It is up to the newly hired building engineer/contractor to turn those plans into a set of purchase orders, and a schedule. It is a requirement that the annex be completed by the end of the setup year. As many affeercianados as needed will be used. Regardless of when purchasing is actually begun, it is recorded in April. The same is true for the hiring of a hospital annex construction team. Hiring of affeercianados can begin in April, is recorded in May, and might not be complete until June, or July, if then.

May
Employees:

Positions	Setup May	Workers	Debit	Credit
May - Build 300 units, 3rd dining hall, begin hospital annex, infrastructure work		0	$0	$0
Utility infrastructure materials (16) [RoadsInfra] AA		16	$83,333	
Road infrastructure materials (10) [RoadsInfra] AA		10	$83,333	
Road signs and signals (12) [RoadsInfra] AA		12	$83,333	
Roads and Infrastructure Project Manager (NA) - Farmhouse		1	$8,333	
Prefab Building Manger/Building Engineer (NA) - Farmhouse		1	$8,333	
Prosperity CEO/City manager (NA) - Farmhouse		1	$12,500	
HR Director of Affeercianado Hiring (NA) - Farmhouse		1	$8,333	
Hospital Annex Building Engineer/Project Manager (NA) - Farmhouse		1	$8,333	
Director of Public Safety (NA) - Farmhouse		1	$8,333	
Doctor/Medical Administrator (NA) - Farmhouse		1	$8,333	
Affeercianado Cooking/Cleaning Farmhouse Maintenance		3	$2,838	
Total Affeercianados/Managers in Farmhouse		10	$0	
Affeercianado full time drivers/security/paramedics/misc.-prefab		16	$15,136	$5,280
Affeercianado Prefab Team - prefab		400	$378,400	$132,000
Affeercianado Road and Infrastructure Team - prefab		120	$113,520	$39,600
Affeercianado Cooking/Cleaning/Dining Hall/Prefab Maintenance - prefab		90	$85,140	$85,140
Total Affeercianados in prefab		626	$0	

Major purchases:

There are no purchases in May that differ from April. Material is ordered for another 300 units, while furnishing and equipment is delivered for the units completed in the previous month. No new dining halls are ordered.

Discussion: This month the prefab team has only 300 motel style units to complete, with no dining halls or other facilities to build, allowing them the chance to catch-up if behind schedule. Two of the three dining halls and most of the units are unused, or used for offices, storage, an infirmary, or meetings. The capacity of the three dining halls is 4,500 at any one time. Use of the halls for socializing might limit total number served. The building of additional dining halls in Year 1 will depend on demand.

The roads and infrastructure team is expanded to 120, as they continue to bring utilities and access to the proposed residential and industrial areas. The prefab team is expanded to 400. Many of these affeercianados will spend only part time on their teams and part time as students building the hospital annex.

Jane Jacobs University:

The ABC Board, with the advice and consent of the contractor heading up the hospital annex project, will select up to 5 affeercianados with exceptional skills in the necessary building trades to be the first instructors at the university. They will each teach one or more courses, three hours a day, up to 5 days a week. Classes will be held in empty units, the farmhouse basement, a cordoned off area of the dining hall or laundry, or other empty building we are lucky enough to acquire at land purchase. Classes will be held in the early morning, allowing most of the day for field work.

Classes will be in foundation, electrical, plumbing, bricklaying, glass, steel, heating systems, drywall, etc., up to an unlikely maximum of 25 courses total. Class size will be limited by the requirements of the hospital annex. Affeercianados on the prefab, or roads and infrastructure teams will be allowed to take up to five courses, 15 hours of credit. When the lecture is over, each student will either go to the annex site for scheduled field duty in one of their courses, or return to work with their respective team. Grades will be based on performance in the field and examinations.

Instructors get an entire day per class for teaching, preparation, and grading. Field duty days are known only a few days in advance. The instructor serves as a liaison between the contractor and students in the field, inspects the work, grades students and prevents errors. In the event of field duty on the day of class, the instructor will receive a second day for preparation and grading. On days when there is no field duty at the hospital annex, or class, the instructor will return to the roads and infrastructure or prefab team.

The hospital annex will have 32 beds, a surgery, a small ER, equipment for basic testing, with first floor offices for doctors' appointments and some outpatient procedures. It is billed as an annex, because an adjacent major hospital will be built in the following year.

Idealistic doctors and other medical professionals often dedicate the first few years of their career, working in free clinics or traveling to third world countries to do their part to save the world. There are a few personal victories, but on a large scale, there is little, if any, improvement. It is completely counter-intuitive to propose that these doctors can end disease, poverty, and even war, in a few generations, not by ministering to the least among us, but by working tirelessly, for as little pay as possible, in service of the wealthy.

The hospital is provided as a free service to those who lease land from the land trust. Following incorporation, the registered voters of Prosperity and their resident families will continue to be entitled to this service. For Medicare patients, the hospital provides a free supplementary policy and will seek to be part of all PPO networks so that non-resident workers covered by another policy can be treated without hassle. Such radically inexpensive medicine is made possible by low cost affeercianado labor. It is anticipated that most hospital employees, even most doctors, will be affeercianados. Revenue from Medicare, PPO's, copays, premiums paid by the municipality, and low-cost premiums paid by county and state residents outside of the land trust will make for a very profitable enterprise.

June, July, August, September, and October

Employees: There is little affeercianado hiring, except several to maintain the additional units, which are mostly unused. A few additional drivers, security, office workers, and other miscellaneous workers are hired.

Major purchases: The major purchases each month are an exact repeat of the previous month: infrastructure materials and signage, 300 more prefabricated motel style units, the furniture to furnish them, and more washers and dryers for future tenants of the units. The purchases are expensed each month, but the actual purchases need not be made until they are needed.

Discussion: The two major teams, roads and infrastructure, and prefab construction, will spend these months working on their respective projects. **By the end of this period, the total number of motel style units completed is 2,300. By the end of November, that number will stand at 2,600, enough for 7,800 tenants.**

Jane Jacobs University will remain in session into November, a full six month semester. During that time, students, under instruction, will complete the hospital annex.

There is a 6 month probationary period before an affeercianado can be a voting member of the Affeercianado Guild. This period does not affect pay or benefits, only voting rights. During these summer months, many of those early affeercianados will gain voting rights. This will be an opportunity to make needed corrections.

Is the plan too ambitious or not ambitious enough? Are there paid managers and executives who are failing to meet their mandate of increasing affeercianado efficiency? Are any ABC board members failing to act in a responsible manner? By a 2/3 majority, the Guild can remove a member of the ABC board. The board will find a replacement that must be approved by a simple majority of the Guild. The top 4 investors are not members of the Guild and cannot be removed from the board by the Guild. The ABC board is expected to implement any recommendation made by a 2/3 majority of the Guild, and take under advisement any recommendation made by a majority of the Guild.

November

Employees: Four tour guides have been added to the staff or taken from elsewhere. Otherwise the other teams continue as they have over the previous six months.

Major purchases: Here are some of the months interesting purchases.

Asset	Setup November	Life	Debit
Computer equip for AMS - office in hospital annex (3) [AMS] EOM		3	$30,000
3 old school buses (not depreciated) EOM			$30,000
Fire engine (8) [Fire]		8	$150,000
Fire pumper (8) [Fire]		8	$40,000
Ambulance (5) [Fire]		5	$50,000
2 squad cars (8) [Police]		8	$100,000
Material for bathhouse (not depreciated)			$300,000
Trailer park electric, water, cable (not depreciated)			$300,000
Supplies			$80,000
Purchase 2 luxury buses (6) [Metrobus] SOM			$800,000
Marketing cost to promote auction			$1,000,000

AMS or Affeercianado Municipal Software is a venture designed to develop municipal applications for the smartcard, a precursor to the VIP. It will also develop protocols for inter-business production control; a veritable internet for physical goods, as well as meet municipal needs in more prosaic applications. Applications will be provided at no cost to the city of Prosperity. Revenue will be generated by sales to other municipalities and corporations. AMS will provide $5 an hour consultation to Prosperity, other affeercianado organizations, and the school district on software packages and computer issues. Minimum bid rate for AMS consultation on computer related projects or problems by Prosperity households, business, and industry will be $18/hour, far higher than the $8/hour minimum bid rate on other labor.

Discussion: The purchase of computer equipment begins the AMS organization in November. We will examine them more closely in a few years.

With the fire engine, fire pumper, ambulance and two squad cars, Prosperity begins the three year journey to incorporation with an investment in public safety. At this time, fire and law enforcement are provided by the county. However, strictly speaking, Prosperity is all private property, owned by the land trust. The police are considered local security guards and are expected to turn over any apprehended miscreants to the county.

The Prosperity fire department too, must defer to county authority, discussed in negotiations with the county board before the land purchase. Local services in conjunction with cooperation between unincorporated Prosperity and the county will have netted us a promised 15% of the rent earmarked for county services.

Material for a much larger bathhouse and trailer park are ordered in November for construction in December by the prefab team. The bathhouse and third dining hall will be central to a field for up to 1000 trailers or RV's. This will complete the accommodations for affeercianados and migrant labor needed during Year 1 for construction.

Three old school buses are purchased for the purpose of taking workers from stations at the trailer park and motel style units to and from active construction sites. This will be provided as a free service.

The luxury bus fleet is rounded out at 6 buses, and put into service. They will transport prospective homesteaders, developers, retailers, industrialists, and other entrepreneurs to and from Old Metropolis in conjunction with a million dollar marketing campaign to advertise the first auction. This includes rental of high powered servers used for both bidding and the first incarnation of the online land system.

As potential citizens take the free bus trip to Prosperity, the tour guide will tell them about:

- Free land, all they do is bid on the ground rent which remains frozen for up to 19 years.
- Cheap labor – Thousands of qualified laborers, construction workers, and even engineers with bids starting at $8/hour
- Reasonable materials – Supply depot with standard building materials, at Old Metropolis retail prices. Import/export from/to ports, rail yards, and wholesalers at a fraction over cost, including delivery of equipment, cargo, and heavy materials directly to site.
- Free medical care for residents at the soon-to-be world class hospital, including an emergency treatment policy and medivac service from anywhere in the country.
- Free luxury bus commuting to Old Metropolis. Free buses also leave throughout the day for shopping and cultural excursions, as well as air travel.
- Energy independence through heavy use of solar in civic design and contributions from waste management. Waste management goal of 99% reuse, recycle, incinerate for municipal, industrial, and medical waste.
- Smart-card access to all municipal services. VIP access expected in the final years of Phase-I.
- Citizens' dividend expected to return municipal profits and grants directly to the citizens by Year 5.
- Reasonably priced general college and a medical school beginning in Year-12. Free tuition for non-affeercianados in Jane Jacobs in Year 1 and nominal tuition for the remainder of Phase-I.
- Unparalleled investment opportunities including municipal and ABC support for import replacement, VIP and smart-card applications, and waste recycling.
- Qualification to take part in the Phase-II homesteader's auctions for basic income, with a free opening bid of $2,000 for every year in residence as a registered voter.

When the buses arrive in the future city of Prosperity, prospects are taken to AFFEERCE a'Cookin, the 24 hour dining hall, and invited to purchase a 24 hour pass for only $22 which includes all they can eat and one free night, double occupancy, in a motel style unit. It is explained how construction workers can enjoy 24 hour access to the dining hall, including morning pickup of custom bag lunches for $560 a month, and lodging in a motel unit for only $233 a month, triple occupancy. Monthly rental in the trailer park is even lower.

In the second dining hall, there will be models of the future medical/educational campus, downtown, community centers, elementary and high school architectures. Hardhat tours of the virtually completed hospital annex should be reassuring. Brochures and maps will be everywhere.

Affeercianados will conduct free private tours of remote neighborhoods designated as residential, industrial, and mixed, helping prospects scout out favorable locations for proposed retail, developments, and industries.

Individual homesteaders will be given the same treatment as developers. They will be shown areas earmarked for individual homesteading, with emphasis placed on the value of import cargo to site and affeercianado consultation and labor.

Affeercianados everywhere will be available to answer questions or direct the prospect to the appropriate party. At night, there will be optional games and discussion groups in the dining hall, with an ice cream and pie bar better than normal. There will be square dancing in the second dining hall and weather permitting there will be a weenie/marshmallow roast. In the rooms there will be on-demand movies and cable TV.

The next morning, after a hearty breakfast at AFFEERCE a'Cookin, perhaps a visit to a prospective site by morning light and getting answers to a few more questions, prospects can board the buses leaving at various times throughout the day for Old Metropolis.

Prospects who establish a line of credit, or place a deposit, are welcome to stay a second day, or return on another date, however, additional nights in the prefab rooms run $45 a night, $195 a week, or $700 a month. Weekly and monthly reduced rates at AFFEERCE a'Cookin are also available. The prospect can also drive down in an RV and use the trailer park and bathhouse for $18 a night. Prospects are welcome to perform minimally invasive tasks on properties such as surveying, measurement, soil testing, and utility verification.

What about pre-auction pricing?

The ground rent is not a major source of revenue in the first few years. In the beginning, almost all of the profit comes from the margin on affeercianado labor. A low rent is preferred early on, since this will accelerate the rate of increase in land values. We expect non-downtown land to fetch ground rent between $2,000 and $5,000 per acre in the first auction and will not be disappointed if it comes in even lower. In the long run, the law of rent always wins.

However, we offer immediate lease in exchange for a tax that is equal to 1/3 projected net rents on a newly constructed 5-story building. In the 200 acre double-level downtown (not available until the end of Year 1), we offer immediate lease in exchange for a tax that is equal to 1/3 projected net rents on a newly constructed 21-story building.

Net rent on 1/2 acre 5-story building	cost/sq ft.	Sq ft./floor	Floors	Total cost	Annual expenses	Annual Revenue
Cost to build (affercianado labor)	$120	21000	5	$12,600,000		
Depreciation over 40 years				$315,000	$315,000	
Interest on loan at 5%				$630,000	$630,000	
Utilities	$1	21000	5	$105,000	$105,000	
Maintenance labor/supplies					$80,000	
Management labor/supplies					$50,000	
Rent first floor retail	$32	21000	1	$672,000		$672,000
Rent upper floors	$12	21000	4	$1,008,000		$1,008,000
Total					$1,180,000	$1,680,000
Net Rent						$500,000
Fair LVT						$166,667

If a developer is willing to pay $166,667 annual rent on ½ acre or a rent of $333,334/acre, they can lease any land they want, any time they want. This is 2 orders of magnitude over what we conservatively expect in the first auction and 1 order of magnitude over conservative predictions for Year 20. Even at this rent, the landlord of a 5-story building can earn $333,333 annually plus another $40,000 management fee, if they are owner/manager.

This pre-auction price is expected to rise over the 20 year period as retail and office rents increase. In some parts of Manhattan, rents are 15 to 25 times as expensive as the $32 1st floor retail, and $12 office/apartment per sq. ft. assumed in this table.

December

Employees: The number of affeercianados hasn't changed but construction of the hospital annex is complete and numbers in the prefab construction and roads and infrastructure teams have dropped by 100 with an equivalent number of affeercianados involved in landscaping, maintenance, and setting up the hospital annex. Some will be the same people. A rich skill set is sought in the hiring process. Affeercianados are not expelled from the Guild without the vote of a 2/3 majority. There is never a lack of work. However, attrition, holiday travel and versatility justify keeping the count constant.

Major purchases:

Item	Setup December		Debit	Credit	Balance
Supplies and bus cargo credits for mail/shipping services	2		$20,000	$1,388	($35,926,600)
Medical Equipment (8) [Hospital]	8		$1,400,000	$0	($37,326,600)
Hospital Furniture/Equipment (10) [Hospital]	10		$140,000	$0	($37,466,600)
Uniforms, Linens, Towels (5) [Hospital]	5		$10,000	$0	($37,476,600)
AFFEERCE a'Cookin Food revenue from prospective bidders	2400		$16,800	$52,800	($37,440,600)
Prefab motel revenue from prospective bidders	1200		$1,200	$54,000	($37,387,800)
Pay agreed county property tax			$100,000		($37,487,800)
Borrow from the land trust				$37,487,800	$0

Discussion: This is the bottom of the Setup Year table, with all columns shown. The last column shows the deficit to date, credits are in the third column, debits in the second, and miscellaneous numbers used for calculations in the first.

Major purchases include equipment for the hospital annex, including MRI and other testing and surgical tools, hospital furniture, and other hospital assets. Initial supplies will be moved from the makeshift infirmary in the motel rooms.

Notice that $100,000 will be paid to the county for property taxes. This will be the property tax on the property before it was purchased, or an amount agreed to during negotiations between the ABC and the county board. Starting in Year 1, the county will get 85% of 30% of ground rent collected. The other 15% of 30% of rent collected goes to the unincorporated city.

The spreadsheet includes profit on food at AFFEERCE a'Cookin, and the much greater profit margin on motel rooms. Over 2000 24-hour passes to the buffet are predicted in light of the marketing campaign, curiosity about AFFEERCE, a way for families of affeercianados to see first-hand what their children are up to, an inexpensive vacation, and, of course, the serious homesteaders, developers, industrialists and retailers.

In the final line, the deficit is borrowed from the land trust, although in reality it will be borrowed as we go. This demonstrates why $65 million is required at start-up, even though only $25 million will be used for the initial land purchase. This is only a loan. It will be repaid and it will be used to purchase more land.

More revenue than you think!

It might seem that revenue from our buffet and motel rooms are the first real instances of revenue. But that isn't true. Careful accounting shows there are credits that need to be recorded. Take affeercianado pay. A full $370 of that pay goes for housing and utilities. But consider that the full cost of the prefabricated housing has already been expensed. Consider too, that with three affeercianados to a small room, and an array of solar panels on the roof, the utility costs per person are apt to be under $10. If one averages in utility costs at the dining hall and laundry, which also have huge arrays of solar panels on their 20,000 sq. ft. flat roofs, then even during high summer air-conditioning season, utility costs are under $12 per person. Property tax of $100,000 divided 500 ways is $200 per person, or $17 a month. There is also an affeercianado who changes the bed linen once a week. This too, is considered part of housing costs. In the course of a week, one person performs maid service for 150 beds. This adds $6 per person per month to housing cost. So out of $370 a month for housing, the actual cost is around $35 a month, maybe $40 to include maintenance. The prefabs are not depreciated. So $330 a month is actual profit. If we fail to take the credit, then we end up expensing the same housing twice.

There is $220 allocated for food. Does this $220 a month handle the 30 kitchen workers? The dining hall serves 1,500 persons. The monthly cost of the kitchen workers is $30,000. That is $20 per person for labor. At these economies of scale, the remaining $200 should cover the cost of food quite well.

This means that affeercianados who work for other affeercianados have their salary paid out of already expensed food and housing. There is no need to expense the salaries of these affeercianados.

Affeercianado full time drivers/security/paramedics/misc.-prefab	24	$22,704	$7,920
Affeercianado Prefab Team - prefab	320	$302,720	$105,600
Affeercianado Road and Infrastructure Team - prefab	100	$94,600	$33,000
Affeercianado Cooking/Cleaning/Dining Hall/Prefab Maintenance - prefab	150	$141,900	$141,900
Affeercianado Hospital setup, landscape, maintenance, medical personnel	100	$94,600	$33,000
Total Affeercianados in prefab	694	$0	

Notice the dining hall, maintenance and cleaning have a credit equal to their debit. The other affeercianados are credited for housing costs saved.

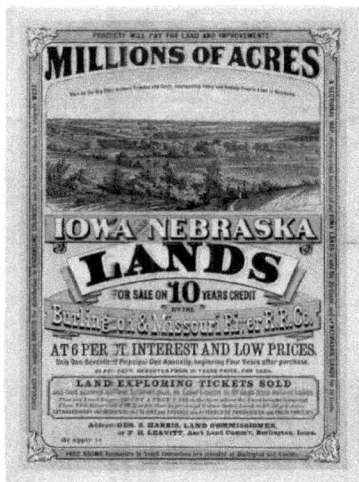

Year 1

Starting in Year 1, detail is confined to the spreadsheets and there is no longer a need for purple-colored text.

The Bid

Once the hospital annex is complete and the roads and infrastructure crew have reached the neighborhoods being promoted, it is time to begin the first auction. Only 650 acres are to be auctioned, and not even this if acres were previously leased in advance for $333,333/acre. While that would yield a whopping $216 million, realistically and conservatively at this early stage of the game, a total ground rent of $2.6 million is predicted.

Bids can be for absolute parcels in dimension and location, or for parcels of absolute dimension that can be moved by the affeercianados to accommodate other bidders, or the city plan. Absolute location bids will compete against moveable bids that are 10% lower.

Bidding is done online. This system will, by the end of Phase IV, hold vast amounts of information about every inch of land in the United States. For the time being, it is sufficient that the system have a map of the land trust's territory, show planned usage in non-biddable regions, show the high-bid on any land parcel and indicate whether it is moveable or non-moveable, and give the user the ability to delineate a property and make a legal bid. Initial development of the online land system will happen at the ABC during the setup year.

If the parcel being bid on overlaps, in whole or in part, any other previously bid land, the new bid must be 10% higher. Bids must be accompanied by a statement of intention on the nature of the development, particularly with regard to hazardous materials and pollution of the air, water, or soil, or noise, light, or odor pollution. The ABC board, or the affeercianados by a 2/3 majority can reject any bid. Any material breach of the statement of intention can result in termination of the lease and no refund of the advance payment.

Overlapping bids. Red must make a bid 10% higher than yellow to be counted

Bidding will last 2 weeks, ideally from Christmas of the Setup Year through January 6th of Year 1. Bidders have 1 business day to insure their deposit or line of credit is equal to or exceeds one year of advance rent. In other words, the deposit or credit must at least equal the bid. Until the additional deposit is made, other bidders can outbid by less than 10%.

Only 650 acres are being auctioned, even though bidders can place bids on over 4,000 acres of land. So the bidder is not only bidding against others who want the same land, but all bidders as a whole. Certain retail slots, listed in advance of the auction, will be filled regardless of bid. For instance, a grocery store, gas station, or department store, will be filled despite bids far lower than the other accepted bids. However, if two grocery stores are in the competition, only the highest would necessarily win, unless both came in above the threshold. Although this feature will be used in the first few auctions to attract necessary services, in future auctions it will be used to support a city building concept called "import replacement."

Residential developers should be aware that they are subject to a developer impact fee of $3,000 per bedroom or den for the purpose of building schools. If the developer bids a rent of $5,000/acre, builds a 3 bedroom home on a quarter acre plot and sells it to a homeowner, there will be $9,000 assessed for impact fees, and the homeowner will pay an annual ground rent of $1,250, equivalent to $5,000/acre.

If a property is moved and the bidder does not accept the new location, the bid is voided and the next highest bidder is accepted. Once all 650 acres are assigned, the auction is over and the deposits are used as a 1-year advance payment of ground rent. At the start of the following month, and every month thereafter, the land rights owner will pay 1/12 of the ground rent, always maintaining a credit balance of one full year's worth of rent.

Although the auction is over, a refund of future rent is still possible if there was a genuine misunderstanding on statement of intention, or the developer's vision is irreconcilable with the city planners. Developers submit plans to the building and planning team for the very reasonable inspection rate of $25/hour. The plans are either approved or negotiations begin. If an impasse in negotiations is reached, and the developer will not accept the decision of building and planning, they will receive a refund of future ground rent provided they vacate in a timely manner.

Once the plans are approved, the transfer is considered complete. There is no longer any liability on the part of the ABC, the affeercianados, or the City of Prosperity in regard to future ground rent payments. They will be refunded only to the extent they are replaced by a subsequent owner.

For the initial bidder, ground rent for land leased in Year 1 is frozen at the bid level for 19 years until the start of universal trebling in Year 20. There is no increase for land transfer, although transfer taxes can be charged. Under normal circumstances, the land cannot be trebled. This treble safety is lost should the lessee be over 1 month in arrears on rent payment. In that case, liens will be placed against the improvements and the property marked as treble-able in the land system. In a treble, liens are reimbursed at 100%, instead of the 150% for unencumbered improvements.

The Jane Jacobs University Chancellery

There are those individuals who are both very charitable and very narcissistic. Despite our present culture's paeans to diversity, they tend to be somewhat ridiculed. This is unfortunate because as discussed in Volume I, a new aristocracy can provide great wealth to the nation. The same is true for our embryo, Prosperity.

The university is critical to our success. It will attract young people into the affeercianados who desire an all-expense paid college education, at a university that will gain acclaim for its intense curriculum, and graduates that excel in their field. At the same time, these young people, in the process of achieving their degrees, will build the urban center, on land that they themselves will own.

Jane Jacobs University is administered by a board of trustees consisting of affeercianados selected by the ABC Board and ratified by the Affeercianado Guild. The paid university president also sits on the board. Major decisions of the Jane Jacobs Board of Trustees must be ratified by the Guild, and the Guild can remove trustees by a 2/3 majority. Bidders or treblers of the chancellery can be prevented from bid or treble, or dethroned by a 2/3 majority of the Jane Jacobs Board of Trustees.

In AFFEERCE, the chancellor of a university is an aristocratic title. The chancellor has no say in curriculum or administration. However, the chancellor hosts major university functions, including graduations, dinners, visiting dignitaries, ribbon cutting, sporting events, sporting team travel, pep rallies, and so forth. There are people who will pay millions to be in this socially notable position. And that is precisely what they will do.

The chancellery is the first incarnation of the university. It will contain classrooms, laboratories, offices, lecture halls, and an assembly hall. On the top two floors will be the palace of the chancellor. The topmost floor will be private, and the penultimate floor designed for entertaining. The assembly hall on the first floor, Proudhon Hall, will also serve as the initial meeting area for the Affeercianado Guild.

At this point we have at least 200 affeercianados who will have had some previous building trades experience, spent a year on prefab construction or roads and infrastructure, took from one to five courses on the building trades, and built a hospital annex. The cost of their labor is less than half of standard labor. The cost of 1 sq. ft. of construction is generally priced at $174. Because the labor in materials transport is also inexpensive, we use the estimate of $100/sq. ft. for all affeercianado projects in this plan, or $85/sq. ft. for materials, if expensed separately.

Our architects will design a chancellery during the setup year. Assume a footprint of 40,000 sq. ft. The first floor will contain the assembly hall, administrative offices, and chancellery entrance with private acre, garage and private elevator. The basement will contain building hardware, machine shops, metal shops, wood shops, and other labs. The second floor will have a library, computers and study area. The third floor will have eight lecture halls, the fourth and fifth floors will each have 60 classrooms. The sixth floor will have 200 offices. The seventh floor will be the lower floor of the chancellor's palace for entertainment and rooftop gardens. The eighth and top floor of the palace will be the private part of the residence and private rooftop gardens. The chancellor's complete residence plus gardens will be 80,000 square feet.

The cost of this 8 story building is estimated at 9 x 40,000 x $100 = $36 million

The first chancellor does not bid on the annual ground rent. It is set initially at the minimum $12/acre by a jurisdictional covenant that restricts the land to a chancellery. Instead, the bidding is on a one-time payment for building construction. When trebled by a new chancellor, the current chancellor receives 150% of the objective depreciated value, or if the full $36 million is bid, $54 million in the first year.

In the first auction, we will take bids on the Chancellery of Jane Jacobs University. With special advertising in the first auction packet, hopefully there will be considerable interest in this prestigious position, this 80,000 square foot home, with minimal ground rent, at least 77% tax deductible bid with possible additional credits for donating to an educational institution, $18 million in profit if somebody else usurps the throne, and the honor of being the first aristocrat in the United States. Unlike properties, in general, during the first 19 years of Phase-I, the chancellery can be trebled as soon as the building is complete.

There is no guarantee we will achieve a $36 million bid. For instance, if we got $20 million, the additional $16 million must come in the form of a loan from the land trust. However, the chancellor, on a treble, will only receive 150% of the objective depreciated value on the portion of their investment.

Should the winning bid exceed $36 million, the new chancellor will be able to work with the architects to add any additions, or luxuries with the additional funds.

This will not be the only chancellery. In Year 2, we will auction off the Chancellery of Thomas Paine Hospital. In Year 3, the palace and title of the Grand Duke or Grand Duchess of Prosperity. Vice-chancelleries of various colleges at the University will be auctioned off starting in Year 8, and the Chancellor of the Medical School in Year 12.

The Financial Situation at the Start of Year 1

Land	Table 1.1 A	Residents	Buildings	Workers	Acres	Rate	Rent
Initial Trust - Setup							$0
Purchase initial 5000 acres							$0
Affeercianado borrowing							$0
Municipal borrowing							$0
Year 1							$0
Affeercianado borrowing							$0
Education borrowing							$0
Municipal borrowing							$0
Affeercianado Rent					200		$0
Municipal Rent					100		$0
Public roads					50		$0
Private Roads					0		$0
Unauctioned land-Rent paid by affeercianados					4000	$250	$0
Auction Rent 650@$4,000			1300	6500	650	$4,000	$2,600,000
Rent 650@$4,000		3250			650	$4,000	$2,600,000

Land –Cont. Table 1.1 B	Rent	10% Rents	40% Rents	Borrowed/ Repaid	On Loan	Land Trust
Initial Trust - Setup	$0				$0	$65,000,000
Purchase initial 5000 acres	$0				$0	$40,000,000
Affeercianado borrowing	$0			($37,487,800)	($37,487,800)	$2,512,200
Municipal borrowing	$0				($37,487,800)	$2,512,200
Year 1	$0				($37,487,800)	$2,512,200
Affeercianado borrowing	$0			$0	($37,487,800)	$2,512,200
Education borrowing	$0			($4,684,133)	($42,171,933)	($2,171,933)
Municipal borrowing	$0				($42,171,933)	($2,171,933)
Affeercianado Rent	$0		$305,600	$0	($42,171,933)	($2,171,933)
Municipal Rent	$0	$237,600			($42,171,933)	($2,171,933)
Public roads	$0				($42,171,933)	($2,171,933)
Private Roads	$0				($42,171,933)	($2,171,933)
Unauctioned land-Rent paid by affeercianado	$0	$0	$400,000	$0	($42,171,933)	($2,171,933)
Auction Rent 650@$4,000	$2,600,000				($42,171,933)	($611,933)
Rent 650@ $4,000	$2,600,000				($42,171,933)	$948,067
Totals	$0				($42,171,933)	$948,067

Table 1.1B is a continuation of Table 1.1A with the initial land and rent column in common. The land trust will have $65 million at the start of the Setup Year. 5000 acres will be purchased at $25 million, leaving $40 million in the land trust as seen on the second row of the table. The deficit during the Setup Year will be over $37 million. This money is borrowed from the land trust leaving it with $2.5 million. Elementary school construction requires an additional $4.6 million from the trust. However, as the year begins, an auction of 650 acres yields an advance payment of $2.6 million. 60% of the rent goes to the land trust, lowering its deficit to $611,933. As additional rent is paid throughout the year, the land trust balance approaches $1 million.   The assumption is that the complete Jane Jacobs University Chancellery will be financed by the new chancellor at auction. Otherwise, investors should be ready to increase their investment by up to $36 million.

Other columns estimate the number of new residents, new buildings, and buildings trade workers, needed as a result of the acres auctioned. By the end of Year 1, Prosperity should have 3,250 residents apart from the affeercianados. With 6,500 workers required for the construction, there will be strong demand for both affeercianado labor and migrant buildings trade workers. It is expected that work on the chancellery and dormitories will be done by Jane Jacobs' students. During down time, affeercianados will rent themselves to developers and others, as described shortly.

Here is how the 40% of Year-1 ground rent that does not go to the land trust gets distributed.

City	County	Admin	Inv Div	Aff Div	Land Broker
$313,380	$1,775,820	$415,936	$233,500	$233,500	$93,400

The county will be paid over 17 times the former property tax, erasing any doubts they had going into negotiations. On the other hand, their sheriff's office must deal with thousands of rowdy construction workers. The contributions of our private police and fire, roads and infrastructure, and municipal hospital warrant our unincorporated municipality getting 15% of the 30% rent tranche, or $313,380.

With the ABC receiving $415,936, a lot of scrip can be redeemed. For many affeercianados at ABC headquarters, this will be the first time they get paid. The investors receive their first dividend of $233,500 and the land-broker their first commission from the land purchase. The affeercianados also get $233,500, from the 50% stipulated ownership in the investment, creating an incentive to increase land value early-on. Affeercianado dividends will be even higher if there are donations.

The third row from the bottom of Table 1.1, labeled "Unauctioned land —rent paid by affeercianados" is rent paid by the affeercianados on all land that has yet to be auctioned off. The county, in particular, expects to receive taxes on all land. The investors, too, should not suffer from a speculative strategy over which they have little control. The land is treated as undeveloped. Its value is its purchase price. This value is then multiplied by 5% to compute the ground rent. The rent on this land purchased for $5,000 an acre is $250/acre. That would be $1,000,000. However, there is no reason for the land trust to get paid for unauctioned land. So the affeercianados only need come up with 40% of that million, or $400,000. Nevertheless, the $233,500 the affeercianados collect from the rent is of little help paying the $400,000 ground rent on unauctioned land and the $305,600 ground rent on affeercianado land.

Why Land Speculation?

We are building a city from scratch. The undeveloped land is worth $5,000 per acre. After putting in our roads, utilities, a municipal hospital, a builder's supply depot and free bus trips to the major city, the land yields a rent of $4,000/acre which translates into a land value of $80,000/acre at an interest rate of 5%. In one year, we have multiplied the value of the land by 16. If this land were owned by some speculator who sat back and ate crumpets while we built our roads and dug our ditches, it would be most unfair for this speculator to profit from our labor. Of course, that is the tragedy that besets the world economy today. Instead, at the beginning 50+% of Prosperity land is owned by the very laborers themselves, with almost 50% owned by the investors who hopefully are actively engaged in planning on the ABC Board. A major improvement over today, with the dynamics designed to radically increase the amount of land owned by the affeercianado laborers. Ultimately, all the land will belong to the people.

As the city grows, the value of the land will continue to rapidly increase. It makes no sense to auction off more land than can be efficiently developed with available resources. When the resources are once again available, the land will have gained in value.

In Year 1, we are getting $4,000/acre in rent frozen for up to 19 years. It is a fantastic economic opportunity for the entrepreneur or resident who wishes to lease. However, auction off too much and we lose significant speculative profits. Auction off too little and the time needed to create the City of Prosperity increases, with diminishing speculative gains.

Factors going into the amount of land to auction are primarily related to labor. Do we have enough affeercianados to adequately fill their role in the massive construction that follows? Do we have enough affeercianados to build the needed schools, and the needed roads and infrastructure? What about fire and police? How prepared is the county with its services? Can we handle the parking? Very critically, can we handle the waste?

Better to err on the side of caution. We can always hold a second auction if affeercianados are going idle. But once the land is auctioned off, we have to live with the zoo that follows. Our current residents will not be pleased, the county won't be pleased, nor will we look good in the eyes of a nation watching the AFFEERCE experiment. There is good news about erring on the side of caution. Even foregoing optimal returns, land speculation always pays off, and in the long run we can expect a huge payoff.

Speculative Ring

Another benefit of land speculation comes from building a speculative ring of undeveloped land around our developed core. The ring gives our land brokers a much larger periphery in which to purchase new land. We are not prey to a small collusion of neighboring property owners, but have a long enough border to generate significant competition in land prices. Every land purchase increases that length. Lack of a community in the undeveloped ring keeps land prices low.

The ring to some extent controls the direction of city growth. One of the competing goals of urban planning is to keep the radius of the ring (the radius of the doughnut minus the radius of the doughnut hole) fixed in all directions. That is if the best prices for land are found to the east, planners will put an eastward bias on city growth. If the ring becomes too lopsided, a new city center can be started to restore balance.

Landowners on the ring's periphery should heed the warning that if they hold out for too high a price, they run the risk of becoming a privately owned island. We will develop around them, and have no further interest in purchasing their land during Phases I or II.

Accommodations

Accommodations	Table 1.2		Debit	Credit	Balance
Setup Year					
Bulldozer/Dump truck (8) INHERIT		8	$50,000	$50,000	0
880 washers/dryers (6) INHERIT		6	$660,000	$660,000	0
3 Kitchens equipment/walk-ins (8) INHERIT		8	$165,000	$165,000	0
Construction tools and equipment (5) INHERIT		5	$2,000,000	$2,000,000	0
Rooftop solar panels (25) INHERIT		25	$1,000,000	$1,000,000	0
Depreciation			$576,875		(576,875)
Year 1		0	$0	$0	(576,875)
Construction tools and equipment (5)		5	$4,000,000	$0	(4,576,875)
Number of kitchens		3	$0	$0	(4,576,875)
Number of buildings to maintain		9	$0	$0	(4,576,875)
Rent			$305,600	$0	(4,882,475)
Number of prefab rooms		2600	$130,000		(5,012,475)
Prefab rooms for affeercianados		1300			(5,012,475)
Number of dorm rooms		0	$0		(5,012,475)
Number of trailer park slots		1000			(5,012,475)
Number of affeercianados in prefab		3900			(5,012,475)
Number of affeercianados in dorms		0			(5,012,475)
Number of affeercianados in trailer park		0			(5,012,475)
Prefab rooms to let		1300			(5,012,475)
Prefab rentals @45 a night		130	$569,400	$2,135,250	(3,446,625)
Prefab rentals @195 a week		780	$1,622,400	$7,909,200	2,840,175
Prefab rentals @700 month		390	$468,000	$3,276,000	5,648,175
Trailer site rentals @22 a day		1000	$3,650,000	$8,030,000	10,028,175
Affeerce A'Cookin @22 a day		1130	$3,299,600	$9,073,900	15,802,475
Affeerce A'Cookin @140 a week		780	$2,068,560	$5,678,400	19,412,315
Affeerce A'Cookin @560 a month		2390	$6,309,600	$16,060,800	29,163,515
Affeercianados working at accommodations		178			29,163,515
Maintenance cost			$540,000		28,623,515
Supply cost			$270,000		28,353,515
Purchase 2 tower cranes (5)		5	$800,000		27,553,515
Materials for City Hall and hospital Dorms (20)		20	$24,000,000		3,553,515
Prefab for 1000 units (not depreciated)			$4,000,000		(446,485)
Rooftop solar panels (25)		25	$1,200,000	$1,200,000	(446,485)
Prefab 4th dining hall			$240,000		(686,485)
Depreciation			$2,784,875		(3,471,360)
Revenue			($3,471,360)		0

In addition to net losses on ground rent, the Affeercianado Accommodations business in Year 1 also suffers a loss. However, much of the loss is depreciation cost.

This affeercianado business continues from the Setup Year. It is responsible for building accommodations for both affeercianados and migrant workers, to realize desired Prosperity growth.

Affeercianado Accommodations has inherited several depreciable assets from the Setup Year. The depreciation for these assets is $576,875. This is taken as an expense. Where does the money go? It goes into a depreciation fund that isn't shown here. The depreciation fund is used to replace assets once they have worn out. It is also a good source of interest free money to fix short term cash flow problems. Using a depreciation fund for anything but asset repair and replacement or a short term loan will never be done in this business plan.

At the end of the Setup Year, there will be 2600 prefabricated motel-style rooms. Arbitrarily, we divide those rooms equally between the affeercianados and migrant workers. With 1300 rooms for affeercianados, 3 to a room, there is space for 3900 affeercianados. Assessing demand stemming from the auction of 650 acres, all rooms need to be filled. The other 1300 rooms are rented out to workers brought in by the development companies, and others who need space until their construction is complete. All 1000 spots in the trailer park are also available to migrant workers and entrepreneurs. There should be no empty rooms or trailer ports. If there are, we can fill them with affeercianados.

What if there are no affeercianados ready to serve? It is the job of the ABC to always have thousands of affeercianados on the waiting list and ready to be deployed. Intense college recruitment, job fair presence, and social media presence, along with an initially large waiting list, should make this a non-issue. While a collective lifestyle is not for everyone, many gravitate to cults and other unhealthy groups just to have this experience. Being an affeercianado offers young people an opportunity to live the collective lifestyle, get a free college education, save the world, learn a diverse set of skills and trades, and end up quite wealthy. Until we are quite certain we can get this message across, we have no business buying the land in the first place.

Major purchases: In Year 1, we purchase $4 million more in construction equipment plus 2 tower cranes for $400,000 each. Most importantly are the materials for 2 luxury affeercianado dormitories (see box, below), one at the city hall site and one at the hospital site. This material costs us $12 million for each dormitory. We are also spending $4 million for 1000 more prefabricated motel-style units, although this cost is variable depending on demand. Given sufficient demand, a fourth dining hall will be built and staffed for $240,000 (ignoring depreciation on the kitchen equipment). Finally, $1.2 million worth of solar panels will supply much of the energy for the finished buildings.

How do we pay for about $30 million worth of material? The Setup Year expenses depleted the land trust of virtually all remaining funds. Even after the advance payment of rent, there is a balance of less than a million, hardly enough to pay for $30 million worth of material.

This $30 million does not come from Accommodation profits as seen in Table 1.2. The affeercianados make a good profit renting out the motel rooms and serving a 24 hour all you can eat buffet at AFFEERCE a'Cookin. Between these and the trailer park, there is almost $27 million in profits. However, with all its expenditures, but not counting affeercianado labor, at the end of the year, "accommodations" is in the hole for $3.4 million.

Estimating the cost of constructing a 300 room dorm

Cost of materials is estimated at $85/sq. ft. The dorm is assumed to be 11 stories, with 30 rooms each on floors, 2 through 11, with a library, game room, storage lockers, 2 utility closets, 3 media rooms and 1 computer room, 2 game rooms, and 2 bathroom/showers and a central stairway in the center of each floor. There are 4 fire stairwells in each corner and exterior elevators stop on one side. The dimensions are 124 feet by 94 feet, with 11 rooms on the two long sides and 9 rooms on the one short side. Other than 4 stairwells, all other rooms and the central staircase are in the middle.

The first floor contains a large meeting/dining room and kitchen. The basement has a laundry, steam, sauna, utility rooms, swimming pool, bowling alley, and gym. Imputed unused space is assumed to be halls and maintenance closets.

Based on these dimensions, the total material cost of the dorm, for 11 stories + basement is $11,949,170. We assume it will take 200 students 1 semester to build. About 30 Jane Jacobs' courses will coordinate each semester to build another dormitory. It is costed at 100 affeercianados working full time for a year.

	Unit price	Quantity	Total Price
Dorm room 10 x 12	$10,200	300	$3,060,000
Stairwell 7 x 7	$4,165	48	$199,920
Bathroom/Shower 28 x 30	$71,400	22	$1,570,800
Central stairway 10 x 8	$6,800	12	$81,600
Media room/Lounge, computer room 12 x 30	$30,600	44	$1,346,400
Game room 20 x 30	$51,000	11	$561,000
Library 20 x 30	$51,000	11	$561,000
Storage lockers 18 x 30	$45,900	11	$504,900
Laundry 8 x 30	$20,400	11	$224,400
Maintenance and supplies 10 x 30	$25,500	11	$280,500
Cafeteria/meeting room 64 x 96	$522,240	1	$522,240
Kitchen/Supplies 40 x 96	$326,400	1	$326,400
Swimming pool 96 x 30	$244,800	1	$244,800
Steam room 15 x 20	$25,500	1	$25,500
Sauna 10 x 20	$17,000	1	$17,000
Gym 89 x 30	$226,950	1	$226,950
Bowling Alley 89 x 24	$181,560	1	$181,560
Utilities/Supplies/Garbage 96 x 18, 20 x 20, 20 x 20	$214,200	1	$214,200
TOTAL			$10,149,170
Imputed hall and maintenance closets	$1,800,000	1	$1,800,000
GRAND TOTAL			$11,949,170

Supply Depot, Import/Export

With Prosperity located in the middle of nowhere, the cost of building materials should be too high for large scale development. Developers do not have the resources to ship at cost, and shipping companies are too expensive to make the job profitable. And if the developer is a few pieces of lumber short, a whole new trip is required.

The Affeercianado Supply Depot will be a giant hardware store of building materials, tools and equipment. At least it will seem that way. While a small build-up of inventory is inevitable, most items will be picked up from wholesalers within a 200 mile radius based on current orders. Because the trucks are dealing with hundreds of orders, and driven by low paid affeercianados, the Supply Depot can charge Old Metropolis retail prices even though a 10% profit is added.

For special imports from ports or rail yards of heavy items ordered directly by the customer, and delivered directly to the customer site, a 15% profit over cost is added. Due to the low cost of affeercianado labor, this is still a bargain.

Although far fewer, exports to the ports or rail yards will minimize the fuel and labor costs of importing. This will be more common once Prosperity develops industry.

This affeercianado business, although not a profit center, is nevertheless one of our most important. Chiefly, low construction costs attract industry and developers. But the affeercianados are also engaged in massive building projects; dormitories, schools, hospitals, community centers, city hall, and so on. Just like the private industry we wish to entice, we too will save hundreds of millions in material cost because of the Supply Depot. But this has already been taken into account in estimating the $30 million the affeercianados need for Year 1. Clearly it does not come from the Supply Depot.

Supply Depot Table 1.3		Debit	Credit	Balance
Setup Year	0	$0	$0	$0
2 Refrigerated Food Trucks (5) INHERIT	5	$80,000	$80,000	$0
3 rigs (5) INHERIT	5	$150,000	$150,000	$0
4 trailers (3) INHERIT	3	$40,000	$40,000	$0
4 flatbed trucks, boom/rollback (5) INHERIT	5	$200,000	$200,000	$0
10 cargo containers (4) INHERIT	4	$30,000	$30,000	$0
Depreciation		$106,833		($106,833)
Year 1	0	$0	$0	($106,833)
Number of rigs and flatbeds	31			($106,833)
Distance to major city in miles	120			($106,833)
Number of refrigerated food trucks	2			($106,833)
Estimate number of trips needed	13206			($106,833)
Number of trips	22630			($106,833)
Miles per gallon rigs and flatbeds	4			($106,833)
Miles per gallon food trucks	5			($106,833)
Fuel cost @$3 per gallon	3	$2,141,820		($2,248,653)
Affeercianado Workers	70	$794,640	$794,640	($2,248,653)
Maintenance parts/utilities		$100,000		($2,348,653)
Cost of trips at 10% profit	42		$1,320,183	($1,028,470)
Cost of trips at 15% profit	37		$1,163,019	$134,548
Profit on 10% trips	10		$132,018	$266,567
Profit on 15% trips	15		$174,453	$441,020
Purchase 12 rigs (5)	5	$600,000		($158,981)
Purchase 10 trailers (3)	3	$100,000		($258,981)
16 flatbed trucks, boom/rollback (5)	5	$800,000		($1,058,981)
40 cargo containers (4)	4	$120,000		($1,178,981)
Purchase Refrigerated Food Truck (5)	5	$40,000		($1,218,981)
Depreciation		$458,167		($1,677,147)
Revenue		($1,677,147)		$0

The Supply Depot inherited a number of trucks from the Setup Year. In addition, in Year 1, it will purchase 12 more rigs, 10 trailers, 16 flatbed trucks, 40 more cargo containers, and another food truck.

In Year 1, 42% of trips are done for 10% over cost and 37% of trips are done for 15% over cost. The other 21% of trips are taken to transport materials for affeercianado projects. In this accounting, the expense for affeercianado transport is taken by the Supply Depot. As the ratio of trips for profit increases over the years, the entire cost of affeercianado material shipment will be absorbed, and a profit will be shown. In Year 1, primarily due to significant vehicle purchases, there is a deficit of $1.7 million.

Suppose you ordered this 1,440 sq. ft. 3-bedroom, 2-bath home from Conestoga Log Cabins for $104,900 with an additional $10,000 to ship to a rail yard 80 miles from Prosperity. The affeercianado supply depot will pick up the cargo and deliver it to your building site for under $300. You might consider bidding on 6 prefab builders for 2 weeks to complete your home. Prefab experts will be in high demand, so assume $12/hour. The cost to build your home would be 6 * $12/hour * 80 hours = $5,760. Developer impact fees would run $7,500, building inspections, an additional $100. Utility connection is free and absorbed in utility delivery charges. A 1/4 acre site might be won for $800 a year, frozen for the next 19, and that includes property tax.

Metrobus

As a free service to our residents, Metrobus makes 6 or more trips to Old Metropolis every day. Four of the trips are timed for commuters who live in Prosperity, but work in the city about 1.5 hours away. The other two are designed for shoppers and those who wish to spend an evening in the city. If demand is greater, more buses will be added.

The notion of hopping on a bus any day of the week and going to Old Metropolis at no charge eliminates the feeling of isolation that might scare away prospective homesteaders. Business persons will find that a free 1.5 hour commute with Wi-Fi, comfortable seats, and a bathroom, beats a 45 minute commute fighting rush hour, paying for gas, and paying exorbitant rates for downtown parking. Metrobus alone could double the number of people interested in buying a home or renting in Prosperity.

This is a slightly profitable business. However, if more buses are added, the margins will grow worse due to a limited number of potential side contracts.

Typically, the affeercianado driver will spend 1.5 hours traveling to the city, four hours unloading and loading cargo, running paid errands (delivering messages or small goods, and purchasing small goods), taking a lunch break, then 1.5 hours on the drive back to prosperity. Time in the city could be longer to accommodate commuters. For a small surcharge, purchased goods can be delivered directly to the home or business who ordered them.

Tips are not accepted

At 8:00 PM, when the nice affeercianado bus driver brings you the gourmet salami and wheel of Gouda cheese she picked up in the city that day the temptation will be to give a nice tip. Ask instead for a donation envelope. These are marked so she collects 1% of any donation you make. The other 99% goes directly to the land trust to increase the affeercianado share of land. Furthermore, any donations you make over the 20 year period add to your free opening bid for selective distribution in the Phase-II homesteader auctions. There is also a free $2,000 opening bid for every year you are registered to vote in Prosperity, so $50,000 of donations in lieu of tips during 20 years of resident citizenship will likely win basic income in the first auction without having to bid any of your own money.

So don't tip the affeercianados, but donate generously in their name and yours.

Metrobus	Table 1.4		Debit	Credit	Balance
Setup Year		0	$0	$0	$0
3 luxury buses (6)		6	$1,200,000	$1,200,000	$0
Depreciation			$200,000		($200,000)
Year 1		0	$0	$0	($200,000)
Total trips		4380	$0		($200,000)
Passenger's cargo-Suitcases assume 100 lbs./trip		10	$0	$87,600	($112,400)
U.S. Mail cargo contract		10	$0	$87,600	($24,800)
Shipping company cargo contract		20	$0	$175,200	$150,400
Business cargo @$1 for 10 lbs., assume 1000 lbs./trip		100	$0	$876,000	$1,026,400
Messenger service average 2/trip (costs extra)		30	$0	$262,800	$1,289,200
Maintenance Cost @$20/trip		20	$87,600		$1,201,600
Tolls/access @$20/trip		20	$87,600		$1,114,000
Fuel cost Total trips * distance*2/4 MPG*$3/gal		4	$788,400		$325,600
3 luxury buses (6)		6	$1,200,000		($874,400)
Depreciation			$400,000		($1,274,400)
Revenue			($1,274,400)		$0

In Year 1, three more luxury buses will be purchased for $400,000 a piece, bringing the total to 6 buses. The loss of just over $1.6 million will be a small gain in subsequent years with few new vehicle purchases plus the increased U.S. Mail and shipping cargo that come with population gains. The depreciation fund is sufficient to replace buses as they wear down. The older vehicles can be reactivated if demand unexpectedly increases.

As you can see from Table 1.4, money is made from contracts with the U.S. Post Office, shipping companies, and a messenger and buyer's service. Metrobus is clearly not the source of the $30 million needed to build the dormitories.

The Affeercianado Hospital

It is the Thomas Paine Hospital as much as the free land and cheap labor offered business that will shape the future growth of Prosperity. Medical care will be our chief export.

Why medical care? Medicine is a monopoly protected by the U.S. Government. Those who compete with the American Medical Association are thrown in prison. Sentences are even worse for those who dare compete with the pharmaceutical industry.

It is not that we plan to defy the government in Phase-I. Deregulation will occur after capitulation. Rather, the monopoly has created a unique opportunity. It has led to so much waste and inefficiency that health care costs have skyrocketed with both higher wages for healthcare workers and huge profits going to corporations that own the hospitals. Recently, even the high wages of health care professionals are being squeezed as hospitals push for greater and greater profits. However, the aura of liability and large capital requirements discourage even legal competition.

By staffing the Thomas Paine Hospital with affeercianados, we gain a fundamental competitive advantage. Medicare and PPO's have agreed to pay for treatment at a rate that includes standard salaries and a built-in profit. Those profits can amount to billions of dollars for a single hospital. Affeercianado wages are significantly lower than the average health care professional. Therefore profits will be significantly higher. After growth, the majority of profits will be invested for the affeercianados in land. As a side benefit, all the citizens of Prosperity will receive free medical care, while county and state residents can buy very inexpensive no-deductible policies. With Affordable Healthcare subsidies, they will be virtually free. Residents on Medicare will receive a free supplementary policy.

There will likely be a shortage of doctors who sign on as affeercianados. Those that do will be treated royally in terms of a short work week, allowing for a private practice on the side. However, all affeercianados receive the same pay. Nevertheless, doctors who put in only 12 hours a week will receive 12 land credits, while the average affeercianado will receive credit for 50 to 60 hours per week.

The hospital administrator and a number of doctors will be on moderately high salary and not members of the Affeercianado Guild. If an affeercianado specialist has the same or greater capabilities than a paid specialist, and is able to assume the workload, the paid specialist will be terminated or phased out. Although not members of the Guild, paid employees receive affeercianado future land monetization benefits, at 37.5 land credits per week. Compensation in land credits acts to keep salaries low. Beyond city department heads, large project managers, and physicians, there will be no paid employees. Unlike department heads and project managers, specialists, surgeons, and other physicians will be replaced by qualified affeercianados, if possible.

The insurance offered by Thomas Paine is an HMO. Included in the premium cost is a policy for emergency treatment anywhere in the country and medivac back to Prosperity for non-critical care. Many of Prosperity's wealthier citizens will find this policy overly restrictive. For this reason, the hospital will be part of as many PPO networks as possible. Because we charge the lowest prices, most networks will allow us in. Citizens that join a PPO network that we are members of will receive a $25 per month subsidy from Prosperity for each policy in the family. This is in addition to subsidies from the Affordable Care Act.

For those in the HMO, ambulance radius will ultimately be 120 miles and include Old Metropolis. Outside of Prosperity, Old Metropolis will be the most likely place illness or injury will strike. After emergency treatment in the city, our ambulances will return the patient to Prosperity for continued care. This substantially reduces the cost of the medivac policy. However, it will be 12 years before the ambulance network is completed.

Medical treatment by the HMO is not completely free. There are $35 copays for various services. However, the copays for residents are placed on the smartcard. If unpaid, they will be charged against future citizen's dividends at a considerable premium.

Affeercianados are exempt from copays. Their treatment is absolutely free. Another powerful motivation for the hospital is the low premium of $100 per month required for HMO membership. Instead of paying $200 to $300 per month per affeercianado for PPO membership, and then having to pay a large deductible if needed, the Affeercianado Guild pays only $100 per month per affeercianado and nothing more. This is shown on Table I2 as $110 per month, but the $10 independently goes for liability insurance.

Like the university, the hospital is administered by a board of trustees consisting of affeercianados selected by the ABC Board and ratified by the Affeercianado Guild. The paid hospital administrator also sits on the board. Major decisions of the Thomas Paine Board of Trustees must be ratified by the Guild, and the Guild can remove trustees by a 2/3 majority. Bidders or treblers of the chancellery can be prevented from bid or treble, or dethroned by a 2/3 majority of the Thomas Paine Board of Trustees.

During the first two years, Thomas Paine will be constrained to the 32-bed hospital annex. In Year 2, however, we will begin construction on a state-of-the-art hospital chancellery.

Thomas Paine Hospital	Table 1.5		Debit	Credit	Balance
Setup Year		1	$0	$0	$0
Materials for 32 bed Hospital Annex (20) INHERIT		20	$4,000,000	$4,000,000	$0
Medical Equipment (8) INHERIT		8	$1,400,000	$1,400,000	$0
Hospital Furniture/Equipment (10) INHERIT		10	$140,000	$140,000	$0
Uniforms, Linens, Towels (5) INHERIT		5	$10,000	$10,000	$0
Depreciation			$391,000		($391,000)
Year 1 -32 beds					($391,000)
Copay Ratio/Premium multiplier		0.05	1.00		($391,001)
Paid doctors + administrator		4	$800,000		($1,191,001)
Total surgery hours		410	$10,250		($1,201,251)
Paid staff surgery hours		205	$61,500		($1,262,751)
Medicare/PPO surgery hours		136.67		$95,667	($1,167,084)
Average beds used per night		1.12	$10,250		($1,177,334)
Medicare/PPO Beds used per night		0.37		$205,000	($972,334)
Average out patients per day		11.23	$41,000	$6,300	($1,007,034)
Average daily ER visits		1.40	$5,125	$1,750	($1,010,409)
Average daily generic drugs prescribed		11.23	$41,000	$36,900	($1,014,509)
Average daily non-generic drugs prescribed		1.12	$24,600	$630	($1,038,479)
Average daily specialty drugs prescribed		0.11	$16,400	$360	($1,054,519)
Medicare/PPO specialty drugs		0.04		$6,833	($1,047,686)
Average tests and procedures per day		4.87	$17,767	$2,730	($1,062,723)
Medicare/PPO tests and procedures per day		1.62		$118,444	($944,278)
Lab work per day		6.74	$49,200	$3,780	($989,698)
Hospital liability		2.53	$50,257		($1,039,956)
Premiums		4100		$4,920,000	$3,880,044
Food			$4,100		$3,875,944
Bandages and Special Appliances			$18,450		$3,857,494
Internal and topical medicines			$500,000		$3,357,494
Prosthesis and Take Home Equipment			$16,400		$3,341,094
Heat, air, electric, cable			$444,000		$2,897,094
Medivac and travel policy			$49,200		$2,847,894
Miscellaneous and unanticipated			$20,000		$2,827,894
Depreciation			$391,000		$2,436,894
Affeercianado Workers		50	$0		$2,436,894
Return to Affeercianados			$2,436,894		$0

In Year 1, Thomas Paine shows a profit of over $2.4 million dollars. Premiums are calculated using the sum of affeercianados and Prosperity homesteaders, all of whom receive free medical coverage. A premium multiplier, assumed to be 1.0 in the first two years, accounts for other county residents taking advantage of the extremely inexpensive medical care. The number of premiums is multiplied by the $1,200 annual premium. There is also the assumption that we have convinced a few PPO's to accept our rather small but very inexpensive hospital. Older residents, who receive free supplemental Medicare policies and $25/month toward their Medicare Part A, are assumed to be exactly balanced in number by other county residents.

Thus $4,920,000 is collected in premiums in Year 1. For local residents who chose to be covered by a PPO, Prosperity will only contribute $75 to premiums, the other $25 returned to the citizen as a subsidy. This is ignored in as much as savings in the other categories and large PPO revenues should more than compensate for the lost $25 a month. Like those insured in a PPO, Medicare patients also receive the $25 monthly subsidy. In addition, they receive free supplemental coverage at the HMO.

All expense categories are computed as a function of annual premiums paid. The number of uninsured is assumed to be negligible. For instance, surgery hours are equal to 10% of premium payers. Beds used per night are set equal to 10% of premium payers/365. Outpatients per day are simply equal to premium payers/365. It is assumed that a premium payer will average 1 outpatient visit per year. But notice that the credit for these visits exceeds the debit. That is due to the $35 copay for a doctor's visit and the virtually free cost of affeercianado labor.

This is the list of copayments. The same copayment (except for ER visit) cannot be charged more than once a month.

Table 1.6 – Proposed Copays	
Doctor visits in any month	$35
Medical testing in any month	$35
ER (each visit)	$35
Ambulance (each use)	$35
Inpatient admission	$35
Surgery or procedure	$35
Generic prescription per month	$10
Non-generic prescription per month	$35
Specialty drug per month	$200
Medical home equipment or cost if lower	$200

Unfortunately we have no leverage over the pharmaceutical industry or their protectionist patents. Once there is capitulation to full AFFEERCE, and possibly as early as Phase-II, patent holders will be rewarded from the intellectual property distribution for the number of people using the drug, which varies inversely with the price charged and directly with its effectiveness. For Phase-I, we are forced to charge $200/month for specialty drugs.

Those over 65 constitute a third of all hospital patients. By assuming 1/3 of all hospital beds and surgeries are Medicare or PPO, we err on the side of extreme caution, since Medicare patients alone should constitute 1/3 of these. Interestingly, the $307,500 brought in from Medicare/PPO beds is dwarfed by the amount brought in by our very low premiums. Clearly insurance companies are sharing in the industry super-profits. Our self-insured HMO is reaping double benefits for both the affeercianados and the citizens.

Surplus Labor

The profit shown by the hospital in Year 1 will be insufficient to cover the losses in Accommodations, Metrobus, and the Supply Depot, although most of the losses are due to the need for rapid capital expansion. Since the land trust has little money at the start of the year, where does the cash come from? The answer is at the heart of Phase-I. Even if there was to be no Thomas Paine Memorial Hospital, no Supply Depot or Metrobus, this alone would give us a better than even shot at success.

It costs $5.50 an hour for an affeercianado including Social Security and Medicare. Leased out at an average $9 an hour, there is $3.50/hour of pure profit. At $13/hour overtime on average, all is profit. The demand for affeercianado labor at these rates in a new city with hundreds, if not thousands, of simultaneous construction projects is predicted to be enormous.

Rates are bid on each affeercianado as an individual. A picture, resume/bio, and updated skillset are presented, usually with a minimum bid of $8/hour. All affeercianados have bids, but those on work teams, in class, or with assigned tasks will have minimum bids that are quite high, perhaps $20/hour or more. If those bids are exceeded, the assigned task will either be delayed or performed by another affeercianado. If an affeercianado gets pulled out of school by a bidder, they must make up the schoolwork on their own time, or retake the course. Affeercianados who have worked over 40 hours in the preceding 7 days will have minimum bids of $13 an hour.

Surplus Labor Table 1.7	Workers	Debit	Credit	Balance
Year 1	0	$0	$0	0
Total Affeercianados	3900	$44,272,800	$9,360,000	(34,912,800)
Affeercianado Businesses				(34,912,800)
Hospital personnel	50			(34,912,800)
University/med school non-construction personnel	78			(34,912,800)
Import/export depot	70			(34,912,800)
Major city Metrobus service	8			(34,912,800)
AMS/Smartcard workers	42			(34,912,800)
Servicing affeercianado accommodations	178		$2,020,656	(32,892,144)
Affeercianado Public Works and all Construction				(32,892,144)
Dorm building crew	200			(32,892,144)
Downtown excavators	100			(32,892,144)
Municipal building crew	0			(32,892,144)
Education building crew	50		$520,000	(32,372,144)
Hospital/JJ University/Medical campus building crew	200		$2,080,000	(30,292,144)
Special projects crew (1000 prefab units)	100			(30,292,144)
Education				(30,292,144)
Teachers, Clerical and maintenance	2		$20,800	(30,271,344)
Municipal Service (no worker charge until Year 3)	0			(30,271,344)
Roads and infrastructure	102		$0	(30,271,344)
Waste management	40			(30,271,344)
City Hall	55			(30,271,344)
Police and public safety	15		$0	(30,271,344)
Fire and paramedic	24		$0	(30,271,344)
Parks and recreation	0			(30,271,344)
Affeercianado Surplus Labor				(30,271,344)
Number to lease @9 with average overtime of 10 hours @13	2586		$65,882,787	35,611,443
Return to Affeercianados		$35,611,443		0

Table 1.7 shows the total number of affeercianados, how many are working in the various businesses and departments, and how many are available for lease.

In Year 1, there is a total of 3900 affeercianados, at an employment cost of $44,272,800. There is a credit of $9,360,000 for low utilities and housing costs expensed elsewhere.

There are 50 affeercianados working the hospital annex, 70 at the supply depot, 8 at Metrobus, 42 at Smartcard, 40 at waste management, and 178 affeercianados serving other affeercianados. Since those 178 are paid from the food and housing allocations, their salary is a credit, $2,020,656, on Table 1.7.

In construction, there are 200 affeercianados building dorms at the hospital and at the future city hall site. 100 are doing downtown excavation, 200 are building the Jane Jacobs' Chancellery, 50 are building an elementary school and another 100 are working on the motel style prefabs. The 50 affeercianados building the elementary school are being rented out to the school district at $5 an hour, hence the credit of $520,000. The 200 building the Chancellery produce a credit of over $2 million. The municipality, the school district, and the University pay for affeercianado labor at $5 an hour; however the Prosperity charge is waived until Year 3 and the onset of incorporation paperwork. Until that time, the city is formally run by the affeercianados. Keep in mind this is all private property, so city management is akin to private property management. The spreadsheets will be modified to reflect standard accounting practices.

In municipal service, there is the roads and infrastructure team with 102 affeercianados, 55 at city hall even though the actual city hall has yet to be built. Most of these are in building and planning to handle the onslaught of new construction. There are 15 police and public safety and 24 fire and paramedic affeercianados.

That leaves 2,586 affeercianados available for leasing. At $9/hour and $13/hour for 10 hours of overtime, this brings in gross revenue of over $65 million! Why is this extremely conservative? Because it does not take into account any of the following:

1. The average wage can be as high as $14/hour with OT at $21/hour before more affeercianados are brought on board. Even this is less than the median cost of a construction worker[FTN1.42].
2. Exceptional wage earners who have valuable skillsets are best removed from the average calculations.
3. Affeercianados, not full-time students or assigned to other tasks, are expected to put in 20 hours of overtime.
4. The numbers only count affeercianados not assigned to other tasks. However, temporarily idled affeercianados are expected to put themselves up for auction during the idle time.

In the end, after all wage expenses and credits are counted, the leasing of affeercianados brings in over $35 million in profit. If there were no affeercianados doing other tasks, the profits would be even higher - near $50 million.

This economic certainty is the essence of the entire business plan. It is literally the force that will change the world.

If high demand pushes the average hourly rate above $14/hour, we will shift priority to new prefabricated housing and fill that housing with affeercianados until the average bid price stabilizes and shows signs of retreating back to $9/hour. Should the average bid price fall below $9/hour, we will auction off more land.

Assuming an endless supply of affeercianados on the waiting list, and enough land to auction, this tool provides a high degree of control over growth.

Here is the complete Year 1 Affeercianado balance sheet:

Affeercianados Table	Debit	Credit	Balance	Borrow	Borrowed
Year 1 with initial debt	$0	$0	$0	$0	$37,487,800
Hospital	$0	$2,436,894	$2,436,894	$0	$37,487,800
Accommodations	$0	($3,471,360)	($1,034,466)	$0	$37,487,800
Supply Depot	$0	($1,677,147)	($2,711,613)	$0	$37,487,800
Surplus Labor	$0	$35,611,443	$32,899,830	$0	$37,487,800
AMS Software	$0	$0	$32,899,830	$0	$37,487,800
Metro Bus Service	$0	($1,274,400)	$31,625,430	$0	$37,487,800
Downtown excavation	$0	($6,200,960)	$25,424,470	$0	$37,487,800
Rent Dividend	$0	$233,500	$25,657,970	$0	$37,487,800
Pay Unauctioned land Rent	$0	($400,000)	$25,257,970	$0	$37,487,800
Borrow from land trust	$0	$0	$25,257,970	$0	$37,487,800
Rent Owed	$305,600	$305,600	$25,257,970	$0	$37,487,800
Grant to municipality	$10,000,000	$0	$15,257,970	$0	$37,487,800

Although we cannot yet pay back the initial debt of $37,487,800 borrowed from the land trust for Setup Year expenses, revenue from leasing out the affeercianados has left us with a credit balance of $25 million at the end of the year. The new municipality is in need of funds, so $10 million is granted as a "gift." The money will be used mostly for medical premiums that increase land value with greater than 100% efficiency and furthermore will be directed to the Thomas Paine Hospital, an affeercianado enterprise.

Downtown Excavation

Like everything in the business plan, the nature of downtown is subject to approval by the ABC Board. However, the downtown plan is also subject to approval by materials and other engineers. One of the two paid professors in Year 1 at Jane Jacobs will be a materials engineer, who will give the go-ahead on any plan.

A 200 acre downtown which includes a 30 acre central park is intended to be the crown jewel of Prosperity. The entire downtown, including the park, is built on a common foundation over a partially excavated 30 ft. high double-decker foundation; an upper-lower and lower-lower level. The size of the foundation is a significant engineering challenge due to stress from earth movement. The final design might involve many foundations connected by a flexible material to appear as a seamless whole.

Passenger elevators in all downtown buildings will go down as far as the upper-lower level, while specialty freight elevators, including large-parcel sized elevators will drop to the lowest level.

The major streets at the upper street level will be mirrored at the upper-lower level to give a strong sense of location. Most of the real estate at the upper-lower level will be taken-up by parking and loading docks. There will be pedways for pedestrians isolated from the traffic lanes and kept at a moderate temperature in the winter. Surrounding the entire perimeter, with the exception of automobile/truck access and egress are buildings that front the upper level downtown on their second floor and the lower level on their first. This too, is an engineering challenge. We do not want the foundation to rip away from a perimeter building with normally insignificant seismic activity. A gap of several feet of compressible soil might be required.

All utilities pass along the roof of the upper-lower level and are easily accessed. Two new utilities are introduced. These are hot air and hot water, obviating the need for buildings to install and maintain boilers. This is called district heating and is both environmentally and economically efficient. It will likely supplement individual rooftop HVAC systems for ventilation and cooling. However, the feasibility of district cooling will be investigated.

The lower-lower level will have additional parking areas. However, it will have several novel features. There will be driverless transportation roadways for inter-business production control, including simple pickup and delivery of merchandise. A simple application might be automated shopping for gifts at four different stores, transportation to a wrapping center, followed by transportation to a shipping firm, all done from home. The driverless roadways will extend from the lower-lower level virtual north-west into the industrial areas. A new concept, a solid waste sewer, runs in the lower-lower level on a conveyer system, and takes all garbage dropped through chutes to a single exit where it is loaded on trucks for the material recovery facility. A solid waste sewer eliminates the odor of garbage on all levels, even in the buildings themselves. However, before the solid waste sewer is complete, the chutes will empty into dumpsters picked up either in normal collection or by the automated vehicles. Just beneath the floor of the lower-lower level is the drainage system whose flow is based on the nature of the watershed.

Soil from the excavation is used to fill upper level parkways and build up hills in the central park to a safe weight. This will allow sledding and skiing during winter months. Excavated soil will also be used to create gentle slopes from the side of the upper level to the ground level where buildings are not yet present.

Streets at the upper level are narrow, often single lane. If feasible, they will be built with solar bricks to help power the grid and automate snow removal. Sidewalks too, will be built from solar bricks for the same purpose. 4-lane boulevards with benched parkways in the middle are used for bus routes. Beyond the boulevards, the streets are created around the building designs of architects. Angles, short streets, and circles could be common, leaving a Greenwich Village like maze. The extent that all of these tiny angled streets are inherited at the lower level is a matter of traffic efficiency. The sense of location need not be exact.

The upper downtown will be free of alleys, garbage, and parking. Light vehicle traffic will be predominantly taxis and jitneys with some tourist.

Land is intended for mixed use 21-story high-rises with first-floor retail, and the remaining floors divided between residences, offices, retail, and clean industry. All buildings should strive for a minimum of 30% residential to insure urban vitality. Sidewalk cafes should be popular owing to the clean downtown environment.

Bids on downtown land will require a general set of building plans and preliminary drawings in addition to the statement of intention. Architects are encouraged to incorporate solar and wind energy into their designs. The building and planning team can reject bids on downtown land that do not meet its goals.

The 100 person downtown excavation and foundation team can create 12 acres of downtown excavation and foundation a year. The first auction of 4 acres is set for the end of Year 1. It likely will prove more efficient to stagger downtown and general land auctions. It is certainly best to err on the side of caution until we better understand the requirements and availability of workers and material.

Excavating Downtown Table 1.9		Debit	Credit	Balance
Year 1	8	$0	$0	$0
Foundation materials cost		$2,000,000		($2,000,000)
Fuel cost 8*24 hrs.*4 gal/hr.*$3/gal*365	4	$840,960		($2,840,960)
8 excavators/dump trucks (5)	5	$800,000		($3,640,960)
Foundation tools and equipment (5)	5	$2,000,000		($5,640,950)
Depreciation		$560,000		($6,200,950)
Borrow from Affeercianados		($6,200,960)		$0

The loss of over $6 million in Year 1 is due in part to the purchase of tools, equipment and vehicles. However, this project has no revenue source, save the possible selling of soil, and will generate an annual loss for the affeercianados.

If the downtown is indeed the crown jewel of Prosperity, it will pay for itself in land value many times over. Revenue from district heat and hot water will bring large profits to Prosperity through the roads and infrastructure team.

The City

Be warned. Planning a city is an interactive process with developers, homesteaders, retailers, and industry. If we build it, they might not come. This beautiful city in China has no residents.

Although Prosperity is unincorporated in Year 1, we are building the infrastructure and organization for a major city. The departments are all under the auspices of the ABC and affeercianados. It will be 4 years before there is an elected city council.

Roads and Infrastructure

In this budget there is no developer impact fee for roads and infrastructure. That is because roads and infrastructure quickly becomes very profitable from utility delivery fees. Delivery fees for cable, electric, water, and gas, and transit fees for drainage and sewage are assumed to total an average $40 per household/business per month. There will be considerable variance, but $40/month would seem to be quite conservative when large retail and industry is included in the total.

For heat and hot water downtown, there are not only delivery fees but supply fees as well. In Year 1, none of downtown has yet been built. It is possible, depending on Prosperity's location that additional costs and revenues will be associated with water supply.

Roads and Infrastructure Table 1.10		Debit	Credit	Balance
Setup Year	0	$0	$0	$0
Road infrastructure tools and equipment (5) INHERIT	5	$4,000,000	$4,000,000	$0
Utility infrastructure materials (16) INHERIT	16	$1,000,000	$1,000,000	$0
Road infrastructure materials (10) INHERIT	10	$1,000,000	$1,000,000	$0
Road signs and signals (12) [RoadsInfra] AA	12	$666,667	$666,667	$0
Depreciation		$1,018,056		($1,018,056)
Year 1	0	$0	$0	($1,018,056)
Road Miles	14			($1,018,056)
Road acres @1 mile = 5 acres	70			($1,018,056)
Rent = $2000/acre*.10		$14,000	$0	($1,032,056)
Affeercianados working at infrastructure	100	$0		($1,032,056)
Maintenance cost		$21,000		($1,053,056)
Gas tax revenue sharing		$0	$4,000	($1,049,056)
Municipal parking subsidiary		$0	($20,000)	($1,069,056)
Utility delivery charge and taxes		$0	$656,000	($413,056)
Office supplies		$20,000		($433,056)
Utility infrastructure materials (16)	16	$1,000,000		($1,433,056)
Road infrastructure materials (10)	10	$1,000,000		($2,433,056)
Road signs and signals (12)	12	$1,000,000		($3,433,056)
Depreciation		$1,263,889		($4,696,944)
Revenue		($4,696,944)		$0

Despite earning $656,000 in utility delivery charges, roads and infrastructure shows a loss of $4.7 million in Year 1. Profitability is not expected until Year 3.

Police and Public Safety

Although police and fire protection will be combined in the plan in a department of public safety, fire and paramedic is broken out in the tables separately. Combined public safety stations are expensed on the police and public safety account.

In Year 1, police and fire will operate out of a room in the hospital annex. In Year's 2 and 3, they will operate from the lower residential floor in the dormitory at city hall. At the end of Year 3, the city hall station will be complete.

In this first year, there are 10 affeercianado police officers and a paid director of public safety who manages police, fire fighters and paramedics. Three more squad cars are purchased to bring the total to 5. There is $2,000 annual maintenance on each vehicle. $10,000 is allocated each officer for uniforms, weapons and supplies. Five additional affeercianados are commanders and/or clerical.

Depending on the laws of the host state, the status of the police prior to incorporation will likely be no higher than that of security guards on private property, which is what they in fact, are. Still the utmost professionalism, dash-cams, and body-cams must be used.

54

Police and Public Safety	Table 1.11		Debit	Credit	Balance
Setup Year		0	$0	$0	$0
2 squad cars (6)		6	$100,000	$0	($100,000)
Depreciation			$0		($100,000)
Year 1		0	$0	$0	($100,000)
Police Chief /Director of public safety includes adjacent fire stations		0	$100,000	$0	($200,000)
Clerical and command affeercianados		3	$0	$0	($200,000)
Police officer affeercianados		10	$100,000	$0	($300,000)
Video surveillance/dash-cams/body-cams/automated ticketing team		0	$1,000	$0	($301,000)
School crossing guards (part time - number is x 3 full time equivalent)		2	$0	$0	($301,000)
Total affeercianados		15	$0	$0	($301,000)
Vehicles		5	$10,000	$0	($311,000)
Police station Rent		0	$0	$0	($311,000)
Number of districts		1	$0	$0	($311,000)
Fuel		0	$27,375	$0	($338,375)
Police station utilities			$0	$0	($338,375)
Fines (from automated ticketing only)		0	$0	$0	($338,375)
Office supplies			$20,000	$0	($358,375)
3 squad cars (6)		6	$150,000	$0	($508,375)
Depreciation			$41,667	$0	($550,042)
Revenue			($550,042)	$0	$0

Fire and Paramedic

Fire and Paramedic	Table 1.12		Debit	Credit	Balance
Setup Year		0	$0	$0	$0
Fire engine (8)		8	$150,000	$0	($150,000)
Fire pumper (8)		8	$40,000	$0	($190,000)
2 Ambulance (5)		5	$100,000	$0	($290,000)
Depreciation			$43,750		($333,750)
Year 1		0	$0	$0	($333,750)
Clerical and command affeercianados		4	$0	$0	($333,750)
Fire fighter affeercianados		10	$100,000	$0	($433,750)
Fire building inspection team, Arson investigators, paramedics		10	$100,000	$0	($533,750)
Total affeercianados		24	$0	$0	($533,750)
Vehicles		5	$10,000	$0	($543,750)
Number of districts		1	$0	$0	($543,750)
Fuel		0	$27,375	$0	($571,125)
Fire station utilities			$0	$0	($571,125)
Inspection fees		0	$0	$390,000	($181,125)
Office supplies			$20,000	$0	($201,125)
Fire engine (8)		8	$150,000	$0	($351,125)
Depreciation			$62,500	$0	($413,625)

In Year 1, an additional fire engine is purchased to bring the total vehicles to 2 engines, a pumper, and 2 ambulances. There are 10 fire fighters and 10 more fire inspectors, paramedics, and arson investigators. $10,000 is allocated per non-clerical employee for uniform and equipment.

The fire department will have a source of income with inspection fees and ambulance copays, but these fees will not make the fire department profitable, unlike the city as a whole.

City Hall

Although city hall exists in a few prefabricated motel rooms in Year 1, it still has important duties, even pre-incorporation.

City Hall Table 1.13		Debit	Credit	Balance
Setup Year	0	$0	0	$0
Underground fuel tank and pumping station (16)	16	$20,000		($20,000)
Computer equip for AMS - office in hospital annex (3)	3	$30,000	$0	($50,000)
Depreciation		$11,250		($61,250)
Year 1	0	$0	$0	($61,250)
City Manager	0	$150,000	$0	($211,250)
City Manager's Office	1	$0	$0	($211,250)
Public Safety liaison	1	$0	$0	($211,250)
Parks and Recreation liaison	0	$0	$0	($211,250)
Roads and Infrastructure liaison	1	$0	$0	($211,250)
Waste Management liaison	1	$0	$0	($211,250)
Transportation liaison	0	$0	$0	($211,250)
City/University Library liaison	0	$0	$0	($211,250)
Hospital/Med campus liaison	1	$0	$0	($211,250)
Janitorial/Maintenance/Garage	2	$0	$0	($211,250)
Building and Planning	18	$0	$390,000	$178,750
City Treasurer	0	$100,000	$0	$78,750
Finance	3	$0	$0	$78,750
Purchasing	4	$0	$0	$78,750
Rent collection, liens and trebling	5	$0	$0	$78,750
City Attorney	0	$100,000	$0	($21,250)
Legal	3	$0	$0	($21,250)
City liability insurance	0	$2,000	$0	($23,250)
Municipal Judge	0	$0	$0	($23,250)
Municipal Judge's Office	0	$0	$0	($23,250)
City Clerk	0	$100,000	$0	($123,250)
City Clerks office	3	$0	$2,000	($121,250)
Gift catalog	2	$0	$0	($121,250)
Software and smartcard AMS liaison	6	$0	$0	($121,250)
Food, health, and sanitation inspectors	2	$0	$200	($121,050)
Voter registration, candidate management, online voting	0	$0	$0	($121,050)
Human resources	2	$0	$0	($121,050)
Total affeercianados	55	$0	$0	($121,050)
City Hall supplies	0	$5,000	$0	($126,050)
City Hall utilities	0	$5,000	$0	($131,050)
Computer equipment (4)	4	$150,000	$0	($281,050)
Depreciation		$48,750	$0	($329,800)
Revenue		($329,800)	$0	$0

Building and planning is the most active department in Year 1, with 18 affeercianados. They will inspect and approve the plans of the 1,300 buildings constructed during the year. At an average of $300 in inspection fees per building, they will bring in revenue of $390,000.

Purchasing for all city supplies, equipment, and materials goes through the treasurer's office where all assets are inventoried and accounted. Prior to Year 4, this office handles affeercianado supplies, equipment, and materials purchasing as well.

The city will be discussed in far greater detail in Year 4, Prosperity's year of incorporation. However, if we look at the city as a whole, it is clear that during Year 1, it operates at a loss.

Prosperity Table 1.14	Debit	Credit	Balance
Year 1	$0	$0	$0
Grant from affeercianados	$0	$10,000,000	$10,000,000
Roads and infrastructure	$0	($4,696,944)	$5,303,056
City Hall	$0	($329,800)	$4,973,256
Parks and Recreation	$0	$0	$4,973,256
Police	$0	($550,042)	$4,423,214
Fire	$0	($413,625)	$4,009,589
Waste Management	$0	($982,250)	$3,027,339
Hospital Premiums	$240,000	$0	$2,787,339
Rent Dividend	$0	$313,380	$3,100,719
Rent Owed (10% only)	$9,600	$9,600	$3,100,719

A $10 million grant from the affeercianados solves the problem, leaving a positive balance of $3 million after expenses. In the years before incorporation, money is borrowed from the land trust by the affeercianados and given as a direct grant from the affeercianados to the municipality. Due to the expense of hospital premiums for all residents, several affeercianado grants will be required during Phase-I.

Prosperity – A Vital City

In rural life, barbarians (and peasants) are the least free of men – bound by traditions, ridden by caste, fettered by superstitions, riddled by suspicion and foreboding of whatever is strange. "City air makes free" was the medieval saying when city air really did free the runaway serf. City air still makes free the runaways from company towns, from plantations, from factory-farms, from subsistence farms, from migrant picker routes, from mining villages, from one-class suburbs. – Jane Jacobs [FTN1.10]

Cheap land, cheap labor, and cheap capital can raise a city from the hills and dales. With free medical care and a citizens' dividend, the rise will be explosive. Complete freedom to experiment is left to Phase-II and beyond when land will be virtually unlimited, and the basic income from selective distribution will limit the negative consequences of mistakes.

In Phase-I, we intend to build Prosperity as a model top-down city. Top-down implies planning in conjunction with local residents, business, and industry. One of the hazards of planning is that it is often at odds with short-term growth. But good planning and long-term growth are always compatible and land monetization over the course of 40+ years is incentive for the affeercianados and investors to support long-term growth through a vital city.

Despite choosing a semi-remote location, it is important to remember that Prosperity will not exist in a vacuum. Our major roads and transportation systems need to fit-in with county, regional and state systems. There are not only the efficiencies of cooperation, but creating a jarring boundary between systems does not generate feelings of good will. Utilities and waste management are also matters for regional planning. Digging a lake and hijacking the watershed might not be the best policy. While building a materials recovery facility is always a good idea, what happens to the non-recyclable waste has regional implications. This is part of the tradeoff we make for being only 1.5 hours from Old Metropolis, as opposed to the complete wilderness.

Planning in Phase-I is accommodative and dynamic. We are not the Comintern. It is rarely, if ever, a question of excluding businesses, but rather one of keeping industries that choose our location from interfering with residents and each other through basic zoning. Once trebling begins in the 19th year, central planning will be greatly eased, and non-existent in the Phase-II AFFEERCE territories.

When the first parcel of land is purchased, the ABC board will examine the context of the land, cognizant of the natural systems that affect environmental qualities and design nuance. This involves relating the virtual map to this parcel, locating the 200 acre downtown commercial center, planning roadways, and designating certain points as industrial centers, residential centers, commercial centers, parks, power, water, sewer and waste management facilities. The virtual map is to be mapped to the actual location in a manner that maximizes the harmony with nature. To this end, the virtual map itself can be tweaked. Once the mapping is complete the entire business plan and set of spreadsheets must be revised to account for the new information. If the input plan is well done, this revision will not have a negative material effect on results. After each auction, land purchase, or unexpected result, a similar revision will take place.

The city will come to be divided into districts and districts into neighborhoods. One of our goals is a cellular democracy, and these districts and neighborhoods will be the initial dominion of level-3 and level-2 cells. (See Volume-I and later discussions.) Future land purchases will determine the direction of growth and location of districts. The statements of intention of bidders will determine neighborhood locations and district boundaries. Bids on moveable plots help the planners organize the disparate bids into a unified vision. Within the district, there should be an architectural and landscaping plan. Walkability, access, and open space, are important at the district level. However, it is how those districts are divided into neighborhoods that assure the viability, livability, and individuality of a city. [FTN1.11]

In this section, many principles of livable cities are examined and related to Prosperity. The next eighteen pages will be an intensive crash course on urban planning concepts. While the hundreds of principles outlined might seem overkill, the reason for their inclusion is to hammer home the importance of urban planning to those of a skeptical libertarian bent who believe the market is sufficient. There will be plenty of time in Phase-II and beyond to test libertarian principles. In Phase-I, however, we will stick with the planners. Non-interested readers should peruse the colorful tables at the very least.

Skidmore, Owings, and Merrill architect John Kriken, in *City Building: Nine Planning Principles for the Twenty-First Century* tells us that successful downtowns are compact and walkable. Work, live, and play in the same place requires high density, and 24 hour operation[FTN1.11]. The most distinctive and flavorful retail is downtown. Expensive shops bring high land values.

We want Michigan Avenue, Fifth Avenue, and Rodeo Drive instead of suburban sprawl. Restaurants and specialty shops should be located on the first floor of mid-rise, mixed use, transit oriented developments.

The collection of ground rents aids this compact vision of downtown by forcing land to be used efficiently. In Hong Kong, lack of space has led to service neighborhoods, where large machinery, trucks and so on are lifted on large elevators to high level loading docks in multi-story service centers[FTN1.12]. This is exactly the density we are striving for.

The best cities tend to have the greatest number of narrow streets, as opposed to a few large ones according to Kriken. Narrow streets are pedestrian friendly with less traffic and easier to cross.

Downtown Sidewalks
In a successful city, Jane Jacobs talks about the importance of the city sidewalk. The bedrock of a successful city is that a person must feel safe on the streets.

Successful city neighborhoods have three main attributes. [FTN1.13]

1. Clear demarcation between public and private space. Public and private spaces cannot ooze into each other as they typically do in suburban spaces or in housing projects.

2. There must be eyes on the street, eyes belonging to those we might call the natural proprietors of the street. The buildings on a street equipped to handle strangers and to insure the safety of both residents and strangers must be oriented to the street.
3. The sidewalk must have users on it fairly continuously, both to add to the number of effective eyes on the street, and to induce the people in the buildings to watch the sidewalk in sufficient numbers….Large numbers of people entertain themselves off and on by watching street activity. [FTN1.13]

Neighborhoods with lively, diverse streets are far safer than high-rise projects with their parks that nobody dare use less they be mugged. These parks do not have the protection of stoops and active sidewalks [FTN1.13]. While the era of stoops has passed, specialty shops and sidewalk cafes, with wide sidewalks expanding into tiny play areas and parks, and benches lining a median parkway, can have the same effect.

In a successful city, according to Jacobs, if there is a problem on the street, people open windows, stick out their heads, the police are called, epithets are yelled. If a rescue is needed, brave men and women will appear simultaneously. In an unsuccessful city, trouble causes lights to go off, and window shades to be pulled.

Jacobs wrote in the days before HVAC, when windows of mid-rises actually opened. However, by bringing lively retail, entertainment, and attractions to street level, the same safe environment is created. There must be sufficient diversity that the sidewalks are populated at all hours of the day, and preferably much of the night. Much of this is a function of city design. Consider a carrousel, a zoological attraction with two docents on duty 24 hours a day, or an affeercianado cop who walks a beat of only 1 or 2 blocks and chats with neighbors and merchants. It is both the cheap labor of the affeercianados, and subsequently, selective distribution empowering entitled citizens to work at what they truly love to do, that makes this throwback to the past possible.

Sidewalk Life[FTN1.14, FTN1.15]	Table 1.15
Anonymity	People move to the city for a certain degree of anonymity.
Limited Privacy	The sidewalk offers neighbors a chance for contact that is not too intimate and respects individual privacy. The tradition is seen today in dog walking and pushing baby strollers.
Limited Contact	According to Jacobs, cities are full of people with whom a certain degree of contact is useful or enjoyable, but you do not want them in your hair. And they do not want you in theirs either.
Trust	The trust of a city street is formed over time from many, many, little public sidewalk contacts. Impersonal streets make anonymous people and anonymous people could be dangerous.
Tolerance	Jacobs goes so far as to say that racism and other forms of bigotry are facilitated by lack of a sidewalk life. When an area of the city lacks a sidewalk life, the people of the place must enlarge their private lives if they are to have anything approaching equivalent contact with their neighbors. People start becoming very choosy about who their neighbors are. However, the most common outcome in cities where people are people are faced with sharing much or nothing is nothing [FTN1.16]
Public Characters	The social life of sidewalks hangs partly on what can be called self-appointed public characters. A public character is anyone who is in frequent contact with a wide circle of people and is sufficiently interested to make himself a public character. [FTN1.17]
Child Play	Sidewalks are a good place for children to socialize under the watchful eyes of adults. There are few eyes in parks and playgrounds where gangs often rule. This means that sidewalks should be wide enough for children to have some play space.

Width Insufficient	However, wide sidewalks in themselves are insufficient. Wide sidewalks failed in the Chicago loop because there were neither children nor residences. At many times, the wide sidewalks made the streets seem even more deserted.
Quick Play	There are brief intervals of time after school, before homework, before dinner, after dinner, when children want to play and cannot play too far from home. The sidewalk fills this role that a distant playground cannot.

Buildings and Space

Open Space[FTN1.18]	Table 1.16
Bad Space	Open spaces are often uncritically venerated in city planning. Yet more often than not, they are public safety hazards. Out of view of parents and merchants, they become turf for gangs.
Good Space	A good park is a small square in the middle of a block of mixed-use buildings with plenty of residences, retail and office space. Parents can see the park from their windows and call out to their children, if needed. During the day, business people eat lunch in the park and surrounding cafes. People cross the park to get from retail to retail. In the evening and during the weekend day, the park is full of kids playing.

Certain types of buildings interfere with a vital neighborhood, and should be excluded from a healthy downtown. [FTN1.18]

- Parking lots
- Large or heavy truck depots
- Gas stations
- Gigantic outdoor advertising (although Times Square is a notable exception to this rule)
- Enterprises that are harmful not because of what they are, but because in certain streets, their scale is wrong.

Generally for lively neighborhoods, controls are not controls on kind of use, but controls on the scale of street frontage permitted to a use. [FTN1.18]

Only a new city can achieve all that urban research has taught us over the past hundred or so years. To not do so is inexcusable. In the issues presented by Kriken and Jacobs above, the proposal for downtown Prosperity does quite well. Light vehicular traffic on the upper level allows for narrow and angled streets that further add to the safety of wide sidewalks by naturally reducing the speed limit. Downtown Prosperity relegates parking, and truck access to the lower level, bringing an unparalleled feeling of cleanliness to the narrow downtown streets. This will cause people to gravitate to sidewalk cafes in warmer weather, making sidewalk play even safer. The central park is surrounded by high-rises, and elevated toward the center to enhance visibility. Because the surrounding buildings are at least 30% residential, the park should be filled with dog walkers, playing children, and office workers on a lunch break at different, but overlapping, hours.

An abundance of affeercianado police officers walking beats in downtown, including the park, add to the safety. Parks and recreation will likely have personnel in the park. Discrete video surveillance cameras in both lower and upper downtown also enhance security.

Beyond the central park, a full 25% of downtown is dedicated to streets, bike paths, sidewalks and parkways. That is actually considered too low for a normal city[FTN1.19], but since downtown Prosperity has no parking, no alleys, many 1-way streets, and no need to worry about traffic congestion, 25% will create the simultaneous impression of spaciousness and efficiency which should be aesthetically pleasing.

Borders

Borders – Both Natural and Man-made[FTN1.20]	Table 1.17
Most Debilitating	Man-made borders such as expressways and rail yards are the most debilitating. By producing vacuums in the nearby general land, they hinder diversity and social vitality.
Divide City	Borders divide up cities into pieces. They set asunder the neighborhoods of "ordinary" city lying to either side of them. In this respect, they behave in a fashion opposite from small parks. Small parks, if they are popular, knit together their neighborhoods from different sides, and mingle users. Borders also behave in a fashion opposite from city streets.
Natural Districts	The sundering, or city-carving, effect of borders is not in itself always detrimental. If each of the localities separated from one another by a border is large enough to form a strong city district, with a sufficiently large and diverse pool of uses and users, the separation effect is apt to be harmless.
Counterforces	Population concentration ought to be made deliberately high (and diverse) near borders, that blocks close to borders should be especially short and potential street use extremely fluid, and the mixtures of primary uses should be abundant.

By siding downtown Prosperity with high-rise buildings that front both the downtown, and the street beyond, the border is invisible everywhere. Because these skyscrapers are supported by their own foundation, they can be arbitrarily tall, even 100 stories. However, they still can take advantage of the downtown utilities available through lower level connections, including heat and hot water.

Automobile Reduction

Automobile Reduction[FTN1.21]	Table 1.18
Insatiable	The more space that is provided for cars in cities, the greater becomes the need for use of cars, and hence for still more space for them.
Public Transit	Jacobs has shown that increased city accessibility by cars is always accompanied by declines in service of public transportation. The declines in transit passengers are always greater than increases in private automobile passengers.
Dullness	Dullness in cities also contributes to traffic congestion. The more territory, planned or unplanned, which is dull the greater becomes the pressure of traffic on lively districts.
Trucks	Trucks are vital to cities. They mean service. They mean jobs. Preference on narrow streets should be given to trucks, not the other way around, according to Jacobs. She feels the fastest lanes in multilane arteries or on wide avenues could be reserved for trucks only.
Taxis	Between taxis and private passenger automobiles, inadequate parking and traffic reduction goals favor taxis. Taxis do many more times the work of equivalent private cars.

Upper downtown is designed with automobile attrition in mind; narrow streets, one-way streets, angled streets, wide sidewalks, and intrusive architecture. It will be primarily the domain of cabs, with transit buses on the wider boulevards.

Downtown Prosperity is built on three levels. The upper-lower level gives trucks ready access to loading docks not seen in other major downtowns. Most of the rest of the upper-lower level space is reserved for parking. Although this parking will not be adequate, it will be expensively priced providing Prosperity with good revenue. A free and continuous stream of buses will transport people from lower downtown to less expensive remote parking and back again.

Because downtown Prosperity will be the liveliest spot for 100 miles in any direction, traffic for the entire area will be efficiently diverted to the ample underground and transit-connected remote parking.

Visual Interruption

Visual Interruption[FTN1.22]	Table 1.19
Beautiful Downtown	Although Jacobs eschews substituting art for life, particularly turning a neighborhood into a disciplined work of art, the device of visual interruption is critical in creating a beautiful downtown.
Highlights Street Life	Cuts off the indefinite distant view and at the same time visually heightening and celebrating intense street use by giving a hint of enclosure and entity.
Additional Streets	If streets of the grid are too far apart
3D	Three-dimensional topography, such as the hills of San Francisco, is the ideal form of visual interruption.
Endless Streets	Straight, "endless" streets can be interrupted, and the street itself divided around a square or plaza forming the interruption; the square can be occupied by a building, or fountain or a grove of trees.
Buildings	The buildings themselves can create the interruption, such as bridges that connect two buildings up above a street. Large buildings can be placed across streets at ground level. Buildings can be set forward from the normal building line with a sidewalk cut underneath. A plaza at one side of the street makes the building beyond stand out as a visual interruption.
Non-intimidating	According to Jacobs, districts with many visual street interruptions do not, in real life, tend to intimidate or overwhelm people; they are more apt to be characterized as friendly.
Away From Borders	Streets that run into borders such as bodies of water, campuses, or large sports grounds should be left without visual interruptions.
Foot Traffic	Actual physical cut-offs to foot traffic in particular are destructive in cities. There should always be a way around the visual interruption, or through it, a way that is obvious as a person reaches it, and that then lays out before the eyes a new street scene.

There must always be an end in view, and the end must not be final. – Eliel Saarinen, Architect [FTN1.22]

Downtown Prosperity is surrounded on all sides by high rises that will exceed the 21 story-maximum of the upper-level foundation floor. At the center is the central park with its high hills from excavated topsoil. Between the high rises at the boundary and the park lies the architectural maze of downtown. This gives the comforting sense of isolation from the real world one gets in a theme park, with no view out. Windows on one side of the surrounding high rises will face inward to the magic kingdom. Windows on the other side will face the distant mountains or prairie.

Landmarks and Character

What will be the landmarks of downtown Prosperity and Prosperity proper?

Landmarks and Character	Table 1.20
Amidst Neighbors	According to Jacobs, as clarifiers of city order, landmarks do best when they are set right amidst their neighbors [FTN1.23]
Not Too Many	Kriken tells us that all cities need landmarks, but when too many buildings strive to be unique, they end up eroding a coherent city. [FTN1.24]
Coherent Pattern	According to municipal theorist Kevin Lynch, one of the most important qualities of good city design is visual and emotional clarity where the parts can be recognized and organized into a coherent pattern [FTN1.24]
Memorable Feel	Historically, the best most renowned cities have a distinctive character, a memorable feel, as well as the ability to function in a civically coordinated way. [FTN1.11]
Unifying Devices	Some city streets need unifying devices to suggest that the street is an entity, often something as simple as a thematic paint color. A strong, but otherwise unobtrusive design element can tie together in orderly fashion much happenstance detail. This unification is most useful on streets that are heavily used or seen, and contain much detail without any real variety of use – such as entirely commercial streets One of the simplest devices is trees along the stretch to be unified, but trees planted close enough together to give a look of continuity when they are seen close up. [FTN1.25]
Street Vendors	Deliberate street arrangements for vendors not only provide a unifying element, but can enhance the sidewalk life and diversity discussed earlier. They create areas that are full of life, attraction, and interest, and because of bargains are excellent stimulators of cross use. [FTN1.25]

Downtown prosperity, itself, is both a landmark and unifying element. The impression should be Dorothy when she first spots the Emerald City of Oz. Within downtown, there is the hilly central park and surrounding wall of tall skyscrapers, enclosing an eclectic collection of mid-rises up to 21 stories located helter-skelter on a maze of narrow streets.

But Prosperity will be more than the 200 acre central wonderland. Beyond downtown is city hall, palace of the Grand Duke or Grand Duchess of Prosperity, with an exciting architecture and a reflecting pool. The pool runs parallel to, and for the length of, downtown. At the base of the reflecting pool lie Jane Jacobs University, Thomas Paine Hospital, palaces for chancellors and vice-chancellors, the medical campus, and other asserted hospitals, laboratories, and colleges. To the other side of downtown are single-family homes and estates. Only one end of downtown overlooks parking garages, warehouses, and clean industrial lots.

An architecture of gross regularity seen on the campus, and near city hall is the dormitory. There are over 60 planned, each 11 stories high. The affeercianado dorms house 600, while the campus dorms house 550, with the first floor dedicated to a lecture hall and classrooms. The dormitories are the combined effort of students from multiple classes at Jane Jacobs, with a new dormitory built every semester. The pressing need for worker housing, the utility of economies of scale, and the introductory nature of the courses, make design variation unlikely. It is here that color might prove useful in aesthetic differentiation. Differences in colors of side solar panels could create a striking contrast. Bold painted numbers that adorn the entire building side could turn a difficult problem into a simple reference. "I live in Red 57," says the inebriated passenger to the cab driver. "My 10 AM anatomy class is in Green 22, so an 11 AM in Orange 40 it too far to walk in 10 minutes," says the student.

The melding of architectures around community centers, where police and fire stations, elementary schools or high schools, and a dormitory are grouped together for resource sharing, creates diverse arrangements of regular parts.

Phase-II will see new architectures and remodeling to accommodate large families motivated by economies of scale made possible through selective distribution. We hope to express a contrast between the individual and the collective in the art and architecture of Prosperity.

Political Organization

As Prosperity grows, the city council will expand into a cellular democracy, to the extent allowed by state law. The closest models we have today are cities divided into horizontal divisions; a 2 dimensional cellular structure.

Jacobs identifies three useful kinds of big city neighborhoods. In the terminology of the cellular democracy, these are districts at levels 2, 3, and 4. She calls them street neighborhoods, district neighborhoods and the neighborhood of the city as a whole. [FTN1.26]

Jacobs' Three Kinds of Neighborhoods [FTN1.26]	Table 1.21
Street	There should be no border to a street neighborhood. They are defined by the families, businesses and characters that populate the street. These neighborhoods have significant overlap and can extend in many directions for some distance. Ideally, there will be few interruptions in these overlapping neighborhoods.
District	The set of street neighborhoods bounded by natural boundaries, highways, industrial or rail yards constitutes a district neighborhood. The district is large enough to fight city hall, and small enough to care about problems in one of its street neighborhoods. These are the administrative districts discussed below.
City	The city as "neighborhood" is usually the most successful as people with common cultural interests are associated with the city's cultural institutions.

The administrative district or district neighborhood would mark the horizontal divisions of city government. Unlike random horizontality, they would be common to the municipal government as a whole. The administrative districts would represent the primary, basic subdivisions made within most city agencies.

The chief officials of an agency, below the top commissioner would be district administrators. Each district administrator would supervise all aspects of his department's service within his district. The same district boundaries would be common to each department which acts directly on district life or planning – such as housing, welfare, schools, police, parks, code enforcement, and health housing subsidy, fire, zoning, and planning. [FTN1.26]

Cheap affeercianado labor is conducive to district management. The city manager, a paid professional, can appoint affeercianados to manage each district. They in turn can appoint liaisons to the various district departments and agencies, with help from a similar hierarchy appointed by the city treasurer and city clerk.

Jacobs stresses that the administrative district and district neighborhood be one and the same; that they operate as both social and political units.

Yet the hierarchy must be maintained. Doctrinaire reorganization of government into pure horizontal administration would be impractical, if for no other reason than that taxation and overall allocation of funds must be centralized city functions. Taxi licenses would be foolish at the district level, but licenses for places of entertainment and vendors are sensibly dealt with at the district level. According to Jacobs, the size of a district should vary between 50,000 to over 100,000 people. [FTN1.26]

In a cellular democracy, a district is defined as a voluntary association of one or more cells at the same level and sharing the same parent. Jacobs' administrative districts would be constituted by 2 to 7 cells at level 3. Her neighborhoods would be one or more cells at level 2, while the major city would be one or more cells at level 4. (See *Volume I – The Vision*, for more details.)

Downtown Prosperity is a bounded district; city hall/university campus is a bounded district, while single family residential areas have evolving district boundaries.

We have the "Law of the single partial" to guide in the creation of top down cells. That is no cell can contain "part of" more than one physical or acknowledged building, neighborhood, or district. So a cell cannot contain part of one building and also part of another. It can contain an arbitrary number of complete entities, but only one partial. So a district in downtown Prosperity cannot extend into the surrounding area, unless the district contains all of downtown Prosperity, which it will in the first few years of the city.

In keeping with Jacobs' principles and the principles of cellular democracy, police and fire districts cannot cross actual district boundaries. Our aim is to have a single police and fire district correspond with a level-3 cell, even though those districts are smaller than Jacobs' administrative district. Formation of administrative districts between cellular levels 3 and 4 will be more of an organic process than a planned one and driven by the economies of scale in consolidating school districts, sanitation districts, water districts, and park districts

A lively city district combines street neighborhood convenience (drug store, laundry) with district wide convenience (cabinet maker, coffee house) with citywide convenience (art galleries, theater, unique specialty shop) – Jane Jacobs. FTN1.18

Nine Principles for Twenty-First Century City Building

Kriken identifies nine principles for 21st Century city building FTN1.11. How will Prosperity succeed in implementing these principles? Some of the implementations mentioned will not be discussed until later in the text.

Sustainability
Sustainability refers to the conservation and protection of natural resources.

Prosperity and Sustainability	Table 1.22
Goal	We are at a disadvantage in that the good city building land has already been taken. Optimally, we wish to build Prosperity on non-prime agricultural and non-essential forest land.
Harmony	Residential development can be in harmony with a forested area.
Vertical Agriculture	Because there is no agricultural rent surcharge prior to Phase-III, vertical agriculture can promote sustainability, lead to new innovation, accelerate import-replacement and increase land value. Vertical agriculture uses drip irrigation and hydroponics to support vertical columns of agriculture. Low wattage LEDs, powered by rooftop solar cells, produce just the wavelengths needed by plants. At the top level is a fish farm, perhaps fed by insects killed with solar electric arcs. The waste from the fish farm is used as fertilizer for the plants below. Money saved on affeercianado food, as well as selling the produce at farmer's market, or to restaurants or supermarkets, can be invested in the land trust.

Air/Water	The air and water quality and capacity are important factors when the land broker chooses the land. The quality and capacity must be sufficient for growth through Phase-III deluxe land expansion. Air basins support certain aircraft properties that affect noise and building height. Watersheds have certain capacities that must be researched by the land broker before the land is purchased.
Energy Efficiency	As a top-down planned city, we can have requirements for energy efficient materials in construction as well as requiring that developers supply energy efficient appliances. This must be balanced against the goal of attracting industry and development. Integration of solar into community architectures will support a maintenance industry, making solar more feasible for private enterprise. Downtown, the hot air and hot water utilities will be highly efficient.
Waste Management	Our aim in waste management is total renewability, or zero waste. This will be reflected in plumbing requirements, garbage collection, recycling programs, and requirements for industrial, medical, or otherwise hazardous waste. Free market solutions will be emphasized. The material recovery facility is expected to be profitable by Year 2. Simplistically, after the removal of all recyclable materials and the production of compost to meet local requirements, wastewater is used to produce gas to burn solid waste where it is purified to potable water. The burning solid waste produces steam that runs generating turbines, producing humus for fertilizer and ash for construction. Little or nothing is left for the sanitary landfill. [FTN1.27]

Accessibility

According to Kriken, design elements to facilitate ease of movement include compact development (minimizes distance people need to travel to work and shop), concentrated destinations (work is found in business parks, assessable to public transit), small blocks and streets, system redundancy (multiple parallel streets prevent traffic congestion and allow faster and safer one-way travel) and multiple modes (pedestrian, bicycle, transit, private vehicle). [FTN1.28]

Design methods to implement these elements include reserving land for movement corridors that may be required in the future, locating corridors at the edge of neighborhoods and districts, without blocking scenic views, considering geometry and scale with broad sidewalks, landscaped medians, narrow streets for slower speed traffic and pedestrian safety, considering utility in street design with medians to provide for pedestrian safety, two medians to allow for local and express traffic, central bicycle or light rail traffic, and street design features that include parallel and diagonal parking, landscaped islands forcing traffic to slow and curve, wide sidewalks at the corners can sport transit shelters, sidewalk cafes, and a tree promenade. [FTN1.28]

Prosperity and Accessibility	Table 1.23
Old Metropolis	Prosperity will be beyond the suburbs, but close enough to Old Metropolis to attract shoppers and long-distance commuters. It is essential we build our city not far from a major highway, and access to that highway be built, even if it involves special land purchases. That means a strip of land, wide enough for a highway and a half-block+ of development on either side, connecting the interstate to Prosperity be included in the initial land purchase. The roads and infrastructure team will build this road early on in the Setup Year.

Metrobus	The Metrobus service scheduling six or more free daily luxury buses between Prosperity and Old Metropolis will provide a new level of accessibility unheard of elsewhere. Commuters who work in Old Metropolis will find commuting from Prosperity to be far easier and less expensive than normal suburban commuting despite the length of the commute. Wi-Fi access and comfortable seating allow the trip to be both productive and relaxing.
Bike Paths and Walkways	Downtown must be bicycle and pedestrian friendly. Bike paths and walkways will lead into upper downtown under archways. Walking paths will lead to wide sidewalks and bike paths follow the same no-parking, low vehicular narrow streets that define upper downtown, as well as bike paths through the central park. Lower downtown pedways will provide protection from inclement weather.
Transportation Depot	All transportation options will merge at a hub just virtual northeast of downtown, with free continuous transportation from the hub to lower downtown. Public transit will follow downtown boulevards.
Schools	Elementary schools should be close enough to residential neighborhoods to eliminate the need for most students to take busses. Free school buses to remote schools, prior to the building of local schools, will begin with the first student resident of Prosperity.
Inter-business Production Control	Automated multi-stop shopping and manufacturing via lower-lower downtown and a driverless highway in the industrial area will vastly improve the life of the disabled and other consumers and stimulate new innovative enterprise.

Diversity

…The interweaving of human patterns. They are full of people doing different things, with different reasons, and different ends in view, and the architecture reflects and expresses this difference – which is one of content rather than form alone. Being human, human beings are what interest us most. In architecture, as in literature and drama, it is the richness of human variation that gives vitality and color to the human setting. Considering the hazard of monotony… the most serious fault in our zoning laws lies in the fact that they permit an entire area to be devoted to a single use. – Jane Jacobs [FTN1.35]

Prosperity must be defined by variety and choice.

Diversity	Table 1.24
Decentralization	People need choices in accommodations, job opportunities, services, cultural and religious activities, visual interest, elements of leisure and recreation. It logically follows that the enemy of diversity is decentralization and the lack of density to begin with. [FTN1.29] Jacobs quotes John Denton, a professor of business at the University of Arizona, "Decentralization produces such a thin population spread that the only effective economic demand that could exist in the suburbs was that of the majority. The only goods and cultural activities available will be those that the majority requires." [FTN1.30]
Walking	According to Jacobs, in dense diversified city areas, people still walk; an activity that is impractical in suburbs and in most gray areas. She believes there is a correlation between close-grained diversity and walking. [FTN1.31]

Many Enterprises	Only a surfeit of enterprises can provide real diversity. For the most part, these enterprises should be small and versatile. When Jacobs says that city diversity itself permits and stimulates more diversity, she is referring to the effects of entrepreneurial mercantilism in creating new import-replacement and exports. In a given geographical territory, half as many people will not support half as many such enterprises spaced at twice the distance. When distance inconvenience sets in, the small, the various, and the personal wither away. [FTN1.32]
Small Enterprise	Jacobs says, "Wherever lively and popular parts of cities are found, the small much outnumber the large." [FTN1.32]
Multiple Functions	The district, and indeed as many of its internal parts as possible, must serve more than one primary function; preferably more than two. These must insure the presence of people who go outdoors on different schedules and are in the place for different purposes, but who are able to use many facilities in common. When a primary use is combined effectively with another that puts people on the street at different times, then the effect can be economically stimulating; a fertile environment for secondary diversity. [FTN1.32]
Short Blocks	Most blocks must be short, that is streets and opportunities to turn corners must be frequent. [FTN1.32]
Mingle Buildings in Various Ages and Conditions	The district must mingle buildings that vary in age and condition, including a good proportion of old ones so they vary in the economic yield produced. The mingling must be fairly close grained. [FTN1.32] If a city area has only new buildings, the enterprises that can exist there are automatically limited to those that can support the high cost of new construction [FTN1.33]
Population Density	There must be sufficiently dense concentration of people, for whatever purposes they may be there. This includes dense concentration in the case of people who are their because of residence. [FTN1.32]

When bidding out land in downtown Prosperity, we need to take into account 4 conditions that, according to Jacobs, help destroy diversity: [FTN1.34]

1. The tendency for outstanding successful diversity in cities to destroy itself.
2. The tendency for massive single elements in cities (many of which are necessary and otherwise desirable) to cast a deadening influence.
3. The tendency of population instability to counter the growth of diversity.
4. The tendency of both public and private money to glut or starve development and change.

If an area is highly successful, new competition for space will represent only a narrow segment of the many uses that together created success. Whichever one or few uses that have emerged as the most profitable in the locality will be repeated and repeated, crowding out and overwhelming less profitable forms of use. If tremendous numbers of people, attracted by convenience and interest, or charmed by vigor and excitement, choose to live or work in the area, again the winners of the competition will form a narrow segment of population of users. In this case, so many want to live in the locality that it becomes profitable to build in excessive and devastating quantity for those who can pay the most. [FTN1.34]

The problem is to hamper excess duplication at one place and divert them instead to other places in which they will not be excess duplications but healthy additions. Zoning for diversity must be thought of differently than the usual zoning for conformity. A park being surrounded by intensive duplications of tall offices or apartments might be zoned for lower buildings along its south side in particular, thus accomplishing two useful purposes at one stroke:

protecting the park's supply of winter sun, and protecting indirectly, to some extent at least, its diversity of surrounding uses. FTN1.34

Prosperity and Diversity	Table 1.25
Achieving Density	For Prosperity, the drive for diversity is in achieving the density in the first place. The compact downtown provides all the density needed to support a strong set of employment, cultural, religious, and recreational options. The nearby medical campus, shared library, and university, enhance those options, as do the community centers and sports fields in the residential neighborhoods.
Trebling	Office and residential towers can easily support 1/3 net rents of the most efficient user while an opera house probably could not. With trebling, the opera house has some protection from land seizure, since the rent must be tripled by a prospective apartment house landlord. However, during Phase-I, a simple outbid will usually win the auction. Businesses that do not get the most rent bang for the buck will never be established. Unfortunately the lack of diversity in winning bidders will lower the land value.
Auction Slots	This is countered by specific and general slots in the auctions. People can bid on land in general, or they can bid on grocery store land, or museum land, or opera house land established by jurisdictional covenant. Winners are the highest bidders in a particular slot. Although slots are very useful in the early years for bringing in needed industry, they must never be used in the opposite sense, to restrict competition. In AFFEERCE proper, jurisdictional covenants are limited to a small percentage of the land.
Building Age	Prosperity will suffer from lack of diversity in building age. Cheap rents in old buildings allow for the development of certain downtown industries that are shut-out by high rents. However, low land lease prices in the early years should help to counter this problem.
No Class Diversity	In a city composed of upper and upper-middle class entrepreneurs and professionals, and the historically-new landlord-working class, the affeercianados, there could be income-related gaps in the range of possible commercial diversification. The retired middle-class and ex-affeercianados might fill these gaps. De-facto discrimination based on class is a necessity of Phase-I and Phase-II. Only when the affeercianados fail to meet the demand will an independent working class arise.

Open Space

Jacobs' vision of good space and bad space can be found in Table 1.16.

Open Space FTN1.36	Table 1.26
Center of Life	Open space is the natural center of a city's civic life. Chicago has the lakefront, New York has Central Park, and Washington has the National Mall.
Crime and Sprawl	Open space can be associated with sprawl in cities such as Los Angeles, or crime and blight in run-down areas of any city, or near housing projects.
Nature	For open spaces at the periphery of a city, Kriken tells us that migratory corridors and watersheds should be respected. Wildlife habitat needs to be somewhat isolated from people and pets.

Per Population	Kriken advocates as much as 2.5 acres of open space per 1000 population, located no more than 15 minutes away by foot.
Human Elements	Specific sports and exercise, walking, biking, picnics, relaxation
Environmental Elements	Cool the air, minimize ozone, consume carbon dioxide, filter polluted water runoff
Equivalents	Large bodies of water or even views of blue sky serve some of the psychological function of open space. Natural landscape features should be protected and preserved, views to and from natural features must be conserved. Spectacular city views reduce the need for open space.
Climate Change	Plans must provide a way to deal with climate change without walling off ocean fronts

The wide open space of the central park is no more than 15 minutes, by foot from any part of downtown. It is less than 1.5 acres per 1000, if office population is included, but more than 2 acres per 1000 actual residents. Additional open space can be found on the wide sidewalks. Roads light on vehicular traffic will add to the feeling of open space.

In Phase-I, Prosperity is required to pay only 10% of the trebled amount for parks and other city space, although if converting developed land they still must pay the full 150% ODV. In Phase-I, jurisdictional covenants are used by the ABC Board, and then the city council, to encourage growth through urban planning.

In Phase-II and afterward, a district of the cellular democracy, by a 2/3 plurality of the citizens will use jurisdictional covenants for parks, zoos, schools, sporting areas, wetlands, and historical landmarks, among others. The total land under jurisdictional covenant cannot exceed 3% at any given level of dominion. Roads, with their driver and utility easements, are not counted in the maximum under jurisdictional covenant.

Compatibility and Context

Compatibility is defined as maintaining harmony and balance. Architecture and city design should blend in with the surrounding environment.

Context is defined by a site's character, both present and historic; its current land use, infrastructure, natural systems, geology, and topography; and the buildings and landscape that surround it. [FTN1.37]

Architectural character and building color determine compatibility. For instance, light colored buildings reflect shadow and sunlight. Their surface character changes throughout the day. In forested areas, dark buildings are hidden and less intrusive. Color ranges of buildings can determine compatibility, such as pinks, reds, browns, and tans in the U.S. Southwest, or dark greens and browns for forests. [FTN1.37]

Repurposing historic buildings to more highly valued retail and entertainment uses in the center of a new development creates a harmonic center for the development; a heart and soul. This adds value to surrounding high-rises.

For Prosperity, these considerations will not be possible until the parcel of land has been selected. One of the principle contextual issues for Prosperity is adapting to the existing utility infrastructure and the extent to which we must develop our own. The latest technology in integrating infrastructure with roads is needed to insure soon-to-be overstressed utilities can be easily expanded without digging up roads.

Incentives

New public buildings provide incentive for private industry, although only a few will be possible in Phase-I. These include airports, seaports, convention centers, ballparks, arenas, museums, performance halls, and theaters, cultural and educational facilities. Each of these buildings is an incentive for one of the others to be built. Convention centers attract hotels and restaurants, which attract more entertainment venues [FTN1.37].

Access improvements provide incentive for both commercial and residential development including transit and street design, bicycle paths, and pedestrian walkways. [FTN1.37]

Prosperity Incentives	Table 1.27
Tax Reduction	Early ground rent will be lower than normal property tax + interest on land value and frozen through Phase-I
Labor Subsidies	Bidding on affeercianado labor greatly increases competitiveness
Site Assembly and Preparation	Supply depot and import to site, low cost affeercianado labor, affeercianado expertise, inexpensive building and fire inspection
New Infrastructure	All infrastructure will be new
Import Replacement	The Mercantile Letter fosters import replacement that will save businesses money and make the local economy more resilient.
Healthcare and Education Services	Thomas Paine Hospital, Jane Jacobs University, medical and regular campus, shared giant municipal/campus library, new schools. All basically free to residents.
Landscape, Parks and Recreation	Top down planning with cheap affeercianado labor
Metrobus	Free Metrobus service to Old Metropolis including messenger and shopping service.
Attractions	Big-10 quality stadium at Jane Jacobs University, downtown convention center, cashless and then card-less economy,
Downtown Utilities	Easy access standard utilities plus hot air, hot water, and dry sewer to MRF
Inter-business Production Control	Automated sophisticated multi-stop transfer of raw and finished goods from business to business, or business to downtown household.
Success	Once the character of the city begins to take shape from the early auction winners, an updated plan reassures subsequent bidders. The more goals that are met, the more likely future goals will be met. The affeercianados are increasingly energized with increased land values, and their control of an increasing share of the land.
Citizens' Dividend	Residents share in the profits from ground rent and affeercianado business.
Hope	Building a future without hunger or homelessness. Residents have advantage for Phase-II selective distribution and take part in great social experiment

Adaptability

Good municipal design should anticipate that unpredictable change will happen over time.

Adaptability [FTN1.38]	Table 1.28
Goal	The unreachable goal is Lego like construction of buildings and utility infrastructure. Snap in another brick, water line, or sewer line. When it comes time to tear down a structure, all the parts can be reused. This allows for dynamic cities, buildings with the latest technology, and efficient full employment.
Rationales	There should be rationales to support every design decision, especially with regard to the future.
Geometry	A city block's geometry, size, and orientation provide a framework that should be adaptable to inevitable changes.

Addresses	All buildings, even those on large campuses should have street addresses, if possible, increasing the adaptability of the building in the event of unforeseen change.
Pedestrian Corridors	Buildings so large they must overflow block size, should maintain indoor public pedestrian corridors.
Reconfigurable	If possible office space should be reconfigurable for different types of tenants, although making the space adaptable to a standard office, a laboratory or a movie theater might be difficult. Buildings should not be too adaptable that it results in a big increase in cost and lowers the resale value. In the case of building adaptability, too much of a good thing is bad. With recyclable parts, the theory would be to optimally build for a specific need and rebuild for a new need.
Open Space	Open space, too, needs to be adaptable. It must provide flexible open areas for sports, community events, and city festivals.
Construction	Construction should be done so early tenants have minimal disruption from later construction. Methods include traffic separation and downwind expansion. New developments should be connected to existing developments, if possible.
	Parts of a project that will be delayed until there is sufficient population should not produce vacant lots but rather should be at the periphery to give the middle a sense of completeness.

Beginning with the start of trebling in the 19th year, building demolition will be more common after depreciation. The more reusable and recyclable construction components, the better we can rebuild cities to adapt to changing needs.

Placing buildings at the edge of parcels, rather than at the center allows the property owner to significantly reduce their ground rent as land becomes increasingly expensive, by letting the vacant edges be trebled away. Even if the land does not become more valuable, having the whole yard together increases its utility.

Most important for Prosperity, a project must have sufficient size to create the necessary economic strength and "gravitational pull" to succeed in a given market. Investors will not be happy if land values fail to rise after 20 years. To facilitate this, according to Kriken, mixed use is essential. [FTN1.38]

Density

Density	**Table 1.29**
Livable	Density must be livable. There must be a comfortable and safe walk from transit to home and transit to a majority of destinations.
Access to Amenities	There must be good access to amenities. According to Kriken, to be successful, high density living must offer their residents amenities such as a short walk to work, exceptional views, close access to support services, cultural, recreational and entertainment venues giving it the exciting buzz of city life. [FTN1.39]
No Overcrowding	According to Jacobs, one reason why low city densities conventionally have a good name, unjustified by the facts, and why high city densities have a bad name, equally unjustified, is that high density of dwellings and overcrowding of dwellings are often confused. [FTN1.40]
Repress Diversity	Densities can begin repressing diversity if they get too high. At some point, to accommodate so many dwellings on the land, standardization of the buildings must set in. This is fatal because great diversity in age and types of buildings has a direct, explicit connection with diversity of population, diversity of enterprises, and diversity of scenes. [FTN1.40]
Minimum Density	Jacobs feels that densities below 100 dwellings per acre are insufficient to produce city liveliness, safety, convenience and interest. [FTN1.40]

In Prosperity, interspersing museums and galleries with Corinthian columns amongst the steel and glass skyscrapers should enhance diversity without seriously impacting density.

A downtown building style that might prove interesting if not overused, is one modeled like a cruise ship, where the cabins are on the sides and all the amenities in the middle. A super market or department store needs no windows. A very thick energy-efficient building can have its retail in the center and its residential units on the periphery. Loud night-time establishments can be on floors where daytime business offices line the periphery. Such a building is also a good candidate for vertical agriculture with plants adding an extra partition between the inner building and apartment/office hallways.

Hong Kong is 50 square miles with 8 million people. That's 32,000 acres. Although our downtown is only a dense 200 acres, during the course of Phase-I, the affeercianados are likely to buy up several hundred thousand acres of land. New dense pockets can develop.

Hong Kong land prices average $100 million/acre If Prosperity had only 50,000 downtown residents, it would achieve the same density. With a projected downtown population of 100,000, downtown Prosperity would have up to twice the density of Hong Kong. Unlike Hong Kong, Prosperity will have hot water, hot air, dry sewage, and automated production control. It would be nice to think downtown Prosperity land prices could equal Hong Kong's. That corresponds to a rent of $5 million/acre and a total downtown ground rent of almost $1 billion.

Our Emerald City will not be surrounded by poppy fields. Land value will be a function of the distance to downtown. Nearby protected residences will give way to giant office buildings and apartment complexes when trebling begins in Year 20. The entire single family residential section could be displaced to the virtual south and east. Areas to the virtual north of downtown, once covered by prefabricated motel units, a trailer park, and dining halls will explode with new construction once they are opened for auction in Phase-II.

What we get is a series of concentric rings around downtown, each increased by 1 downtown radius of about 1500 feet, and each with a rent averaging half of the rent in the next inner ring, until the final ring has a ground rent equal to the rent bid at the margin. By subtracting areas, one sees that the acres in each subsequent ring increases by 2 downtowns. Because of the central park, only 170 acres is used for downtown. With an additional 25% for sidewalks and roads, there is a buildable 125 acres, with the peripheral skyscrapers raising the buildable acreage to 150. For greater accuracy over distance, we treat the downtown area as a circle rather than a rectangle, and ignore conversion to square feet giving the identity $150 = \pi R^2$.

Formula	Acres	Rent/acre decreasing at 50%	Total Rent
πR^2	1*150	$5,000,000	$750,000,000
$\pi(2R)^2 = 4\pi R^2$	3*150	2,500,000	$1,125,000,000
$\pi(3R)^2 = 9\pi R^2$	5*150	1,250,000	$937,500,000
$\pi(4R)^2 = 16\pi R^2$	7*150	625,000	656,250,000
$\pi(5R)^2 = 25\pi R^2$	9*150	312,500	421,875,000
$\pi(6R)^2 = 36\pi R^2$	11*150	156,250	257,812,500
$\pi(7R)^2 = 49\pi R^2$	13*150	78,125	152,343,750
$\pi(8R)^2 = 64\pi R^2$	15*150	39,062	87,889,500
$\pi(9R)^2 = 81\pi R^2$	17*150	19,531	49,804,050
Total projected rent for 5 mile radius from center of downtown			$4,438,475,925

In year 20, $19,531 is close to our marginal rent, so downtown loses its effect at the 5 mile radius. Interestingly, the closest two rings have an even greater total ground rent than downtown itself, due to their relative increase in acreage. The total rent for the complete circle of 5 mile radius is over $4 billion. This is over 4 times the predicted rent in the conservative spreadsheets. Using the spreadsheet numbers is best for the following reasons:

1. The decline in land value of 50% per radius is a guess. The actual decrease could be faster or slower.
2. Expected densities might not be realized.
3. The law of rent takes time to work. Our residents moved to Prosperity for a great deal on land. Even after trebling takes effect, there will be significant discounts on land.

Identity

Identity FTN1.41	Table 1.30
Water	Water is the natural feature most closely associated with memorable cities. Freshwater is also a necessity that must be preserved, adding to the cities identification with the waterway.
Terrain	Hills or mountains create distinct city memories.
Invented Identity	Without such identifying features, it is a good idea to invent these features with man-made lakes and lagoons, which have added value as filters of gray water, irrigate farms, serve as a source of potable water, control flooding and can be used for recreational boating.
Access	According to Kriken, there should be visual and physical access to natural resources, roads, trails, bicycle paths and walkways. View corridors to natural resources or man-made identity, such as spectacular buildings or bridges, should be preserved.
Climate Based Identity	Climate based identity such as interior skyways between buildings in Minneapolis, shading of sidewalks in hot climates, ski themes and surf themes, light colored buildings to reflect the sun's heat, design to catch the afternoon breeze in warm climates, and climate-protected pedestrian walkways.
Culture Based Identity	There is identity by culture. For instance, private cultures have few windows shuttered to the public, with open windows to a private courtyard, while open cultures have homes with many windows to the outside. Themed areas of a city also can create an identity, like a Chinatown, old town, or a themed architecture.

We are not expecting true believers to come to Prosperity and live in cinderblock homes built up to the sky, drab outposts with one grocery store, one shoe store, one gas station, etc. waiting for the 20 year payout to investors and affeercianados. If we did, the payout would never come and AFFEERCE would fail. Instead, we must build a unique wonderful city that will survive and thrive, even if unforeseen events somehow prevent Phase-II.

We must preserve the areas uniqueness over the interests that threaten it. Although the best development areas have already been taken, many of the areas we can purchase will have unique geographical features. Rather than tear them down or ignore those features, we need to honor them and incorporate those features into the development theme.

In modifications to the business plan following initial land purchase, conservation of natural identity is important. The municipality might be on land where identifying natural resources have been destroyed by what used to occupy the brownfield. Repair of these features should be part of the plan.

To have a downtown and campus town sharing the same space results in a vibrant downtown. One need only look at downtown Evanston, Illinois, home of Northwestern University to see rapid growth and vitality. We hope to capture that same diversity in Prosperity.

AFFEERCE – Volume II, The Plan, 4.1.5

Virtual Prosperity is restricted to an identity by design. We have upper and lower downtown, rising like an emerald city out of the prairie, with a hilly central park rising as if from a cavern. A distinct city hall/palace overlooks a reflecting pool that extends down to the campus with its chancelleries and other architecturally significant buildings. Until we instantiate virtual Prosperity with an actual land purchase, that is our identity.

Year 2

The completion of 1000 prefabricated units and two affeercianado dorms, one at the city hall site and the other at the hospital site, will allow us to significantly increase the number of affeercianados from 3900 to 6600.

The year will begin with a land auction. We will auction off 700 acres and conservatively estimate the land value will increase by 50% from Year 1 to $120,000 an acre. That is, the ground rent people are willing to pay will go from $4,000 an acre to $6,000.

For the first time, we will auction off 4 acres of our downtown foundation, getting $100,000 of rent per acre. This might seem overly optimistic for a downtown acre so early in the game, but should we achieve projected densities the land could rent as high as $5 million/acre in 20 years. Not only does that represent a gain of 50x, but the $100,000 bid in Year 2 includes property tax and is frozen for 15 years. Should the developer build a 21-story office/residential tower on one acre and achieve an average $1/sq. ft. net rent/month, they will profit by over $10 million per year, paying only $100,000 per year for the ground rent. Clearly this is a great investment if the developer believes we can deliver on the promised growth. Even if we are only partially successful, the investment will be a good one.

Hospital

The population of Prosperity will have grown over the year from 200 non-affeercianado residents to 3,250, although affeercianados will still outnumber residents 2 to 1. The hospital will receive a $100 premium for each resident from the city, and a $100 premium for each affeercianado from the Guild. There will also be premiums from county residents who wish to take advantage of the no-deductible policy. This number will be minimal until the new state of the art hospital/trauma center is completed at the start of Year 3.

To that end, the special item in our land auction during Year 2 is the Thomas Paine Hospital Chancellery. This plan assumes the same 40,000 sq. ft. footprint, for a chancellor's palace on the top two floors, equal in size to the palace in the Jane Jacobs' Chancellery. The first floor is all outpatient doctors' examination rooms, a few administrative offices, waiting rooms and the ER. With 100 examination rooms, each serving 14 people per 12 hour day, and assuming an average of 2 doctor's visits per year, and a 7-day schedule, 1,400 people can be seen in a day, 504,000 per year which is equal to 252,000 premiums. This will be sufficient through Year 11.

The basement has testing rooms, some labs, offices, and a snack bar. The second and third floors will have 50 hospital rooms along the periphery with 20 ICU rooms, nurses' stations, supplies, and some labs. The fourth floor is for surgeries, procedures, supplies, labs, lounges, offices. These 240 beds will bring the total with the hospital annex to 272 beds.

The top fifth and sixth floors will be the chancellor's palace.

The total cost of this 6 story building is 7 x 40,000 x $100 = $28 million. In this case, we are assuming that the chancellery is only able to obtain a bid of $16 million at auction, leaving $12 million in expenses that must be covered by the affeercianados.

In that case, the most the chancellor could expect to receive in compensation if the chancellery were to be trebled is 150% of $16 million plus subsequent renovation. The depreciation fund is maintained by the Board of Trustees. If the chancellor fails to maintain the chancellery, depreciation funds will be used. The chancellor's portion of the ODV will continue to decrease.

At this point the hospital is rather empty with an average of only 4 beds used per night, 57 affeercianado employees, 4 salaried doctors and a salaried administrator.

Thomas Paine Hospital	Table 2.1		Debit	Credit	Balance
Year 2					$0
Copay Ratio/Premium multiplier	0.33		1.01		$0
Paid doctors + administrator	5		$1,000,000		($1,000,000)
Total surgery hours	994.85		$24,871		($1,024,871)
Paid staff surgery hours	497.43		$149,228		($1,174,099)
Medicare/PPO surgery hours	331.62			$232,132	($941,967)
Average beds used per night	2.73		$24,871		($966,838)
Medicare/PPO Beds used per night	0.91			$497,425	($469,413)
Average out patients per day	55.27		$201,733	$211,070	($460,077)
Average daily ER visits	3.41		$12,436	$28,914	($443,599)
Average daily generic drugs prescribed	49.67		$181,284	$163,155	($461,727)
Average daily non-generic drugs prescribed	4.97		$181,284	$18,967	($624,044)
Medicare/PPO non-generic drugs	1.66			$60,428	($563,616)
Average daily specialty drugs prescribed	0.50		$72,514	$10,839	($625,291)
Medicare/PPO specialty drugs	0.17			$30,214	($595,077)
Average tests and procedures per day	21.15		$77,193	$80,766	($591,504)
Medicare/PPO tests and procedures per day	7.05			$514,620	($76,884)
Hospital liability	6.13		$122,292		($199,176)
Lab work per day	30.36		$221,630	$115,944	($304,863)
Premiums	9949			$11,938,200	$11,633,337
Food			$9,949		$11,623,389
Bandages and Special Appliances			$44,768		$11,578,620
Internal and topical medicines			$323,326		$11,255,294
Prosthesis and Take Home Equipment			$39,794		$11,215,500
Heat,air,electric,cable			$444,000		$10,771,500
Medivac and travel policy			$119,382		$10,652,118
Miscellaneous and unanticipated			$20,000		$10,632,118
Materials for 240 bed hospital - Chancellery (20)	20		$28,000,000	$16,000,000	($1,367,882)
Construction tools and equipment (5)	5		$3,000,000		($4,367,882)
Purchase crane (5)	5		$800,000		($5,167,882)
Depreciation			$2,551,000		($7,718,882)
Affeercianado Workers	54		$0	$0	($7,718,882)
Return to Affeercianados			($7,718,882)		$0

Surplus Labor

In Year 2, there will be 6600 affeercianados with base pay of $74 million. From that almost $16 million is saved on utilities, with another $3.6 million saved because affeercianados serving other affeercianados are paid directly out of the affeercianado food and housing allocations.

The school district pays for affeercianados at the rate of $5 per hour. This returns a $1.56 million credit for the school building crews, and a $488,880 credit for teachers, administrators, and maintenance of the elementary school built in Year 1. Also paid at this rate are school bus drivers to and from the county high school. With savings on utilities,

$5/hour is very close to the subsistence cost of labor. Surplus labor all goes to land value in the form of great value for education.

Unincorporated Prosperity is using about the same affeercianado resources as in Year 1, and those resources are still provided at no charge.

Surplus Labor Table 2.2	Workers	Debit	Credit	Balance
Year 2	0	$0	$0	0
Total Affeercianados	6600	$74,923,200	$15,840,000	(59,083,200)
Affeercianado Businesses				(59,083,200)
Hospital personnel	54			(59,083,200)
University/med school non-construction personnel	91		$946,400	(58,136,800)
Import/export depot	71			(58,136,800)
Major city Metrobus service	8			(58,136,800)
AMS/Smartcard workers	42			(58,136,800)
Servicing affeercianado accommodations	328		$3,723,456	(54,413,344)
Affeercianado Public Works				(54,413,344)
Dorm building crew	200			(54,413,344)
Downtown excavators	100			(54,413,344)
Education building crew	150		$1,560,000	(52,853,344)
Hospital/University/Medical campus building crew	0		$0	(52,853,344)
Education				(52,853,344)
Teachers, Clerical and maintenance	47		$488,800	(52,364,544)
Municipal Service	0			(52,364,544)
Roads and infrastructure	102		$0	(52,364,544)
Waste management	27			(52,364,544)
City Hall	60			(52,364,544)
Police and public safety	18		$0	(52,364,544)
Fire and paramedic	24		$0	(52,364,544)
Parks and recreation	0			(52,364,544)
Affeercianado Surplus Labor				(52,364,544)
Number to lease @9 with average overtime of 10 hours @13	5277		$134,469,649	82,105,105
Return to Affeercianados		$82,105,105		0

This leaves 5277 affeercianados with no other jobs than to be leased out to local business, industry and homesteaders. With a starting bid of $8/hour, we assume an average bid of $9/hour with an average of 10 hours overtime at $13/hour. In any case, demand will exhaust 100% of supply. Most of that demand will be in the building trades, however, household jobs including babysitting, cleaning, party service, home healthcare, and errands, will quickly absorb any unexpected residual supply.

The affeercianados can bring tools and machinery to a job. Their value is enhanced many fold because of that. The client only pays for depreciation and fuel with a 15% surcharge. Utilities supplied by the client are not subject to the surcharge. If tools are required and depreciation is under $1, then the client is charged a minimum of $1 depreciation per day. Significant machinery will bring in much higher amounts. For instance, the depreciation on a dump truck is $9/day + fuel + surcharge. The depreciation on a large crane is $219/day + fuel + surcharge. These charges are not reflected in Table 2.2, but add to leased income. If the average hourly bid for affeercianados is under $14/hour, and these charges create an effective hourly rate over $14/hour, this will not trigger a priority effort to increase the number of affeercianados over plan that a flat out bid rate over $14/hour would.

Clients bid for affeercianados online. Search can be done on name, skills, minimum bid, and available machinery. Except for teachers during the school week, and most police and fire personnel, and any other position deemed absolutely essential by the Affeercianado Guild, all affeercianados that are part of active teams will have a minimum bid, albeit, some will be quite high. Work will simply stop on non-essential endeavors if the needs of Prosperity business and industry are too high. Once average hourly rate exceeds $14/hour, the most essential task will be the building of new prefab motel style units. A cot can be temporarily placed in each dormitory room to allow an immediate increase of 1,200 affeercianados.   Affeercianado growth will continue at planned rates for bid rates between $9/hour and $14/hour.

The minimum bid on an affeercianado for an entire week is $10/hour. The minimum bid on an affeercianado for an entire month is $11/hour. Weekly and monthly bids override daily bids of the same amount. Once an affeercianado is bid on for a week, they are no longer eligible for daily bids during that week. Once an affeercianado is bid on for a month, they are no longer eligible for daily or weekly bids during that month. Weekly bids imply a minimum of 40 hours work in 7 days. Monthly bids require a minimum of 168 hours work in 30 days. These $2 and $3 surcharges are not used in determining the average hourly bid. Clients need not retain the affeercianados for the entire period. If the affeercianado is released before the full number of hours, 8 additional hours of surcharge are assessed.

The client is charged for affeercianados on their smartcard (discussed later). Clients who are non-residents, have smartcard debts over 30 days old, or who are contracting for an amount in excess of previous contracts will be required to deposit some or all of the funds on the smartcard in advance.

In Table 2.2, we see that leasing the affeercianados in Year 2 has resulted in almost $135 million in revenue with a profit of $82.1 million. This profit has exceeded the entire initial investment. Here is the affeercianado balance sheet for Year 2.

Affeercianados Table 2.3	Debit	Credit	Balance	Borrow	Borrowed
Year 2	$0	$0	$15,257,970	$0	$37,487,800
Hospital	$0	($7,718,882)	$7,539,088	$0	$37,487,800
Accommodations	$0	$7,549,758	$15,088,846	$0	$37,487,800
Supply Depot	$0	$484,526	$15,573,372	$0	$37,487,800
Surplus Labor	$0	$82,105,105	$97,678,478	$0	$37,487,800
AMS Software	$0	$0	$97,678,478	$0	$37,487,800
Metro Bus Service	$0	$651,200	$98,329,678	$0	$37,487,800
Downtown excavation	$0	($3,400,960)	$94,928,718	$0	$37,487,800
Rent Dividend	$0	$397,550	$95,326,268	$0	$37,487,800
Pay Unauctioned land Rent	$0	($329,600)	$94,996,668	$0	$37,487,800
Repay land trust	$0	$0	$57,508,868	$37,487,800	$0
Rent Owed	$333,600	$333,600	$57,508,868	$0	$0
Grant to municipality	$15,000,000	$0	$42,508,868	$0	$0

With the $82+ million from the surplus labor of affeercianados, the $37.4 million loan from the land trust is easily repaid. Unincorporated Prosperity is granted $15 million, and that still leaves a positive balance of $42.5 million. Furthermore, all of these numbers are based on conservative estimates. The affeercianados are probably anxious for that first significant land trust contribution to increase percentage of land ownership, but prudence dictates insuring early growth needs are met first. Nevertheless, the Affeercianado Guild will be asserting its authority in Year 2, especially if the business plan as modified by the ABC board has failed to live up to expectations.

Education

Let's take a closer look at primary and secondary education in Year 1 and Year 2.

Primary/Secondary Education Table 2.4		Debit	Credit	Balance
Year 1	0	$0	$0	$0
Number of elementary school students at county schools	24	$0		$0
Number of high school students at county schools	12	$0		$0
Number of elementary school students local students possible	0	$0		$0
Number of high school local students possible	0	$0		$0
Number of elementary school students at local schools	0	$0		$0
Number of high school students at local schools	0	$0		$0
Number of elementary schools	0	$0		$0
Number of high schools	0	$0		$0
Number of school buses needed	2	$0		$0
Number of school buses	4	$0		$0
Number of elementary school teachers	0	$0		$0
Number of high school teachers	0	$0		$0
Non-teaching staff	2	$0		$0
Total Educational Staff	2	$20,800		($20,800)
Construction workers needed	50	$520,000		($540,800)
Fed, state county revenue sharing	0	$0	$0	($540,800)
Developer impact fees	0	$0	$10,400,000	$9,859,200
4 School buses (6)	6	$400,000		$9,459,200
Construction tools and equipment (5)	6	$4,000,000	$0	$5,459,200
Building Material Elementary School (20)	20	$5,000,000		$459,200
Depreciation		$983,333		($524,133)
Revenue		($524,133)		$0
Year 2	0	$0	$0	$0
Number of elementary school students at county schools	0	$0		$0
Number of high school students at county schools	195	$0		$0
Number of elementary school students local students possible	594	$0		$0
Number of high school local students possible	0	$0		$0
Number of elementary school students at local schools	390	$0		$0
Number of high school students at local schools	0	$0		$0
Number of elementary schools	1	$0		$0
Number of high schools	0	$0		$0
Elementary school texts/supplies	0	$78,000		($78,000)
High school texts/supplies	0	$0		($78,000)
Elementary school utilities	0	$50,000		($128,000)
High school utilities	0	$0		($128,000)
Rent	0	$34,800		($162,800)
Number of school buses needed	4	$0		($162,800)
Number of school buses	8	$0		($162,800)
Number of elementary school teachers	27	$0		($162,800)
Number of high school teachers	0	$0		($162,800)
Non-teaching staff	20	$0		($162,800)
Total Educational Staff	47	$488,800		($651,600)
Construction workers needed	150	$1,560,000		($2,211,600)
Developer impact fees	0	$0	$11,264,000	$9,052,400
Fed, state, county revenue sharing	0	$0	$1,170,000	$10,222,400
Building Material 2 Elementary School (20)	20	$10,000,000		$222,400
Building Material High School (20)	20	$24,000,000		($23,777,600)
4 School buses (6)	6	$400,000		($24,177,600)
Depreciation		$2,750,000		($26,927,600)
Revenue		($26,927,600)		$0

In Year 1 we purchased 4 school buses to take the few students in unincorporated Prosperity to county schools. Two affeercianado bus drivers drove the students to county schools. We used 50 affeercianado construction workers to build an elementary school centrally located in the residential area. The building material for the school cost $5 million, and the construction tools and equipment, $4 million, but we only suffered a loss of $524,133 for the year due to developer impact fees.

Grade school student growth accelerates in Year 2, as many residential developments are completed. So much so, we need to build a high school and two more elementary schools. This is based on the guestimate that 6% of the population is in secondary school (9-12) and 12% in primary school (K-8). The maximum number of students in one high school is 3000, average 30 per class, although we build new schools before that limit is reached. There is a maximum of 594 students per elementary school, average 22 per class.

At least one elementary school will be built each semester. Like dormitories, elementary schools are the responsibility of Jane Jacobs' building trade students. Some classes will employ their specialty in multiple projects, such as 2 dormitories, or a dormitory and an elementary school, during the semester.

In Year 2, the total cost of the school materials is $34 million. Notice that 150 affeercianado construction workers add a cost of $1,560,000 at the billable rate of $5 per hour. Developer impact fees of $11+ million, and the $1.17 million in state revenue sharing, are hardly sufficient to turn the year profitable. Revenue sharing is only figured on the students currently enrolled, not the schools being built. Any state or federal construction grants will be added revenue.

Here is the education account at the high level. It includes grade school, high school and all the university colleges and schools.

Education Table 2.5	Debit	Credit	Balance	Borrow	Borrowed
Year 1 with initial debt	$0	$0	$0	$0	$0
Lower Education	$0	($524,133)	($524,133)	$0	$0
Higher Education	$0	($4,160,000)	($4,684,133)	$0	$0
Rent Dividend	$0	$0	($4,684,133)	$0	$0
Rent Owed	$228,000	$228,000	($4,684,133)	$0	$0
Borrow from land trust	$0	$0	$0	$4,684,133	$4,684,133
Year 2	$0	$0	$0	$0	$4,684,133
Lower Education	$0	($26,927,600)	($26,927,600)	$0	$4,684,133
Higher Education	$0	$3,400,000	($23,527,600)	$0	$4,684,133
Rent Dividend	$0	$0	($23,527,600)	$0	$4,684,133
Rent Owed	$234,800	$234,800	($23,527,600)	$0	$4,684,133
Borrow from land trust	$0	$0	$0	$23,527,600	$28,211,733

The combined deficit of Year 1 and Year 2 is $28,211,733. It is borrowed from the land trust as needed. So while the affeercianados are paying back $37 million to the land trust, the educational district is borrowing over $28 million.

Land Trust
Here is the land trust for Year 2:

Land Trust Table 2.6	Rent	10% Rents	40% Rents	Borrow	On Loan	Balance
Year 2	$0				($42,171,933)	$948,067
Affeercianado repayment	$0			$37,487,800	($4,684,133)	$38,435,867
Education borrowing	$0			($23,527,600)	($28,211,733)	$14,908,267
Municipal borrowing	$0			$0	($28,211,733)	$14,908,267
Affeercianado Rent	$0		$333,600	$0	($28,211,733)	$14,908,267
Municipal Rent	$0	$244,400			($28,211,733)	$14,908,267
Public roads	$0				($28,211,733)	$14,908,267
Private Roads	$0				($28,211,733)	$14,908,267
Unauctioned land-Rent paid by affeercianado	$0	$0	$329,600	$0	($28,211,733)	$14,908,267
Auction Rent 700@$6,000	$4,200,000				($28,211,733)	$17,428,267
Downtown auction Rent 4@$100,000	$400,000				($28,211,733)	$17,668,267
Rent 650@$4,000	$2,600,000				($28,211,733)	$19,228,267
Rent 700@$6,000	$4,200,000				($28,211,733)	$21,748,267
Rent 4@$100,000	$400,000				($28,211,733)	$21,988,267
Totals	$0				($28,211,733)	$21,988,267

The land trust begins Year 2 with $42 million on loan that is lowered to $4.6 million after the affeercianados pay their debt. Education then borrows $23.5 million. The Year 2 land auction and monthly ground rent on all developed land brings the land trust cash balance to almost $22 million by the end of the year.

Year 3

With the opening of 2 more affeercianado dormitories, the number of affeercianados can increase to 7,800. In the interest of fairness, seniority dictates which affeercianados have the opportunity to live in the dorms versus the prefab motel rooms, unless where one resides is a function of job requirements. However, all affeercianados can use the swimming pool, steam room, sauna, and gym in each of the dormitories.

Growth

Year 3 is a good time to examine planned growth. All of growth hinges on the quantity of land auctioned each year. That translates into new buildings and increases in population. However, new buildings are constructed by workers in the building trades or those able to function as an apprentice in the building trades. These workers, in turn, are a function of the population, the student body at Jane Jacobs, the number of affeercianados available for lease, and the number of migrant workers. Yet the number of affeercianados and migrant workers are a direct function of the available housing. The growth process is a collection of these and other circular dependencies including schools, retail, and infrastructure.

In Table 3.1, the estimate of buildings to be constructed that year is a function of the amount of land auctioned, at 2 buildings per acre. The estimate of workers needed is very crudely assumed to be 5 worker-years per building. Prefabricated homes, where 6 workers can put the home together in 2 weeks' time, require only .23 worker-years, while office buildings, apartment complexes and large retail could easily require 50 to 100 worker-years or more. However, these large entities tend to occupy more than a half-acre, reducing the building count. Because of division of labor and economies of scale, a community developer can build a single home for 1-2 worker-years. Therefore 5 worker-years, is an unstable median and definitely not a mode. The number must be watched closely as the plan unfolds.

Year Table 3.1	Estimate of total Population – non affeercianado	Estimate of buildings constructed per year	10% of population + affeercianados for lease + vacancies for migrant workers	Estimate of worker-years needed
1	200	1,300	8,584	6,500
2	3,250	1,408	13,093	7,800
3	7,550	1,608	13,909	8,800
4	12,350	2,008	15,065	10,800
5	18,150	2,808	16,465	14,800
6	25,950	3,708	19,736	19,300
7	36,000	4,008	21,100	20,800
8	46,800	4,308	22,454	22,300
9	58,350	4,768	24,734	24,600
10	71,050	5,210	27,641	27,000
11	85,050	5,632	31,292	31,200
12	102,250	6,032	33,231	33,200
13	120,450	6,032	33,202	33,200
14	138,650	6,632	36,331	36,200
15	158,350	6,632	40,684	36,200
16	178,050	6,832	45,339	37,200
17	198,250	6,814	48,940	35,400
18	216,650	6,814	50,343	35,400
19	235,050	6,814	54,530	35,400
20	253,450	6,812	58,664	35,200

The number of estimated worker-years is matched against 10% of the local population, reasonably assumed to be in the building trades in a new city, plus the number of affeercianados available for lease, plus the number of prefabricated motel rooms and trailer park slots available for migrant workers. There are ample workers for the job, although Year 13 cuts it rather close. In years 1, 2, and 3, there is a good cushion, to hone the parameters and modify growth accordingly.

Beginning in Year 12, we hold the rate of growth fairly constant, as school and infrastructure expansion begin to push the limits of credibility. There will also be resident backlash against the rough and tumble prefab and trailer park village. Migrant buildings trade workers need to be phased out in favor of local businesses, Jane Jacobs' students, and affeercianados. In Year 11, affeercianados will start replacing migrant workers in the prefabs and trailer park. They will be needed for work in households, industry, and retail, more so than the building trades. Then in the event we have reasons to slow the rate of growth earlier on, Years 15-20, where workers available significantly exceeds workers needed, can be used to catch up.

Critically, a final population of 253,450 plus the affeercianados is almost 300,000 and sufficiently large to support a local currency, the VIP$, in Phase-II.

Auction

Success in meeting the plan will lead to a projected increase in land values of 50%. We will auction off 800 acres at an estimated rent of $9,000 per acre. Another 4 acres of downtown should be auctioned for $150,000 in rent/acre. Ironically, a rapid increase in the ground rents each year does not work to our advantage. For one, it makes the land less appealing to future homesteaders and industry. Secondly, it raises the value of outlying land that we have yet to purchase. In Year 3, there is no speculative ring of undeveloped land. For these reasons, we want to keep the apparent land value as low as possible, even as we raise the actual value of the land.

In the first year, we need a critical level of interest, and this is initiated with the $1 million marketing campaign before the first auction. Once the first year goal of $4,000 rent/acre is met, there is no need for additional marketing. Word of mouth alone will be sufficient to push land prices too high, too fast. Nor can we increase the supply by auctioning off more land without creating a severe labor shortage in the building trades.

For these reasons, the amount of rent obtained in auction is a non-critical parameter. A low rent attracts people and industry, and allows for cheaper land accumulation by the affeercianados. A high rent generates a citizens' dividend that attracts people and industry, and provides the affeercianados with more funds to purchase land, although of little significance in comparison to the vast sums generated by the surplus labor of affeercianados and profits from Thomas Paine Hospital.

Just prior to opening up the land for trebling in Year 20, a media campaign, in the unlikely event it is needed, can be undertaken to promote the true value of the land.

Prosperity and the Aristocracy

You won't find a spreadsheet for the aristocracy, because there would be no debit entries and their balance is their own business. However, recall from *Volume I, The Vision*, that the cellular aristocracy plays a vital role in AFFEERCE. Many consider an aristocracy to be preposterous in a modern democracy so let me review the important points from Volume I.

1. Title is only a function of paying the highest ground rents. For example, the land baron of a given district will lose their title, if a resident of the district, paying a higher rent, wishes to assume the title.
2. Title is completely voluntary. If you do not wish a title, it passes to the next highest payer of ground rent. If at a later time you change your mind, and you are still paying a higher ground rent than the current holder of the title, you can usurp the title at will.
3. Title carries with it many responsibilities of a pecuniary nature. Most members of the aristocracy enjoy these responsibilities. They include hosting parties for legislators, sponsoring fact-finding trips out of state or out of country, paying for airfare, and hotels for your delegation, hosting evening entertainment, choosing restaurants, serving as a social ambassador, arranging schedules, leading sightseeing expeditions.
4. If there is a government building/palace provided by the citizens, pecuniary duties include paying the ground rent, maintenance, depreciation, and utilities on the entire property.
5. Title can be removed by a 2/3 vote of the associated cell, if the aristocrat is deemed an embarrassment to the district, city, state, or nation.

The aristocracy saves the taxpayer a fortune in financing boondoggles, entertaining visiting dignitaries, and maintaining embassies. But more than that, in a cellular democracy, higher offices will tend to be filled by the best qualified person. Knowledge of spreadsheets and budgeting will be far more important than charisma and good looks. To put it simply, in AFFEERCE, our legislators will be a rather boring bunch. And the higher they get, the more boring they will be. Rising through 7 cellular levels, they will not be part of royal families with names like Clinton, Bush, or Kennedy, but ordinary people first elected by their neighbors. This will be very, very, good for democracy and good government, but kind of lifeless. Enter the aristocracy, with no real power except to make the nerds look good; to surround them with enough fluff and falderal to generate an aura of importance.

Even before the cellular democracy, we will implement an aristocracy in Prosperity. The chancellors at the University and Hospital are considered aristocrats. But the highest level titles go to those paying the greatest ground rent in a dominion. Unlike titles of old, our titles are very gender neutral. One can be a baron or baroness, duke or duchess, even king or queen, based on personal gender preference.

The Grand Duke of Prosperity is the highest rent payer who volunteers to be duke. Although duke is a title reserved for aristocracy at the level of cellular level-5, a large state, Prosperity is like a city that will grow to fill the entire host-state. The Grand Duke of Prosperity or her heirs could ride the entire wave of Phases I, I, and III, if the family remains the top taxpayer, or are deferred to by the top taxpayer. Alternative family members of the Grand Duke of Prosperity are referred to by the title of count or countess.

Each of Prosperity's three districts will be served by a baron. With names far more eloquent than these, they will be the Baron of the Medical District, Campus and Southern Downtown, the Baron of City Hall and Large Retail, and the Baron of Prosperity Residential Estates. These will be offered first to the highest rent payer in each district, besides the Grand Duke. Alternative family members can choose between the titles, lord or lady. Needless to say, an aristocracy will also be very good for tourism.

In all seriousness, there will be many outside dignitaries, U.S. and foreign, interested in our experiment. Who are our leaders? The mayor and city council members are affeercianados paid $25/week plus room/board/medical. The school board and county board are affeercianados paid $25/week plus room/board/medical. They are hard workers who got their positions through knowledge of what needs to be done. It would be grossly unfair to them to have them host U.S. senators, big city mayors and even world leaders, unaided. The aristocracy will host the receptions, make the introductions, arrange the meetings, and serve as Prosperity ambassadors with members of their own social class. Our affeercianado leaders can get as involved as their comfort level allows, or quickly withdraw if they feel they are in over their heads.

Early on, Prosperity will be very involved in smartcard and VIP standards. This will involve travel to ANSI and ISO meetings around the country and around the world. An interested member of the aristocracy can support our delegation in style, paying for expensive transportation, room and board, even throwing evening parties for all the delegates at the meeting. Everyone will look forward to the arrival of the Prosperity delegation, and that will help us win important votes in the standards' bodies.

The Grand Duke or Grand Duchess of Prosperity

At this point, there isn't much ground rent, so the title of Grand Duke of Prosperity will likely be won simply by bidding the highest rent on the city hall/palace. Unlike the chancelleries whose rent is minimal because the chancellor's pay for their construction, city hall construction is paid for by the city, so high rents are likely, especially when there are no large land rights holders at this early stage of the game. This is specified in the jurisdictional covenant.

The auction brochure lists the minimum bid needed on the palace to become the largest ground rent payer in the dominion. Current land rights holders can subtract their total ground rent from this amount to find their minimum bid. However, minimum bids are not likely to win this prestigious title. This is the highest aristocratic title that will exist in the United States for perhaps 50 years. When Prosperity is a success, the Grand Duke as chief ambassador, will host visiting world leaders and travel the world as a dignitary to social events.

Because the results of the land auction will affect the minimum bid needed to be Grand Duke, the auction for the title will be held after the land auction has settled. At that point, a temporary Grand Duke will be crowned from the largest payer of ground rent who agrees to be Grand Duke. Bidders must exceed the total ground rent of the temporary Grand Duke, and future treblers must exceed with their trebles the total ground rent of the current Grand Duke.

A 2/3 vote of the ABC Board can withhold permission to bid or permission to treble, or dethrone the crowned Grand Duke, should they prove an embarrassment or fail to perform their duties.

Duties of the Grand Duke include payment of ground rent, maintenance, depreciation, and utilities of the city hall/palace. Unlike a chancellery, there is no objective depreciated value returned to the Grand Duke on a treble, so renovations or any contributions to the building fund beyond replacing depreciated assets are done as a donation, one that will likely increase ground rent. Unlike a chancellor, the Grand Duke has hosting, entertainment, boosterism, and travel obligations, where the failure to perform these obligations can result in dismissal by the ABC Board, or later the city council. However, the very reason wealthy people become aristocrats, is because it is a lifetime dream to perform these obligations. (For more details, see *Volume I – Cellular Aristocracy*)

It is not unreasonable to expect a bid of $2 million in ground rent for the title and palace. As Prosperity grows in prominence, that number could easily be trebled to $6 million or more. However, none of this is reflected in the conservative spreadsheets, except the saved depreciation, maintenance and utility costs.

Accommodations

Due to the large number of migrant workers, the affeercianados will have enough business renting out the motel rooms and feeding the workers that two affeercianado dorms being built in Year 3 are completely covered, with a positive ending balance of $7 million.

Accommodations Table 3.2		Debit	Credit	Balance
Prefab rooms to let	1800			(345,600)
Prefab rentals @45 a night	180	$788,400	$2,956,500	1,822,500
Prefab rentals @195 a week	1080	$2,246,400	$10,951,200	10,527,300
Prefab rentals @700 a month	540	$648,000	$4,536,000	14,415,300
Trailer size rentals @18 a day	1000	$3,650,000	$6,570,000	17,335,300
AFFEERCE a'Cookin @22 a day	1180	$3,230,250	$9,475,400	23,580,450
AFFEERCE a'Cookin @140 a week	1080	$2,808,000	$7,862,400	28,634,850
AFFEERCE a'Cookin @560 a month	2540	$6,705,600	$17,068,800	38,998,050
Affeercianados working at accommodations	442			38,998,050
Maintenance cost		$1,140,000		37,858,050
Supply cost		$570,000		37,288,050
Purchase 60 washes/dryers (6)	6	$40,000		37,248,050
Purchase kitchen equipment (8)	8	$70,000		37,178,050
Dorm furnishings (10)	10	$600,000		36,578,050
Materials for 2 Dorms(20)	20	$24,000,000		12,578,050
Depreciation		$5,385,708		7,192,342
Revenue		$7,192,342		0

Affeercianados

The Year 3 balance sheet for the affeercianados is quite impressive.

Affeercianados Table 3.3	Debit	Credit	Balance
Year 3	$0	$0	$42,508,868
Hospital	$0	$16,773,432	$59,282,299
Accommodations	$0	$7,192,342	$66,474,641
Supply Depot	$0	$542,368	$67,017,009
Surplus Labor	$0	$87,746,624	$154,763,633
AMS Software	$0	$0	$154,763,633
Metro Bus Service	$0	$651,200	$155,414,833
Downtown excavation	$0	($3,400,960)	$152,013,873
Rent Dividend	$0	$706,331	$152,720,204
Pay Unauctioned land Rent	$0	($244,200)	$152,476,004
Grant to municipality	$140,000,000	$0	$12,476,004
Rent Owed	$345,600	$345,600	$12,476,004

The hospital will generate over $16 million, accommodations $7 million, and the gem of Phase-I, leasing out affeercianados, is predicted to generate over $87 million! Although the temptation to purchase land will be great, incorporation of Prosperity is only one year away. A beautiful city hall that will double as a palace for the Duke or Duchess of Prosperity, overlooking a reflecting pool, will be a landmark. And Prosperity must pay a $100 medical premium for every resident (premiums that come right back to the affeercianados). So rather than buy land, the affeercianados grant the municipality $140 million.

Why is this a grant instead of a loan? The grant will increase land value by $140 million or more. Although the affeercianados own just over 50% of the land, they will ultimately own over 94% of the land, and while ownership is time weighted, land value is not. Furthermore, most of this money will go right back to the affeercianados in the form of medical premiums and paid labor. There is no reason to saddle the new city with debt. Such a debt would eliminate the citizens' dividend in Years 4-9. These CDs are even more valuable to the affeercianados than the citizens at large as a source of discretionary income. So in a sense, this $140 million grant gives the affeercianados an actual increase in salary at the same time it increases land values. After the grant, the affeercianados are left with only $12.2 million on their balance sheet.

Affeercianado Recruitment

It is expected there will be a surplus of applicants for affeercianados due to media publicity over the first AFFEERCE land purchase and excitement generated by this book. Many college students will see the collectivist affeercianado dorms as a continuation of the campus lifestyle; a way to hide from the real world for 20 more years and then be presented with over a million dollars as a reward in addition to a large pension, while those who could not afford college will jump at the chance of a free education.

For some, it will be a dream lifestyle, however, all but the most dedicated will want to get married, have children, buy an expensive automobile, and live in a home with pets and a yard, etc. after 4 or 5 years of tiny bedrooms, hard work, and little pay. Some will not easily handle the frequent demotions. (We will always move the best skilled person into the higher job without regard to seniority.) Many of the businesses that lease affeercianados at low pay will want to hire the best and brightest at large salaries. The take the money and run option returns a severance of $30,000 after five years of service, more than enough for a down payment on that beautiful home. Or the departing affeercianado can take severance for three years, $18,000, and remain vested in the final two years for an expected payout of over $120,000, 15 years later in today's dollars.

It is best to be prepared and assume a chronic shortage of affeercianados. Recruiters from the ABC will attend job fairs, campus career-days, and advertise on the AFFEERCE web page and through social media. There is much to be said for becoming an affeercianado. Besides the campus lifestyle and free education, there is the camaraderie, the belief that one is saving the world, opportunities to run for political office, continual education, and last but not least, the giant pot of gold at the end of the rainbow.

Once vetted by the ABC Board, resumes are turned over to the HR department of the municipality if the affeercianado will fill a municipal position.

Once hired, the new affeercianado goes through a 6 month probationary period. On completion, they are judged by supervisors, peers, and possibly business owners. A bad leasing history over the period could be a serious warning sign. If leased by different businesses at the start of the period, and then never leased again, or leased for lower amounts each day, then there is strong evidence of poor performance.

If the probationary period is passed, the new affeercianado becomes a member of the Affeercianado Guild and can only be removed by a super-plurality vote of the entire Guild.

The City

City hall
The city hall/palace of the Grand Duke of Prosperity is being built in preparation for incorporation.

Here are the expected city hall purchases for Year 3. A temporary city hall will be located in the hospital annex, as it is in Years 1 and 2. The only depreciation taken is the 5 year depreciation on tools and equipment.

City Hall (purchases Year 3) Table 3.4		Debit	Credit	Balance
Total affeercianados (includes 200 construction)	274	$0	$0	$341,950
City Hall supplies	0	$100,000	$0	$241,950
City Hall utilities	0	$60,000	$0	$181,950
Construction tools and equipment (5) (used by parks and recreation/police)	5	$4,000,000	$0	($3,818,050)
Material for City Hall (30)-Depreciation paid by Duke	30	$18,000,000	$0	($21,818,050)
Depreciation		$848,750	$0	($22,666,800)
Revenue		($22,666,800)	$0	$0

There will be 200 affeercianados working on the city hall with a materials cost of $18 million. The additional $4 million of construction tools and equipment purchased will be later used by parks and recreation and police/fire.

Police

Police Table 3.5		Debit	Credit	Balance
Year 3	0	$0	$0	$0
Police Chief /Director of public safety includes adjacent fire stations	0	$100,000	$0	($100,000)
Clerical and command affeercianados	8	$0	$0	($100,000)
Police officer affeercianados	25	$251,667	$0	($351,667)
Video surveillance/dash-cams/body-cams/automated ticketing team	0	$2,517	$0	($354,184)
School crossing guards (part time - number is x 3 full time equivalent)	8	$0	$0	($354,184)
Total affeercianados	41	$0	$0	($354,184)
Vehicles	19	$38,000	$0	($392,184)
Police station Rent	0	$0	$0	($392,184)
Number of districts	1	$0	$0	($392,184)
Fuel	0	$104,025	$0	($496,209)
Police station utilities		$0	$0	($496,209)
Fines (from automated ticketing only)	0	$0	$0	($496,209)
Office supplies		$20,000	$0	($516,209)
9 squad cars (6)	6	$450,000	$0	($966,209)
1 police wagon (6)	6	$100,000	$0	($1,066,209)
1 animal control wagon (6)	6	$50,000	$0	($1,116,209)
Materials for new police/fire station-City hall (20)	20	$6,000,000	$0	($7,116,209)
Depreciation		$600,000	$0	($7,716,209)
Revenue		($7,716,209)	$0	$0

Side by side with the new city hall will be a police and fire station with a material cost of $6 million. By the end of Year 3, there will be 2 affeercianado dormitories at the city hall site. These will house all municipal employees including public safety. As the population grows and new districts form, there will be a dormitory at each police/fire/municipal substation.

The director of public safety, a non-affeercianado earning $100,000 per year, and building costs for joint police/fire stations are accounted for on this spreadsheet. Otherwise, the fire department maintains its own account (below). By the end of Year 3, the police will have 19 vehicles including 9 squad cars, a police wagon, and an animal control wagon purchased during the year. At this point in time, the police department is still covered by state laws regulating private security. All of Prosperity is private property owned by the land trust as proxy for the affeercianados and investors. This provides both benefits and limitations that will be lost in Year 4 with incorporation.

Fire Department

Fire and Paramedic Table 3.6		Debit	Credit	Balance
Year 3	0	$0	$0	$0
Clerical and command affeercianados	4	$0	$0	$0
Fire fighter affeercianados	13	$188,750	$0	($188,750)
Fire building inspection team, Arson investigators, paramedics	10	$20,000	$0	($208,750)
Total affeercianados	27	$0	$0	($208,750)
Vehicles	5	$10,000	$0	($218,750)
Number of districts	1	$0	$0	($218,750)
Fuel	0	$27,375	$0	($246,125)
Fire station utilities		$10,000	$0	($256,125)
Inspection fees	0	$0	$482,400	$226,275
Fire station supplies		$80,000	$0	$146,275
Depreciation		$62,500	$0	$83,775
Revenue		$83,775	$0	$0

The firefighters are able to eke out a small profit thanks to the $482,400 of inspection fees generated from new construction. Profits won't last from Year 4 on, when they begin paying the affeercianados $5/hour for labor. There are also no new vehicle purchases in Year 3.

The $138,750 charged for the 13 firefighters is for uniforms, supplies, and equipment.

Parks and Recreation

Parks and Recreation Table 3.7		Debit	Credit	Balance
Year 3	0	$0	$0	$0
Parks and Recreation Manager	0	$100,000	$0	($100,000)
Manager's Office	3	$0	$0	($100,000)
Public Safety liaison	1	$0	$0	($100,000)
Landscaping	30	$0	$0	($100,000)
Lights and electrical	8	$0	$0	($100,000)
Playground repair	3	$0	$0	($100,000)
Bike paths and walking trails	8	$0	$0	($100,000)
Water fountain maintenance	3	$0	$0	($100,000)
Total general employees	56	$0	$0	($100,000)
General supplies	0	$500,000	$0	($600,000)
Annual pass for community centers	0	$0	$0	($600,000)
Per Community Center employees	0	$0	$0	($600,000)
Lifeguards and swim instructors	4	$0	$0	($600,000)
Coaches	5	$0	$0	($600,000)
General officer, reception, scheduling, grants	6	$0	$0	($600,000)
Day care center	8	$0	$0	($600,000)
Senior center	4	$0	$0	($600,000)
Youth center	6	$0	$0	($600,000)
Social workers/counseling/victims advocates	6	$0	$0	($600,000)
Trainers	3	$0	$0	($600,000)
First aid	2	$0	$0	($600,000)
Arts and craft instructors	6	$0	$0	($600,000)
Library	2	$0	$0	($600,000)
Kitchen	8	$0	$0	($600,000)
Janitorial/Maintenance/Security	6	$0	$0	($600,000)
Community center supplies	0	$0	$0	($600,000)
Revenue from rental of meeting rooms, theater	0	$0	$0	($600,000)
Catering income	0	$0	$0	($600,000)
Anchor tenant rent	0	$0	$0	($600,000)
Total affeercianados per community center	66	$0	$0	($600,000)
Number of community centers	0	$0	$0	($600,000)
Total community center supplies	0	$0	$0	($600,000)
Total community center affeercianados	0	$0	$0	($600,000)
Total affeercianados	56	$0	$0	($600,000)
Community center utilities	0	$0	$0	($600,000)
Parks and rec tools and equipment (5)	5	$6,000,000	$0	($6,600,000)
Depreciation		$1,200,000	$0	($7,800,000)
Revenue		($7,800,000)	$0	$0

Most of Table 3.7 describes the makeup of a community center, of which there are currently none. However, a manager is hired in Year 3 for $100,000. There are 30 landscapers and assorted other personnel. The big expenses in Year 3 for parks and recreation are tools and equipment costing $6 million that depreciate over a rapid 5 years. By this time, the pattern of bids will suggest areas for bike paths, walking trails, and the upcoming first community center.

Let's look at the balance sheet of the city in its last year before incorporation.

Prosperity Table 3.8	Debit	Credit	Balance
Year 3	$0	$0	$12,194,549
Grant from affeercianados	$0	$140,000,000	$152,194,549
Roads and infrastructure	$0	$188,284	$152,382,834
City Hall	$0	($22,666,800)	$129,716,034
Parks and Recreation	$0	($7,800,000)	$121,916,034
Police	$0	($7,716,209)	$114,199,825
Fire	$0	$83,775	$114,283,600
Waste Management	$0	$393,875	$114,677,475
Hospital Premiums	$9,060,000	$0	$105,617,475
Rent Dividend	$0	$1,807,470	$107,424,945
Rent Owed (10% only)	$9,600	$9,600	$107,424,945

The $140 million grant from the affeercianados leaves the city quite solvent in preparation for incorporation. There is an ending balance of $107 million even after huge charges for city hall, parks and recreation, and police. Roads and infrastructure, and waste management are both showing profits. Those departments will continue to grow more profitable as utility delivery charges, and sale of recyclable product, respectively increase.

Take a look at the $1.8 million rent dividend tranche for the city. Per agreement with the county, the city's share of the 30% rent for services will rise from 20% in Year 3 to 60% in Year 4, with incorporation. Therefore we can expect a considerable increase to over $5 million in the following year, which takes into account an additional land auction.

Higher Education

Higher Education (Year 3) Table 3.9		Debit	Credit	Balance
Year 3	0	$0	$0	$0
Affeercianados enrolled full time at Jane Jacobs/quarter	1248	$0	$0	$0
Prosperity resident students enrolled full time/quarter	0	$0	$0	$0
In-state nonresident students enrolled full time/quarter	0	$0	$0	$0
Medical school students	0	$0	$0	$0
Medical student lab costs	0	$0	$0	$0
Jane Jacobs affeercianado instructors	80	$0	$0	$0
Jane Jacobs affeercianado non-dorm staff	24	$0	$0	$0
State grant @5000 per full time college year	0	$0	$6,240,000	$6,240,000
Paid university professors/Department heads	4	$400,000	$0	$5,840,000
Med school affeercianado instructors not hospital affiliated	0	$0	$0	$5,840,000
Hospital affiliated med school instructors	0	$0	$0	$5,840,000
Paid med school instructors not hospital affiliated	0	$0	$0	$5,840,000
Med school affeercianado non-dorm staff	0	$0	$0	$5,840,000
Total affeercianado educators and staff	104	$0	$0	$5,840,000
Number of student dorms of 250 rooms for 2 + paid room debits/credits	0	$0	$0	$5,840,000
Rent Owed	0	$200,000	$0	$5,640,000
Dorm Staff (counted in accommodations)	0	$0	$0	$5,640,000
Construction workers	100	$1,040,000	$0	$4,600,000
Materials for 1 Student Dorm s(20)	20	$12,000,000		($7,400,000)
Depreciation		$2,160,000		($9,560,000)
Revenue		($9,560,000)		$0

The enormous Jane Jacobs University chancellery is still mostly empty classrooms. In order to have a student population that goes beyond nearby residents and affeercianados, student dormitories are needed. Student dorms, like elementary schools and affeercianado dorms are handled as part of the Jane Jacobs curriculum. The regularity allows the same courses to be taught each semester and gain new insights into division of labor and economies of scale. In a slight variation with the affeercianado dorm, each student dorm houses 550, with a floor dedicated to classrooms and a lecture hall, in keeping with the spirit of mixed usage. There is no waste. Before housing outside students, the rooms will be used to house affeercianados or migrant laborers at a profit. One dormitory will be built in Year 3. Each year thereafter will see two new student dorms built.

Year 4

This is the year of incorporation, when Prosperity becomes a real city. Our population is projected to be 10,800 homesteaders plus 9,000 affeercianados. In most states, that is a sufficient number of citizens for incorporation.

City Hall

The text below on city structure and function is meant to be a starting point for discussions. It combines mostly conventional city organization with a few concepts unique to Prosperity, but is a far cry from the organic structures that will emerge from the cellular democracies of Phase-II. In addition to the desirability of structure in Phase-I, we are also limited by the regulations of the host state. The Affeercianado Guild will have three years to hammer out the details before we go live.

The City Council

City hall opens as parks and recreation complete the landscaping around the reflecting pool. Electing a city council will be the first order of business. To that end, the Affeercianado Guild will hold a primary convention, with candidates submitting their resumes, speaking to the assembled Guild, and answering questions. In the end, a full slate will be chosen.

An election, by district, transitions easily into a cellular democracy. Prosperity is initialized as a level-5 cell, complete with a Grand Duke. This purposely orphans all lower level cells so they can have maximum freedom to grow in Phase-II and Phase-III. During the previous three years, we will have built six affeercianado dormitories. Two at city hall, one at the hospital and the other three scattered in different parts of the city. These will correspond to the five districts established in the city charter. There is no mayor. The ceremonial role will be played by the Grand Duke of Prosperity.

The affeercianado slate might have competition from homesteaders in the general election, but it is doubtful we will have serious competition, at least not yet. We will have made many promises to our homesteaders, promises that for the most part will have been kept. Their economic future is tied up with ours. Business does not want to lose cheap affeercianado labor. Homesteaders do not want any rent increase before the freeze officially ends in Year 20. Unless and until we seriously fail our citizens, winning in the Affeercianado Guild primary, will be tantamount to winning the general election. Although affeercianado control will be true for the city council from the start, it will become increasingly true for the school board, county offices, and state and federal legislative offices.

That is a powerful reason for paid non-affeercianado department heads. Without them, it would be difficult, if not impossible, to form an efficient hierarchy. With an affeercianado city council, an affeercianado city manager, and affeercianado city workers, there would be no locus of authority to grow a department. That is why the city manager, and many of the department heads beneath the city manager, are well paid, and are not Guild members.

City Manager

The city council can hire and fire a city manager. The original city manager will be hired by the ABC board and Prosperity CEO and will be retained if the council is satisfied with their performance.

City Manager – City Hall – Year 4 Table 4.1	#EMP	Debit	Credit	Balance
City Manager	0	$150,000	$0	($150,000)
City Manager's Office	2	$0	$0	($150,000)
Public Safety liaison	1	$0	$0	($150,000)
Parks and Recreation liaison	0	$0	$0	($150,000)
Roads and infrastructure liaison	1	$0	$0	($150,000)
Waste Management liaison	1	$0	$0	($150,000)
Transportation liaison	0	$0	$0	($150,000)
City/University Library liaison	0	$0	$0	($150,000)
Hospital/Med campus liaison	1	$0	$0	($150,000)
Janitorial/Maintenance/Garage	10	$0	$0	($150,000)
Building and Planning	21	$0	$602,400	$452,400

The paid city manager manages paid or affeercianado department heads and a number of affeercianados in the office, such as secretary, receptionist, filing clerk, computer aid, and assistants. In Year 4, these roles are filled by 2 staff members with the aid of the liaisons. These are liaisons to municipal or municipal-related departments headquartered outside of city hall. The employee count appears higher than it actually is, as there will be considerable redundancy between liaisons and workers in the city manager's office.

The city manager, with the advice and consent of the city council, can hire and fire a city treasurer, city attorney, city clerk, director of public safety, director of parks and recreation, director of roads and infrastructure, and director of waste management. Some of these positions can be filled by qualified affeercianados at the discretion of the city manager. The city manager cannot fire an affeercianado, only remove them from the team, or demote them.

With the advent of cellular democracy, the city manager will appoint district managers with the advice and consent of district councils. Because the cellular democracy is a template for government, details of retrofitting Prosperity will be found in the city charter.

The city manager chairs the building and planning team, and appoints team leaders. The $602,400 revenue earned from building inspections is shown as a credit for building and planning.

The city manager appoints an affeercianado director of maintenance and janitorial services for the upkeep of city hall, the city yard, and garage.

City Clerk

The city clerk is the public face of city business. The clerk is hired by the city manager. The city clerk should be professionally certified by International Institute of Municipal Clerks (IIMC). Some of the more interesting projects of the City of Prosperity can be found in the clerk's office. These include the smartcard (later the VIP), and the city gift shop.

City Clerk – City Hall – Year 4 Table 4.2	#EMP	Debit	Credit	Balance
City Clerks office	6	$0	$123,500	($47,600)
Gift catalog	4	$0	$494,000	$446,400
Software and smartcard AMS liaison	10	$0	$0	$446,400
Food, health, and sanitation inspectors	3	$0	$12,350	$458,750
Voter registration, candidate management, online voting	4	$0	$0	$458,750

The clerk's office is a revenue generator for Prosperity, collecting money for fines, fees, licenses, permits, gift shop purchases, and food inspections.

Inspections out of the clerk's office include sanitary conditions in restaurants, rodent infestations, swimming pool inspections, nuisance hoarding and nuisance noise, accumulation of garbage, accumulation of debris. However, stray and wild animal control is handled by the department of public safety.

Although most software is developed at AMS (Affeercianado Municipal Software), usage requirements and acceptability come from the city clerk's office for the smartcard, online gift shop, online land system, and online voting, as well as internal software.

The following tasks are performed by the city clerk's office:

- Issue birth, marriage, and death certificates
- Answer municipal queries from citizens (press 0 to talk with a live operator).
- Register alternative families, record modified family charters, grant union and divorce
- Maintain deeds in online land system. Handle property transfers via purchase, treble, auction, or gift.
- Maintain an archive of all city documents.
- Certify the ballot petitions of all candidates for council, taxation petitions, and local legislation
- Oversee voting on community legislation, certifying the necessary 2/3 or 5/6 pluralities.
- Oversee standard state and federal elections
- Register voters and maintain voter registration lists
- Take minutes at all council and other public meetings
- Prepares agendas for meetings organizing input from council members, department managers, and other stakeholders throughout the period between meetings.
- Register and issue jitney cab identifiers
- Accept cash for and distribute cash from smartcard accounts (mostly done online)
- Issue permits and licenses. Contract with state and county to issue state permits and licenses
- Keep copies of all city laws
- Work with police on their responsibility under recent ordinances. (Legal handles older ordinances).
- Manage city charter that maintains relationship between the city council, the affeercianados, the ABC, the city manager and other hired department heads.
- Copy city documents on request
- Handle inquiries from other cities, counties, the state or federal government as well as citizens
- The certification of documents is a small revenue generator.
- Issue dog licenses so that loose dogs can be returned.
- Sell auto stickers for reduced parking rate.
- Record liens on property for failure to pay ground rent and lift rent freezes on these properties.
- Record and archive documents for citizens, such as removal of liens, military discharge, and other papers.
- Codify ordinances by reviewing changes, approving and backing up final wording.
- Distribute citizens' dividend after applying smartcard deficits
- Have good working knowledge of latest software packages.

Smartcard

Drivers' licenses and state ID cards are usually issued by the county. However, the smartcard is a precursor to the VIP and very important to the future of Prosperity and AFFEERCE. We will push in negotiations for a single card and would be happy to provide reduced-price card service for county residents outside of Prosperity in return.

As of this writing, smartcard technology allows money, debit accounts, passes, tickets, permits and licenses to be accessed through a single card. If that card is an application on a smart phone, biometric identification can be added as a safeguard for all uses.

Prior to the external biometric identities required for the VIP, all citizens should register for a city card or city card smart phone application. The card itself electronically contains the owner's unique name and ID, biometric identity, and a headshot photo. Contact information is kept by the city clerk. Actual balances and other items placed on the card are also stored remotely on city computers. If a card is reported lost or stolen, it will set off an alarm if an attempt is made to use it. A replacement card with a new unique ID will be issued for $5.

Prosperity Smartcard	Table 4.3
Identity	A sophisticated smartcard reader can use the biometrics on the card to verify that the person using the card and the card owner are one and the same, even if the card is not on a smart phone. Card also contains photo for human verification.
Voter Registration	In addition to holding the drivers' license and state ID, the smartcard is a voter registration card. With smartcard readers on a home computer, the card can be used for online voting if legal by state and federal law.
Paying Traffic Fines	For moving violations, and other civil infractions where the citizen is present and does not plan to contest the ticket in court, there is a 25% discount of the fine, if the officer places the fine directly on the smartcard.
Show Tickets	Paper tickets of the good kind can also be avoided. Vendors can place tickets to shows directly on the card, and the card or smart-phone display can be presented at the door. The card can be used to direct you to your seat in a crowded theater or stadium.
Library Card	The smartcard is required to check out library books and for inter-library loan. Library fines are added to the card.
Jitney Mutual Identity	Jitney cab safety requires both the driver and passenger to have verified identities. If the registered driver installs a smartcard reader, mutual identity app (MIA) verifies both driver and passenger are who they say they are. It also verifies that the person driving the vehicle is authorized to do so, revolutionizing ride-sharing safety.
Debit Card	A smartcard can be used as a general debit card for money stored with the city clerk. Deficits on the card are not allowed when used for non-municipal purposes. Deficits for fines, permits, inspections, copays, and fees that are over 60 days old will be applied against any citizens' dividend at two to one. That is, if you owe $50 in fees, $100 will be deducted from your CD before it is paid out. While a deficit exists, use of the card for certain municipal services will require cash up front, and up to 10% of that cash will be used to pay down the deficit.
Credit Cards	A smartcard can be tied to multiple credit cards, so only the single smartcard with picture ID and biometrics need be carried.
Parks and Recreation	A smartcard is required for all community center services.

Medical Care	The smartcard is needed for medical care with doctors at the municipal hospital. It can be used for copays if there is no deficit over 60 days old. Otherwise, cash for non-emergencies and an additional 10% is required to pay down the deficit. All medical records, including high-resolution test results will be "stored on the card," so as you move from doctor to doctor, your records will move with you.
City Passes	A city pass, good for discounts or free admission at many venues in the city can be placed on the card. These venues receive monthly pro-rated revenue from the card based on the time you enter their place of business, until the card is used again outside their place of business.
Parking	Monthly and weekly passes for remote, lower downtown, and metered parking can be placed on the card, as well as parking by the hour.
Transit Pass	In this business plan, public transit is relegated to jitneys. The assumption is that a sufficient number of jitney buses and cars can be persuaded to accept a monthly pass on the smartcard for all or most of their fare. If not, public transit using affeercianado labor should at the very least break even, making it a non-issue for the business plan at this stage. Monthly passes can be added to the card online manually or automatically every month for only $20 a month. The pass allows free 15 minute bicycle rental and 10 cent/half hour thereafter, 10 cent/ride intra-city bus, free bus rides to and from high school. Luxury bus rides to Old Metropolis will remain completely free, although a smartcard might be required for boarding at some point.

Prepare the VIP

The smartcard is the first step toward the VIP. With the VIP, Prosperity can be a card-less, cashless, even key-less. The only real difference between the VIP and the smartcard is that with the VIP, there is no card. Tourists will be anxious to experience such a society, adding tourism to medical tourism and education, as chief exports.

Phase-II cannot occur unless the VIP is safe, secure, and flawless. A VIP VSG will be formed in Phase-I, and will be open to industries interested in VIP development. The ABC board of directors in conjunction with Affeercianado Municipal Software (AMS) will lay down usability requirements for the VSG, although it is expected that implementation will involve customization of existing technology. AMS representatives will be certified as experts in hardware, software, VIP technology, and security.

The VSG chosen technology will likely alter the marketplace, as Prosperity will be a major consumer initially, and by capitulation, all U.S. citizens will be bound to this technology. AMS representatives will serve on any related ANSI (American National Standards Institute) or ISO (International Standards Organization) committees.

Phase-I implementations of the VIP will use the U.S. dollar as default account currency, as the VIP$ will not exist until the land monetization at the start of Phase-II. Nevertheless, before Phase-I is complete, the VIP$ must be fully functional and pass the following benchmarks: (This is a preliminary list of technical requirements and can be skipped by the casual reader.)

1. The creation of the AFFEERCE Central Bank (precursor to the Treasury at capitulation).
2. VIP handling of U.S. dollar accounts must be functional in most Prosperity businesses.
3. The advance creation of several hundred VIP$ for testing VIP$ accounts.
4. PCA, PSA, FCA, FSA, and CA must be able to be established at the Central Bank and assigned to private banks. (P = Personal, F = Family, C = Corporate, S = Spending, A = Account)
5. Banks can establish individual, family, and business CCAs (credit corporate accounts).

6. Food and housing distribution accounts and advance rent accounts using the U.S. dollar must be functional.
7. Personal distribution accounts must be able to be established at the Central Bank with immediate pass through via discretionary and annuity distribution trees, including roots to other distribution trees.
8. Ability to group food and housing distribution accounts by family and ability to specify group access rules.
9. Consumption tax must be moved to the Central Bank, whenever money is moved from a corporate account to a spending account or spent directly.
10. Allow spending from corporate accounts if marked as capital expenditure.
11. Scripted VIP application accounts to meet citizen investor requirements.
12. Ability to store an open identity in a trinket or smartphone for offline identity verification that can be used for property access. (A key or weapon that can be used only by one person.)
13. Point of sale transactions with arbitrary account configurations.
14. Record of every VIP transaction stored in multiple locations
15. Ability to restore and replay VIP transactions without shutting down the system.

On completion of the VIP specification, all industries are encouraged to compete in the production of readers for ATM's, doors, computers, phones, cabs, retail outlets, etc. These readers should not require a significant outlay, as several incarnations might be needed before Phase-II, and then capitulation.

Once the VIP is operational, the smartcard can be disposed of and the city clerk will simply register identities. The city clerk will open an office so tourists can take advantage of free identity registration.

Obviously, those who fear Big Brother will not be residents or even tourists in Prosperity. It will take decades to prove that the information is both secure and can only be used responsibly. Our honesty and transparency is critical to that end. In the meanwhile, the Prosperity monopoly on biometric identity will create life benefits of great convenience for those who trust us and lead to immense profit.

City Gift shop and Warehouse

The city clerk's office is in charge of the gift shop and warehouse. This serves several valuable purposes. First of all, when donated items are purchased, the proceeds go to the city. Secondly, the city can encourage volunteerism, by paying volunteers $2 gift shop scrip for every hour volunteered. This is a nice way to thank neighborhood patrols, community center volunteers, those who check up on seniors, volunteers in day care centers, and so on. The scrip can be placed directly on the smartcard. Finally, the affeercianados who are paid next to nothing can be given perhaps $50 of gift shop scrip a month to buy clothing, games, cool stuff, or dorm furnishings.

The online software is designed by AMS. Donated items are photographed and described for the online catalog. Inferior items will be rejected. The price is set relatively high for the condition and original purchase price. Every week the price drops by 20% until the item is sold.

The city should feel free to use the gift shop for its own furnishings and decorations. Sports equipment and other items for the community center can also be purchased from the gift shop.

Legal

The city attorney is hired by the city manager. There are many unique legal issues that an AFFEERCE Phase-I municipality must deal with such as labor issues, conflict of interest, interdependence between usually independent agents, leasing of land, auction of leases, special contracts with the county and state, details of the city charter, disputed state and federal tax liability, and trebling. This is in addition to standard duties. The city attorney probably will have been actively involved in drafting the city charter and will have a long history with the ABC.

City Attorney – City Hall – Year 4	Table 4.4	#EMP	Debit	Credit	Balance
City Attorney		0	$100,000	$0	$252,400
Legal		4	$0	$0	$252,400
City liability insurance		0	$123,500	$0	$128,900

The city attorney has 4 paralegal/clerical assistants. The cities liability policy cost $123,500 for the year, calculated at $10 per resident. The affeercianados have their own liability policy.

The following tasks are performed by the city attorney's office:

- Provides legal opinions to all department heads and the city council.
- Prepares all ordinances based on drafts by council members or department managers
- Reviews all leases, contracts, etc. before they are signed.
- Reviews questions of conflict of interest.
- Acts as parliamentarian during uncontrolled meetings (should know Robert's Rules of order).
- Serves as legal advocate with the host-state.
- Maintains integrity of our standard land leases in keeping with state law.
- Keeps track of legal issues with trebling and self-assessment.
- Insures city, land-trust, and affeercianados are completely non-liable for events on leased land.
- Advises on issues relating to private vs. public property.
- Advises on compliance with state and federal regulations.

Indemnity

Those who disagree with the AFFEERCE concept might be more tempted to initiate lawsuits, or in the case of a hostile judiciary, unjustifiably rule in favor of plaintiffs. The city attorney will search for the best possible liability and indemnification plans and policies.

We will do everything we can, including intense lobbying at the state level, to limit liability. However, if there is clear negligence on the part of an affeercianado in municipal service, we will negotiate in good faith once foul play has been excluded. Affeercianado negligence that results in a lawsuit will be cause for dismissal from the Guild.

There is a high potential for claims from the affeercianados themselves against the Guild, Prosperity and the ABC. Free medical care for affeercianados and residents should help limit liability. The affeercianado also agrees at hiring that a lawsuit resulting in a disability settlement negates any claim to land monetization.

The legal staff will conduct and recommend safety and risk reduction programs for the affeercianados.

Affeercianados can support indemnifying organizations with claims investigations, such as taking photos of fraudulent accident victims. The quick response of the affeercianados to any malfunction or damage should keep the city free from real negligence.

We must never cover up, no matter what the cost. If the city is negligent, we confess as a matter of good government and try and reach a fair settlement, including suggesting binding arbitration. There must be nothing less than pure transparency.

Finance

The city treasurer is hired by the city manager and certified in municipal finance.

City Treasurer – City Hall – Year 4 Table 4.5	#EMP	Debit	Credit	Balance
City Treasurer	0	$100,000	$0	$456,400
Finance	4	$0	$0	$456,400
Purchasing	7	$0	$0	$456,400
Rent collection, liens and trebling	6	$0	$0	$456,400

There are 17 affeercianados working for the treasurer in Year 4. Four manage the books and budgets; seven are in purchasing, and six deal with rent collection.

At least two of the affeercianados are CPA's. The affeercianado in charge of purchasing should be a certified purchasing manager (CPM). The purchasing manager should be familiar with life-cycle costing. How much will the purchase cost in terms of training, maintenance, etc., not just the lowest bid price. Much of the purchasing has to do with building materials, and construction equipment and tools. Expertise in this area is a requirement.

If a land rights owner is more than 1 month in arrears on ground rent, treble-safety will be removed and liens placed on the improvements. Property, to the extent it is encumbered, is available to the trebler at 100% objective depreciated value, rather than 150%. The land rights owner will lose rights to a citizens' dividend, and the smartcard will impose 10% surcharges and cash demands for many services. In addition to rent scofflaws, flagrant code violators also lose treble-safety. Treble-safety and all rights are restored once the liens are repaid with 4% interest and/or code violations are fixed. These cases of limited trebling in the first 20 years, along with trebling of the chancelleries and other palaces allow us to judiciously build up a body of treble law before trebling becomes widespread.

The following additional tasks are performed by the finance department:

- Receipts: ground rent, city card payments for services and fines, developer impact fees, gift shop receipts, state and federal revenue sharing, code violation fines for non-residents
- Forward 70% of rent to the ABC
- Forward county share of 30% rent revenue to county
- Collect revenue sharing funds from the state
- Invest city funds in safe instruments in keeping with sound investment practices
- Compute productivity of each Prosperity program, including its expected effect on land value.
- Set developer impact fees in conjunction with county and school districts, if separate.
- Review pricing for the city gift store and audits for fraud on smartcard accounts.
- Review deficit for each department and suggest ways to help make departments cost covering.
- Suggest changes to user fees, utility delivery fees, and fines to city council.
- Make payroll and benefit payments
- Monitor department budgets and purchases
- Write all checks over $100.
- Maintain up-to-date inventory records of all municipal property.
- Pay city land 10% ground rent payment to the ABC.
- Put together the next year's capital and operating budgets with department heads for city council approval
- Schedule depreciation and maintain depreciation funds for all capital expenditures
- Consolidate purchases between departments, and other cities and districts, for bulk savings of equipment, vehicles and computers.
- Conduct annual financial audit
- Conduct performance audits as needed

- Research and apply for federal, state, and private grants
- Prepare multi-year budget forecasts

Fire Department

Fire fighters and paramedics are part of the department of public safety along with the police. Stations are connected to police stations and financed as one. There will also be an affeercianado dorm with rapid access to the station. There is one fire station for every 20,000 of population and three mile radius, whichever is less. The first fire station is at city hall. This central location is within 2.5 miles of any point in the initial 5000 acre purchase.

Fire and Paramedic	Table 4.6		Debit	Credit	Balance
Year 4 Incorporation and city hall station	0		$0	$0	$0
Clerical and command affeercianados	4		$0	$0	$0
Fire fighter affeercianados	25		$375,000	$0	($375,000)
Fire building inspection team, Arson investigators, paramedics	10		$20,000	$0	($395,000)
Total affeercianados	39		$405,600	$0	($800,600)
Vehicles	6		$12,000	$0	($812,500)
Number of districts	1		$0	$0	($812,500)
Fuel	0		$32,850	$0	($845,450)
Fire station utilities			$10,000	$0	($855,450)
Inspection fees	0		$0	$602,400	($253,050)
Fire station supplies			$80,000	$0	($333,050)
Fire engine (8)	8		$150,000	$0	($483,050)
Furnishing/supplies for fire station (5)	5		$600,000	$0	($1,083,050)
Depreciation			$201,250	$0	($1,284,300)
Revenue			($1,284,300)	$0	$0

Each station has 39 affeercianados, with groups of 12 working 24 hours on, 48 hours off. Vehicles include 3 engines, 2 ambulances and a pumper. The extra ambulance and engine are for emergency maintenance issues. All fire fighters can be called in on cell phones for 3-alarm fires or greater. Additional volunteer gift scrip will be issued for overtime. Affeercianado firefighters are expected to spend up to 8 of their 48 hours off on fire inspection and other duties related to their specialty, or leased out on weeks without overtime.

All affeercianado fire fighters are expected to have graduated from the fire academy. Specialties should include hazardous materials, fire inspection, and arson investigation. Paramedics are certified EMS workers.

Firefighters report to the director of public safety, a non-affeercianado $100,000 paid position. The director of public safety also heads the police department, and is responsible for all disaster coordination.

The breakdown per shift is 8 fire fighters and 1 battalion chief, with 1 floater. There are also 2 paramedics per shift.

There are several duties of the firefighters that bring in revenue, although the department as a whole is not expected to be profitable. Revenue generators are indicated by ($)

Duties of the firefighters include:

- Review all development plans and architectures for fire safety ($)
- Conduct fire inspections of buildings and certify there are no impacts to ODV. ($)
- Fire safety certification for insurance companies ($)
- Enter fire violations into online land system.
- Preliminary building code violation checks ($)
- Disposal of hazardous materials in coordination with waste management ($)

- Hazardous materials annual fees ($)
- Maintain hazardous materials database
- Maintain database of fires and responses
- Work with police on arson investigations
- Supply fire extinguishers and smoke detectors at reasonable but slightly profitable price ($)
- Developer consultations ($)
- Ambulance service ($)

Fire certification will mitigate liability even in current state and municipal courts. Thus certification of fire and buildings standards is a service offered by Fire at a fee. Insurance companies will offer a significant discount with such certification, reducing liability cost.

The following fees are 1/8 the cost of similar services elsewhere. They will not only encourage development, but should be very popular, as they will reduce business insurance rates by more than their cost. These services could help the fire department break even. They are not fully accounted for in Table 4.6. Firefighters perform these services during their 8 hours off in 48. This should not be an excessive imposition, since the 24 hours on will usually allow plenty of time for napping, eating, playing cards, etc. These charges are based on charges by the Seattle Fire Department, at considerably less expense. [FTN2.10]

Fire Inspection Fees	Table 4.7
Fire Department review of building plans and fire protection system designs	$24 per hour (one hour minimum)
Fire Alarm Systems	$58 plus $1 per device > 6 devices
Fire Alarm Systems with more than 6 devices and no new control panel installation or major modification to the system.	$29 plus $1 per device > 6 devices
Fire Extinguishing System - Pre-Engineered	$25
Fire Sprinkler Systems	$35 plus $1 per sprinkler head > 6 sprinkler heads
Standpipe	$25 plus $1 per landing with PRVs (pressure reducing valves)
Fire Pump	$25 per pump
Sprinkler System Supply Main	$31
Tenant Improvement (TI) Inspection without modification of fire protection systems, Or TI with 6 or less sprinkler heads and 6 or less fire alarm devices.	$23
Emergency Responder Radio System Coverage - Systems Testing	$24 per hour (one hour minimum)
Knox Box Inspection	$23
Ambulance Service	$35 copay
Hazardous Materials Fee	$200 - $10,000 annually
Request for Temporary Certificate of Occupancy recommendation	$27 plus time charge for all related inspection and review.

Qualified firefighting affeercianados will be available as consultants to developers or anyone requiring fire safety consultation for a low price of $24 per hour. They will be expert on sprinkler system and life safety system design, as well as have familiarity with all state and county standards.

Every week, it is possible each firefighter will put in 16 hours of fire inspection and other paid services at $24 per hour or $384. With monthly affeercianado cost of $946, this is over $700 a month in profit per firefighter. Even so, inspection fees pay only half the department cost.

Fire responds to search and rescue, emergency response, simulated emergency exercises for public safety, including weather and other natural emergencies, as well as war and civil unrest. None of these can generate income.

Affeercianados who engage in corrupt practices will be fired immediately and prosecuted. It is their job to help the developer be compliant with standards at the lowest cost. If an affeercianado is contracted by a developer, another affeercianado must do the paid inspection.

If an inspection uncovers coding violations, the building can schedule a second inspection within a prescribed warning period. If the warning period expires without an inspection showing the violations fixed, the violations are reported in the online land system. The city council has the right to open for trebling, before Year 20, any building where the owner refuses to fix fire violations. Once the coding violations are corrected, the ODV is increased in the land system and treble-safety is restored.

Companies that deal with hazardous materials must have adequate liability insurance and pay an annual hazardous materials fee to support the local fire department. This fee is based on potential community risk, and supports database maintenance. The fee also covers periodic inspection by trained affeercianados.

There might be small fines for false alarms that are not motivated by any safety concerns.

Because all buildings in Prosperity will be built to standard, the incidence of fires should be low and major fires should be very few. Fire equipment must be consistent with growth. High-rise equipment must be purchased before downtown buildings can be occupied. Prosperity will support all federal and state regulations on firefighter safety.

Mutual assistance agreements exist between neighboring cities for handling disasters. In such an emergency, the director of public safety will serve in the role of emergency management coordinator.

Centralizing certain low frequency functions can achieve economy of scale. Because of the large number of affeercianados, the municipality can rent out affeercianados for fire inspection, and support neighboring cities for rare types of hazardous materials and poisonous gas fires and other contract services. A good regional command can supply choppers, and other region level equipment to neighboring cities. This can add considerable revenue to the fire department. Arson investigators can be contracted to neighboring cities, as well.

Police Department

The police are commanded by the director of public safety who also commands the fire department and coordinates disaster relief.

In Year 4 there will be 77 affeercianados working for the police department. It will be the department's first year as an official law enforcement agency. As of the end of Year 4, there will be 29 vehicles, including 10 squad cars purchased during the year.

All affeercianado officers will be academy trained, with specialties in detection, criminology, communications, and forensics. In Year 4, there will be a single investigative unit, with new units added as needed in the future. As multiple units develop, they will be assigned certain areas such as fraud and commercial crimes, homicide, stolen vehicles, juvenile crime, etc. As the size of Prosperity increases, investigative units will become increasingly specialized. In Year 4, the single unit will work directly under the director of public safety, and cover all investigative areas. Because of the low cost of affeercianado labor, foot patrols will be common, especially in downtown areas. Police will be assigned to certain neighborhoods, so they get to know the residents and merchants.

Police and Public Safety	Table 4.8		Debit	Credit	Balance
Year 4 (Incorporation)		0	$0	$0	$0
Police Chief /Director of public safety includes adjacent fire stations		0	$100,000	$0	($100,000)
Clerical and command affeercianados, municipal prosecution		14	$0	$0	($100,000)
Police officer affeercianados		41	$411,667	$0	($511,667)
Video surveillance/dash-cams/body-cams/automated ticketing team		10	$4,117	$0	($515,784)
School crossing guards (part time - number is x 3 full time equivalent)		12	$0	$0	($515,784)
Total affeercianados		77	$803,284	$0	($1,319,068)
Vehicles		29	$58,000	$0	($1,377,068)
Police station Rent		0	$0	$0	($1,377,068)
Number of districts		1	$0	$0	($1,377,068)
Fuel		0	$158,775	$0	($1,535,843)
Police station utilities			$30,000	$0	($1,565,843)
Fines (from automated ticketing only)		0	$0	$0	($1,565,843)
Office supplies			$20,000	$0	($1,585,843)
10 squad cars (6)		6	$500,000	$0	($2,085,843)
Video surveillance command center in city hall station (14)		14	$800,000	$0	($2,885,843)
10 video surveillance cameras (5)		5	$400,000	$0	($3,285,843)
4 automated speed violation detector (5)		5	$240,000	$0	($3,525,843)
4 automated red light detector (5)		5	$200,000	$0	($3,725,843)
Furnishing/supplies for police station (5)		5	$600,000	$0	($4,325,843)
Depreciation			$1,028,476	$0	($5,354,319)
Revenue			($5,354,319)	$0	$0

Although not shown on the spreadsheets, there are still many grants for increasing police presence and Prosperity might be eligible for some of those grants. With a force almost twice the size of the national average, it follows that a less stressed force, with officers more involved in the community, is less prone to violence and other problems. With the advent of the VIP in Year 16, crime in Prosperity should virtually disappear.

Any community that assists in its own policing is entitled to gift shop vouchers for walking beats and otherwise assisting the police. Non-sworn affeercianados and volunteers are used for police functions such as accident monitoring, crowd control, issuing traffic and other citations. Non-sworn personnel are responsible for cleaning squad cars and entering routine reports into the computer, further relieving officers of stress.

Prosperity will be divided into patrol areas based on geography, population, and building densities, or some combination of these. Walking patrols will be used in the downtown and migrant worker areas. Patrols work 24 hours a day in three 8 hour shifts, although police days slightly exceed 8 hours to allow for full readiness during shift change.

Because of the low cost of affeercianado labor, minor crimes can receive a full investigation, outside of an investigative unit. Interested and responsible non-sworn affeercianados and volunteers can take training courses at Jane Jacobs to become involved in minor crime investigation. Non-sworn affeercianados are also responsible for traffic control and enforcement. Non-sworn personnel should be allowed to carry stun guns but will be prosecuted for misuse.

Internal affairs will be a separate division under the municipal judiciary. It shall consist of ABC hired investigators answerable to the state attorney general who are not affeercianados or entitled to any affeercianado benefits. Their job will be to root out corruption and misbehavior in the police department. Sworn or non-sworn affeercianados who fail to cooperate with internal affairs will be recommended to the Guild for expulsion.

Prosperity will make heavy use of surveillance cameras. Body-cams and dash-cams will be standard. A video command center will be established in the city hall station in Year 4, and the first of 10 cameras installed. In addition, automated red light detectors and speed detectors will be used with a total of 8 installed in Year 4. Fines from automated violation detection can help finance police operations without creating a conflict of interest and jeopardizing the integrity of officers.

Affeercianados in community policing efforts will also work on crime prevention, including neighborhood watch, helping with object identification, education on preventing bicycle theft, and training of volunteer neighborhood patrols. They will give talks on the heavy toll of drug and alcohol abuse, and teach seniors how to remain street safe and what to do if they are suspicious of any scams. Police can sponsor athletic teams at the first community center completed in Year 6.

Frequent outside training for sworn affeercianados can be financed by an aristocratic patron of the police. If not, it must be included in the budget. This includes firearms, self-defense, using the latest technology, investigative and interrogative techniques, crisis intervention, communication skills, and hostage negotiation. Training is also mandated by law in most states.

Non-sworn affeercianados manage the records of the police. Complete and accurate documentation is required to win cases. Data from body-cams and dash-cams must be effectively indexed and archived. For major crimes, the data will be sent to the National Crime Information Center, accessible to law enforcement throughout the nation. Records will be stored on databases, along with pictures of all evidence. Because sworn officers carry lethal force and non-sworn personnel carry stun-guns, no interaction between the police and citizens will go unrecorded. All of these recording must be accessible from relevant cases and also archived independently.

Prosperity will want the latest in advanced communication technology so it is likely that we will replace the county's 911 dispatch system, if inadequate. Dispatch will be located at the central city hall station. It is assumed that some of the 18 clerical and command affeercianados will be in dispatch, as well as school crossing guards when not on duty. No capital expenditures for dispatch are currently included on the spreadsheets.

Dispatchers check records for officers in the field, verify emergencies, prioritize responses, and provide emergency medical advice before first responders arrive. Dispatchers initially determine the level of the municipal response required and coordinate the sharing of police and fire resources between communities.

Affeercianados who are proficient in hostage negotiation, police artistry, working with K-9 units, forensic analysis, and arson investigation can be used as revenue sources by renting them out to neighboring municipalities.

Police should represent the community in make-up, and all segments of the community should be treated the same regardless of race, religion, creed, or socio-economic status. Police officers should maintain high ethical standards. Affeercianados who fail to do this could be terminated or transferred.

Regardless of state laws permitting it, Prosperity will never engage in asset seizure and forfeiture absent a sentencing agreement in a criminal trial. We will lobby to forbid its practice everywhere, even before the capitulation. Nor will Prosperity police officers ever arrest anybody for using or abusing drugs in the privacy of their own home, unless there is domestic abuse or gross disturbance of the peace. However, there will be zero tolerance for driving under the influence of drugs or alcohol.

Police will introduce victims to victim advocates at the community center for counseling, regaining stolen assets, and suing in civil court.

Consolidation of police and fire into a department of public safety has synergy beyond arson investigations, including crowd and traffic control in the vicinity of traffic accidents and fires, emergency preparedness and disaster recovery, vehicle maintenance, landscaping and building maintenance, janitorial service, uniform laundering, procurement, coffee and break rooms, and code enforcement.

Sharing Responsibility

Although affeercianados are tied to specific jobs, or simply members of the business pool, they must be prepared to take on added responsibility in emergencies, such as large fires, conventions, major auto accidents, hurricanes, snowstorms and natural disasters. Every supervising affeercianado will have a special supervisor in the department of public safety. In the event of an emergency or a preparedness drill, that chain of command will kick in.

Animal Collective

A Prosperity animal collective, a subsidiary of the department of public safety, staffed by affeercianados, will take in strays, do spaying and neutering for a price and sponsor adoptions. They will issue dog and cat licenses, so that owners of stray animals can be quickly found. They will try and maintain a minimal kill shelter. They will deal with all wild animal calls and will have stun guns, tranquilizer darts, etc., if necessary. Between licensing, spay and neuter services, and adoption services, and donations, the animal collective should be self-supporting. The collective will be located in the city hall yard.

Prosperity Incorporated

Let's conclude Year 4, by looking at the balance sheet of our newly incorporated city.

Prosperity Table 4.9	Debit	Credit	Balance
Year 4	$0	$0	$107,424,945
Roads and infrastructure	$0	($281,466)	$107,143,480
City Hall	$0	($5,853,983)	$101,289,496
Parks and Recreation	$0	($8,222,400)	$93,067,096
Police	$0	($5,354,319)	$87,712,777
Fire	$0	($1,284,300)	$86,428,477
Waste Management	$0	$469,825	$86,898,302
Hospital Premiums	$1,235,000	$0	$85,663,302
Rent Dividend	$0	$7,650,180	$93,313,482
Rent Owed (10% only)	$3,600	$3,600	$93,313,482
Payment for affeercianado labor	$4,838,484	$4,838,484	$93,313,482
CD issued for $162 to each citizen.	$2,000,000	$0	$91,313,482

We expect to begin the year with a balance of $107 million and end with a balance of $91 million. We will pay $1.2 million in hospital premiums for our citizens, and almost $5 million for affeercianado labor, which is no longer provided gratis. Because of incorporation, the ground rent tranche has increased to $7.6 million from $1.8 million the year before. Roads and infrastructure showed a small loss for increased spending and affeercianado labor, but that will turn positive in Year 5 with increased utility delivery fees and parking revenue. Parks and recreation's money will be spent on the reflecting pool and the associated park stretching from city hall to the campus.

With all the exciting things going on in Year 4, for some citizens, the most exciting thing will be the last line in Table 4.9: the citizens' dividend. With only $162 given to each registered voter, it isn't much, but it is the start of something that will grow every single year of Phase-I. For the low-paid affeercianados, it is especially welcome.

Year 5

There are a few highlights in Year 5. But the most important, at least to an affeercianado, is what they have been waiting for, for 5 long years. Their dream is one significant step closer to reality. They will be buying land!

Give Me Land!

Affeercianados Table 5.1	Debit	Credit	Balance
Year 5	$0	$0	$149,691,554
Donate to land trust	$100,000,000	$0	$49,691,554
Hospital	$0	$40,612,596	$90,304,150
Accommodations	$0	$4,077,508	$94,381,658
Supply Depot	$0	$1,602,139	$95,983,797
Surplus Labor	$0	$117,817,220	$213,801,018
AMS Software	$0	$0	$213,801,018
Metro Bus Service	$0	$651,200	$214,452,218
Downtown excavation	$0	($3,400,960)	$211,051,258
Rent Dividend	$0	$3,259,217	$214,310,475
Pay Unauctioned land Rent	$0	($2,986,800)	$211,323,675
Repay land trust	$0	$0	$211,323,675
Rent Owed	$369,600	$369,600	$211,323,675

Beginning the year with a balance over $149 million, the affeercianados donate $100 million to the land trust. Their share until this point is 50% of the original investment, not counting donations.

In Year 5, with the $100 million donation, the affeercianados will own 74% of the land.

Let's see what the land trust does with this $100,000,000.

The $100 million donation brought the land trust up to $137 million. They purchased land for $150 million, leaving a $12 million deficit in the trust. However, the deficit is an artifact of Table 5.2 ordering. Rent payments bring the land trust balance to over $20 million during Year 5.

With the $150 million, 15,000 acres will be purchased at $10,000 per acre. This land costs 2 times the amount of the initial land purchase of $5,000 per acre. This is to be expected. There is still no speculative ring. Land values in the center of Prosperity have been driven up much more than 2 times. The auction in Year 5 brought in $16,000 of rent per non-downtown acre. That is a land value of $320,000 per acre, an increase of 64 times over the $5,000/acre purchase price. Even undeveloped land at the margin will shoot up in price. It will take skill and serious negotiation on the part of the land broker to get it for $10,000 per acre.

What negotiations? Actually there is quite a bit to negotiate. Landowners often live and farm on the land. Do they receive Prosperity benefits? What kind of rent will they have to pay? Cropland surtax goes into effect in Year 20. The land value of cropland is simply too low for us to pay $10,000/acre. Perhaps the farmer has 200 acres free and clear and is ready to retire, but wants to keep 5 acres for the farmhouse, some crops and livestock. We pay the farmer $2 million for the land at $10,000 an acre. We set aside 195 acres for a future auction. As for the 5 acres the farmer chooses to keep, we merely quadruple the land value to $40,000/acre fixing the rent at a very low $2,000/acre for the next 14 years. The farmer pays $10,000/year for the 5 acres, gets free Prosperity medical care for the entire family, and retires with $2 million. If auctions are firmly established to fall in the winter months, we can even offer the farmer use of any un-auctioned land for spring planting and autumn harvesting at a very low rent. The affeercianados must pay $500/acre rent for un-auctioned land purchased at $10,000/acre, so if the farmer is willing to pay $100/acre each year to plant on this land, the affeercianados save some money. Rent on un-auctioned land is the biggest affeercianado expense in the final years of Phase-I when the holdings become increasingly speculative. Any rent received on speculative land is a bonus.

Land Trust Table 5.2	Balance	Donation	Buy Land	Acres	$/Acre
Year 5	$37,604,758				$0
Affeercianado Donation	$137,604,758	$100,000,000			$0
Purchase Land	($12,395,242)		$150,000,000	15,000	$10,000
Affeercianado repayment	($12,395,242)				$0
Education borrowing	($25,250,367)				0
Municipal borrowing	($25,250,367)				$0
Affeercianado Rent	($25,250,367)				$0
Municipal Rent	($25,250,367)				$0
Public roads	($25,250,367)				$0
Private Roads	($25,250,367)				$0
Unauctioned land-Rent paid by affeercianado	($25,250,367)				$0
Auction Rent 1400@$16,000	($11,810,367)				$0
Downtown auction Rent 4@$250,000	($11,210,367)				$0
Rent 650@$4,000	($9,650,367)				0
Rent 700@$6,000	($7,130,367)				0
Rent 4@$100,000	($6,890,367)				0
Rent 800@$9,000	($2,570,367)				0
Rent 4@$150,000	($2,210,367)				0
Rent 1000@$13,500	$5,889,633				0
Rent 4@$150,000	$6,249,633				0
Rent 1400@$16,000	$19,689,633				0
Rent 4@$250,000	$20,289,633				0
Totals	$20,289,633				

In general, there is more room for negotiation when the landowner is willing to surrender the vast majority of their land to auction and keep only a few acres for personal use. A small landowner would not benefit much from selling us their land at $10,000/acre and then paying a minimal rent of $2,000/acre for the next 15 years unless we brought in water, sewer, fiber, and electric to replace a well, septic system, antenna, and propane generator. For us, $2,000 rents are not exciting when the prevailing bid is for a rent of $16,000/acre, so there is no reason to make the deal unless the land is a corridor to a much more exciting purchase and the landowner is willing to surrender a small portion, at once, for a highway.

The rural land owners we are offering $10,000/acre, paid $5,000/acre or less for their holdings. They are being offered this high price solely because of the existence of Prosperity, not through any of their own doings. As Henry George pointed out, this is the very nature of land speculation. In a few years, the price might even rise to $40,000/acre. Our land brokers will try to be fair based on the prevailing market, however, those who holdout for more, will find their land encircled by Prosperity. They will receive none of the municipal benefits, nor will we have any need or desire to purchase their land once our margins have extended beyond them. Only decades later, in Phase-III deluxe land expansion, will they have a second opportunity to sell the land. If they refuse then, they will ultimately be reimbursed for their land at capitulation, in a manner specified by constitutional amendment, when all land shall be the common wealth of the nation.

Thomas Paine Hospital – The Ambulance Network

In Year 5, the hospital's insurance branch collects 37,422 premiums. Prosperity pays the premium for all residents and the Affeercianado Guild pays the premium for all affeercianados. The actual mechanics of payment will be engineered to either maximize subsidies or to get a major concession from the IRS on some other tax question.

37,422 = the population of Prosperity plus the number of affeercianados multiplied by 1.32. Why the 1.32? We assume that many of the county residents and even some in neighboring counties will want to take advantage of the no-deductible, $100/month policy. With federal subsidies, most people, even outside of Prosperity and the county won't pay a penny for medical care beyond the co-pays.

However, in order for the hospital to be a true export, our reach must extend beyond the county. It must extend all the way to Old Metropolis, 120 miles away in the worst case, as well as other small and mid-sized communities within that radius.

Obviously, in the case of trauma, patients must be treated at the nearest hospital, but otherwise we will consider the economics.

For ordinary doctor visits, testing, scheduled procedures and surgeries, the free luxury Metrobus leaves 8 times a day or more from Old Metropolis. We hope to have the fine dining, accommodations, and retail to motivate people to spend the night and return home the next day, turning medical tourists into actual ones.

Uninsured visits to a doctor can cost $200 per person with lab tests, while PPO visits cost $100 with lab tests, and PPOs have higher monthly premiums, certainly far more than our $100 premium discounted by federal subsidies. At Thomas Paine, there is $35 copay for a doctor's visit and $35 copay for lab tests. That is a maximum charge of $70 and if you need to return within the next 30 days, it is free. For a family of 4 who schedules their doctor appointments together, there is a minimum savings of $120 over the PPO, not counting premium savings. If Prosperity is an exciting enough city, people will look more favorably at the free 1.5 hour bus trip each way.

Of course, if the only savings were for doctors' appointments, nobody in Old Metropolis would tolerate the inconvenience, no matter how nice it will be to visit Prosperity. Scheduled tests, procedures, and surgeries, however, can easily cost the full out of pocket maximum of $6,000 found on most reasonably priced medical plans. Compare this to $35 or $70 for the same tests, surgery, or procedure at Thomas Paine, with premiums that are virtually free and the 3 hour round trip bus ride becomes a pleasure.

What about trauma? The policy will cover emergency care at PPO hospitals in Old Metropolis and covered communities with a $2,000 deductible/day. As soon as the patient is able to be transported by ambulance to Thomas Paine, medical care continues for free. For instance, a cardiac patient might be rushed to the nearest hospital. Once the immediate danger passes, they are transported in a cardiac care ambulance, sedated for a comfortable ride, to Thomas Paine where angioplasty is scheduled.

For non-traumatic injuries like many sports injuries, or illnesses like pneumonia, the patient might wish to avoid the $2,000 charge and be transported directly to Thomas Paine. A doctor will instruct the paramedics over the phone to administer painkillers, sedatives, and other medications to make the trip more comfortable.

How much does an ambulance trip cost the patient? The copay for an ambulance is $35. If the patient is being transported from a PPO hospital, that is the only cost. If the patient is being transported from home, an accident site, or elsewhere, the charge is $35 plus $24/hour of travel (at 90 MPH) plus twice fuel cost. If fuel costs $3 gallon and the ambulance gets 30 miles to the gallon, the cost from Old Metropolis will be approximately $35 + $24 + 3 x $3 = $68. Compare this to most ambulance services that charge $600 to go a few miles.

But how long will an accident victim have to wait for an ambulance? Not long at all. Thomas Paine Hospital will maintain an ambulance network in every city that coverage is offered. Beginning in Year 5, and every year through Year 12, 4 ambulances are purchased for the fleet. Of the 32 ambulances by Year 12, at least 30 will be in the field at any one time. Suppose there are 5 ambulances in Old Metropolis, 90 miles from Prosperity. Along a direct line, there are 2 ambulances in a large suburb, 75 miles from Prosperity. Following the same line, 50 miles from Prosperity there is city with 30,000 residents and 2 ambulances. A single ambulance is parked in a small town of 600, 20 miles from Prosperity along the same line.

Suppose one of the ambulances in Old Metropolis picks up a patient and heads for Thomas Paine. A chain reaction is initiated. One of the 2 suburban ambulances heads for Old Metropolis, reaching it in 25 minutes at normal speeds. Once again there are 5 ambulances in Old Metropolis. One of the two ambulances in the city 50 miles from Prosperity heads for the suburb 75 miles away. At high speeds it reaches the suburb in 25 minutes. The ambulance parked in the small town of 600 heads for the city with 30,000 residents 30 miles away, reaching it in less than 30 minutes. Meanwhile, an ambulance heads out from Prosperity to the small town of 600. Within 30 minutes, the entire network is restored. As for the ambulance carrying a patient from Old Metropolis, it arrives at Thomas Paine in one hours' time at high speeds. It is restocked, the shift changed if appropriate, and it is sent onto one of the network paths to indirectly replace an ambulance called into service. The full implementation of this network is unlikely before Year 12.

The shifts will be brutal, although most of the time is spent waiting, or driving into position at the far end of the network. Of course these are affeercianados and they are turning Thomas Paine into a major exporter of medical care.

In Year 5, the multiplier for guesstimating premiums is 1.32 and Prosperity's population is small. By Year 20, the multiplier for guesstimating premiums is 2.6 and Prosperity's population is large which means a significant amount of exporting is projected to take place.

Waste Management

Waste management is a low-cost service of the city of Prosperity. Bags for general waste and those for highly specific waste are freely available around town. The specific bags are at least partially transparent. A full bag of general waste costs $2 for pickup. A half-bag of specific waste pays .50; a full bag pays $1. An additional .50 is paid for highly specific waste. With two full bags of specific waste for every bag of general waste, collection is free. Recycle more than that and collection will lead to a smartcard credit. Special collection of non-bagged items is $1 plus $1 for every 100 pounds.

There's gold in them thar circuit boards

Barcode adhesive labels, red for general waste, white for special collection items, and green for specific waste can be printed with the smartcard. These bar codes indicate the smartcard to charge or credit for refuse collection and connect contents with an owner in the event of problems.

Bags are taken by truck to the materials recovery facility (MRF) where they are sorted by general, specific, and special collection items.

Waste Management Table 5.3		Debit	Credit	Balance
Year 5	0	$0	$0	$0
Garbage collectors	18	$180,000	$0	($180,000)
MRF Workers	24	$240,000	$0	($420,000)
Product drivers	6	$0	$0	($420,000)
Total affeercianados (+ 30 new facility builders)	78	$811,200	$0	($1,231,200)
Vehicles	21	$42,000	$0	($1,273,200)
Recycle bags 12 product + generic product	2835000	$141,750	$0	($1,414,950)
Product sales	0	$0	$283,500	($1,131,450)
Smartcard revenue	0	$0	$2,178,000	$1,046,550
Special collections revenue	0	$0	$280,800	$1,327,350
Fuel	0	$114,975	$0	$1,212,375
Office supplies	0	$20,000	$0	$1,192,375
Dump truck for large pickups (8)	8	$25,000	$0	$1,167,375
Garbage Truck - Roll off (8)	8	$130,000	$130,000	$1,167,375
Garbage Truck - Front load (8)	8	$225,000	$225,000	$1,167,375
1 Flatbed (8)	8	$50,000	$0	$1,117,375
State of the art MRF Zero Waste facility (20)	20	$2,000,000	$0	($882,525)
Automated separating equipment (6)	6	$1,000,000	$0	($1,882,525)
Depreciation		$631,667	$0	($2,514,292)
Revenue		($2,514,292)	$0	$0

The waste management team has been working out of a prefabricated materials recovery facility, about 2 miles north of the industrial area. In Year 5, we will be spending $2 million on a state of the art MRF and a million on separating and processing equipment. Once complete, we will be able to do the following.

- Specific waste goes through the clean MRF process. The bags are placed on conveyors, ripped apart for inspection, and the contents, if clean, will be manually placed in the appropriate bins by affeercianados working the line. If the contents are too contaminated for easy sorting, the barcode is scanned to place a warning on the associated smartcard (3 warnings = $20 fine), and the bag is routed to the manual sorting stage of the dirty MRF. Empty waste and transparent bags go to separate bins for recycling.

- Special collection items are sent to a reuse engineer who assigns a workflow which includes manual separation and disassembly, crushers, shredders, smelters, chemical baths, separators and screens, with the output going to different bins.

- General waste goes through dirty MRF processing. Bags are broken open on a much slower conveyor belt (15 ft./minute) where affeercianados are tasked with removing specific items from the stream. These items are placed in bins or on conveyor belts for further processing. What is left goes through screens where large objects, initially missed by the affeercianados are re-sent to manual sorting. A magnet separates out ferrous metals and with a different process, non-ferrous metals. The remainder is shredded and screened, and used for fuel or compost. Fuel is burned for energy creation and/or materials processing.[FTN5.10]

The output from an MRF can be thought of in the same way as the output from mining; raw materials for either our production process or to be exported. Here are some of the outputs[FTN5.11]:

We don't expect residents to break things down any finer than the first column; however, businesses that deal with specific outputs and residents with time on their hands can earn extra income by bagging some of the more specific types. Generally, large non-bagged items pay nothing regardless of content.

Category	Recovered Resource			
Paper	Newspaper	Corrugated boxes	WM garbage bags	Office papers
	Standard mail	Paper towels	Folding cartons	Paper plates/cups
Container glass	Beer/soft drink	Wine/liquor	Other bottles/jars	Green glass
	Amber glass	Blue glass	Non-container	Ceramics
Aluminum	Cans	Foils	Window frames	Building siding
Steel	Cans	Small appliances	Large appliances	Demolition
Plastics	PETE (1)	HDPE (2)	PVC (3)	LDPE (4)
	Polypropylene (5)	Polystyrene (6)	Other (7)	
Yard Waste	Grass	Leaves	Brush	
Rubber	Tires	Footwear	Sports equipment	
Leather	Clothing	Footwear	Furniture	
Electronics	Cell phones	Computers	TV's	Audio players
Batteries	Nickle-Cadmium	Mercury	Carbon	

A Few Facts on Year 5

- $18 million will be spent on materials for a community center and athletic field in the heart of the residential area. It will be built by 200 affeercianados, with another 100 building an attached affeercianado dormitory.
- Prosperity will have 4 elementary schools with 2 more being built, 1 high school, 8 school buses, 162 elementary school teachers, 100 high school teachers, 122 non-teaching staff, and all affeercianados.
- The affeercianados will have built a total of 10 dormitories by the end of Year 5. Each houses 600 and has luxury amenities.
- AFFEERCE a'Cookin is bringing in over $22 million in profits with 24 hour all-you-can-eat buffet service for migrant building trade workers.
- The citizens' dividend is $220 for every registered voter

Year 6

Community Center

Year 6, marks a few exciting Prosperity milestones, but none more so than the first community center. The survey of community center activities listed below, like many aspects of this plan, is meant to generate discussion and like most everything in this plan, should not be seen as definitive.

The plan calls for Prosperity to have a community center for every 40,000 to 50,000 residents. This is similar to the number of residents needed to support a high school. In many cases, the high school will be built beside the community center so the two can share resources. Our first high school, Henry George High, will have been built on the Jane Jacobs campus. The second, to be built in Year 6, will be beside this community center. If geographically convenient, one of the 3 elementary schools planned for Year 6 can also be built on the community center campus. Rounding out the campus will be an affeercianado dorm, where affeercianados who staff the center and schools reside. Passageways shall connect all the buildings for use in inclement weather.

Athletic fields might include a football/soccer field with bleachers, 4 baseball diamonds with bleachers, lights for night play, a skate-board park, tennis courts, and a running track. An indoor gymnasium features basketball, volleyball, gymnastics, exercise, etc. There might be two pools, a lap pool and one for relaxing swims. In surveys, neighbors of the center should indicate which athletic facilities they place the highest priority on, in the likely event of space limitations.

Parks and Recreation Table 6.1		Debit	Credit	Balance
Year 6	0	$0	$0	$0
Parks and Recreation Manager	0	$100,000	$0	($100,000)
Manager's Office	3	$0	$0	($100,000)
Public Safety liaison	1	$0	$0	($100,000)
Landscaping	30	$0	$0	($100,000)
Lights and electrical	8	$0	$0	($100,000)
Playground repair	3	$0	$0	($100,000)
Bike paths and walking trails	8	$0	$0	($100,000)
Water fountain maintenance	3	$0	$0	($100,000)
Total general employees	56	$0	$0	($100,000)
General supplies	0	$500,000	$0	($600,000)
Annual pass for community centers	0	$0	$454,125	($145,875)
Per Community Center employees	0	$0	$0	($145,875)
Lifeguards and swim instructors	4	$0	$0	($145,875)
Coaches	5	$0	$0	($145,875)
General officer, reception, scheduling, grants	6	$0	$0	($145,875)
Day care center	8	$0	$42,000	($103,875)
Senior center	4	$0	$0	($103,875)
Youth center	6	$0	$0	($103,875)
Social workers/counseling/victims advocates	6	$0	$0	($103,875)
Trainers	3	$0	$0	($103,875)
First aid	2	$0	$0	($103,875)
Arts and craft instructors	6	$0	$0	($103,875)
Library	2	$0	$0	($103,875)
Kitchen	8	$0	$0	($103,875)
Janitorial/Maintenance/Security	6	$0	$0	($103,375)
Community center supplies	0	$0	$0	($103,375)
Revenue from rental of meeting rooms, theater	0	$0	$127,750	$23,375
Catering income	0	$0	$52,000	$75,375
Anchor tenant rent	0	$0	$120,000	$195,375
Total affeercianados per community center	66	$0	$0	$195,875
Number of community centers	1	$0	$0	$195,875
Total community center supplies	0	$200,000	$0	($4,125)
Total community center affeercianados	66	$0	$0	($4,125)
Total affeercianados	122	$1,268,800	$0	($1,272,925)
Community center utilities	0	$200,000	$0	($1,472,925)
Furniture/Equipment/Gym/Lockers/Kitchen for community center(6)	6	$1,000,000	$0	($2,472,925)
Depreciation		$3,066,667	$0	($5,539,592)
Revenue		($5,539,592)	$0	$0

During the school day, most of the athletic facilities will be reserved, or the number of non-student guests will be limited. This also applies to the library, auditorium, wood shop, metal shop, home economics shop, and various arts and crafts. However, the full center could be open from 5 AM to 9 AM for all residents and again from 4 PM to 11 PM, as well as 5 AM to 11 PM on weekends and school holidays.

A $35 1-year pass for residents to use the center facilities is projected. The pass will be placed on all residents' smartcards, but only activated with first use and good for the next 365 days. If the fee is not paid within 60 days, it will be deducted from the resident or resident's parent's CD in the normal manner of deducting unpaid fees and fines. Non-residents might get a 2-week pass for $35 and a 1-year pass for $200. The 2-week pass could be attractive to tourists.

In addition to the pass, there likely will be small materials' fees for some classes, services, and activities. All of these shall be placed on the smartcard. Sources of revenue include metered parking at the center, and charges to sports leagues for field maintenance and lights for night games. In general, the community center should interface with the community using coproduction, cosponsorship and facilitation of services.

Table 6.1 assumes liberally that half the residents of Prosperity will use the community center and conservatively that no non-residents will use the facility.

Revenue for the center will include rent from an anchor tenant, such as a restaurant or grocery store. This diversity of retail, entertainment, learning, and residential enhances the vitality of the campus. Table 6.1 shows annual rent of $120,000.

The library might feature best-selling fiction, non-fiction, and classics for adults. The thrust should be fiction, non-fiction, and classics geared to preschool through 12th grade. Adults doing serious research should check out the main city/university library also to be built in Year 6, and discussed below. The smartcard will be required to check out books and for all community center access.

The community center should feature a senior center, youth center, and day-care center, each with its own private space. The senior center might have a lunch program, group outings, group shopping, games, and other activities. The youth center should provide after-school and weekend activities, especially valuable for latch-key kids. The day-care center should provide care and activities for preschoolers of working parents, as well as breakfast and lunch. There will be a cost-covering charge for day care and meal service, placed on the smartcard. Federal and state subsidies and grants might reduce or eliminate these charges.

The community center could work in conjunction with Thomas Paine Hospital for health and human services. The center will seek federal, state, and corporate grants to fund various programs. Programs could include such things as: prevention and control of disease, health concerns of the young and senior citizens, environmental health issues such as exposure to hazardous materials, safe drinking water, and programs for cleaning the air. Because Prosperity will be a new community, there will be little need for programs related to asbestos and lead-based paints. Services might include educational programs for proper exercise and nutrition, immunization, alcohol and drug abuse, weight loss, sexually transmitted diseases, antismoking, high blood pressure, proper dental and body hygiene, pregnancy, cholesterol, hearing and eyesight, etc.

The community center should be a good place to learn how to use computers and the latest technology. Job and career counseling should be an important function of the center, with employers using the facility to seek applicants. New arrivals in town can be given information on housing, shopping, and other guidance.

Rooms in the community center can be adopted by persons and business. Trebling of annual adoption fee is required to seize an adoption. If an auditorium is adopted for $1000 a year, a $3000 a year treble would be required to seize the adoption. Adoption fees go directly to the community center. There might also be a one-time fee for changing signage.

Government grants often fund construction costs. Such a possibility is not included on the spreadsheet.

The community center should have a domestic violence and victim advocacy group. All victims of domestic violence should receive temporary quarter and permanent judicial quarter in a women-and-children only shelter. The abused partner can seek refuge as an affeercianado.

Meeting rooms and an auditorium will be available for community center sponsored lectures, events, forums, and entertainment. Private groups can rent these rooms for meetings or events for a small charge, if they are not otherwise scheduled.

The cafeteria can be reserved at night for catered events. Events are either non-alcoholic or wine can be served with the meal. The charge is not nominal and meant to generate revenue for the center. Affeercianados can be leased out at normal bid rates for catering. Table 6.1 conservatively shows a profit from catered events at $52,000.

At the pools, affeercianados could lead general swim classes, swim classes for toddlers, and elderly pool exercise. There might be a nominal fee for these classes.

The center should also provide counseling, domestic violence support, addiction support, and general victim support. These services are free to residents. Social workers should be available to help residents obtain city, state, and federal benefits, obtain caretakers, and be connected to the right person who can help with a problem.

The community center might contribute to holiday celebrations with themed decorations, fireworks on July 4th and other special occasions. Community festivals can also be held at the centers and surrounding fields in keeping with the ethnic or other characteristics of the neighborhood. Concerts in the park and movies outdoors might coincide with festivals.

It is projected that only 66 affeercianados will work a community center apart from the overlap with an adjoining high school. The community center should offer many opportunities for volunteers. Volunteers might receive $2 toward purchase in the city gift shop for every hour worked.

Last but not least, first time users of the community center shall sign a release from liability for any injuries suffered when using any of the facilities before they are allowed access. However, there are always paramedics on duty, and health care for residents is free. Much effort will go into reducing sports injury liability. Playgrounds will be use the latest in safety equipment. There will be plenty of safety signage and safety instruction from the coaches and trainers.

Currently there is no developer impact fee for parks and recreation. A small one can be considered if rigorous planning reveals unexpected expenses. A rural set-aside of 30% of all community development block grant funds will favor Prosperity, and can be used to help fund the building of community centers. State funds might also be available. Table 6.1 conservatively assumes no grants or room adoptions.

The Main City/University Library

As you can see, Year 6 is a good one for the affeercianados.

The year begins with a balance of $211 million. The hospital brings in $57.4 million and leasing affeercianados (surplus labor) brings in a huge $144.6 million. The year ends with a balance over $64 million higher than it began. And that is after a $140 million grant to higher education, in part for a joint city/Jane Jacobs University/medical school world class library.

Affeercianados Table 6.2	Debit	Credit	Balance
Year 6	$0	$0	$211,323,675
Hospital	$0	$57,482,267	$268,805,941
Accommodations	$0	$2,614,092	$271,420,033
Supply Depot	$0	$531,122	$271,951,155
Surplus Labor	$0	$144,639,659	$416,590,814
AMS Software	$0	$0	$416,590,814
Metro Bus Service	$0	$651,200	$417,242,014
Downtown excavation	$0	($3,400,960)	$413,841,054
Rent Dividend	$0	$4,763,046	$418,604,099
Pay Unauctioned land Rent	$0	($2,576,000)	$416,028,099
Repay land trust	$0	$0	$416,028,099
Rent Owed	$377,600	$377,600	$416,028,099
Grant for higher education	$140,000,000	$0	$276,028,099

Like the community center, a shared library is an example of cost-savings through sharing. Here is the table for higher education in Year 6:

Higher Education Table 6.3		Debit	Credit	Balance
Year 6	0	$0	$0	$0
Affeercianados enrolled full time at Jane Jacobs/quarter	1596	$0	$0	$0
Prosperity resident students enrolled full time/quarter	120	$0	$76,800	$76,800
In-state nonresident students enrolled full time/quarter	0	$0	$0	$76,800
Medical school students	0	$0	$0	$76,800
Medical student lab costs	0	$0	$0	$76,800
Jane Jacobs affeercianado instructors	110	$0	$0	$76,800
Jane Jacobs affeercianado non-dorm staff	33	$0	$0	$76,800
State grant @5000 per full time college year	0	$0	$8,580,000	$8,656,800
Paid university professors/Department heads	7	$700,000	$0	$7,956,800
Med school affeercianado instructors not hospital affiliated	0	$0	$0	$7,956,800
Hospital affiliated med school instructors	0	$0	$0	$7,956,800
Paid med school instructors not hospital affiliated	0	$0	$0	$7,956,800
Med school affeercianado non-dorm staff	0	$0	$0	$7,956,800
Total affeercianado educators and staff	143	$1,487,200	$0	$6,469,600
Number of student dorms of 250 rooms for 2 + paid room debits/credits	5	$6,487,200	$9,740,880	$9,723,280
Rent Owed	0	$290,000	$0	$9,433,280
Dorm Staff	225	$2,340,000	$0	$7,093,280
Construction workers	200	$2,080,000	$0	$5,013,280
Purchase 60 washes/dryers (6)	6	$40,000		$4,973,280
Purchase kitchen equipment (8)	8	$70,000		$4,903,280
Dorm furnishings (10)	10	$600,000		$4,303,280
Materials for city/university library w/affeercianado grant (30)	30	$40,000,000	$140,000,000	$104,303,280
Depreciation		$6,081,875		$98,221,405
Revenue		$98,221,405		$0

$40 million will be spent on materials to build the library, completely supported by the $140 million affeercianado grant shown as a credit on the same line. The 200 affeercianado construction workers will have several years of experience building dorms and elementary schools through Jane Jacobs University. With such a large amount of money spent on the building alone (books, periodicals, equipment, and furniture will be expensed in Year 7), it should be a grand edifice on the university/medical campus.

Notice that higher education is generating significant revenue by renting out the dorms to migrant buildings trades workers which includes 24-hour all you can eat buffet in the dorm cafeteria. In Year 6, 120 Prosperity residents are enrolled in Jane Jacobs University in addition to the 1,596 affeercianados.

College resident cost 5 unit course w/2 online lecture	$40
College non-resident cost 5 unit course w/2 online lecture	$250

Once building schedules are mastered, Jane Jacobs University will transition from a semester to quarter system. This will allow students multiple roles in construction of a single building. Courses with significant field construction will remain tuition free for affeercianados, residents and non-residents alike. However, as the curriculum is extended into engineering and urban planning, residents and non-residents will find the fees for these courses very reasonable. A 5 unit course (5 hours/week) costs residents $40 per 10 week quarter. Two hours per week are spent viewing online lectures from top professors in the nation, while 3 hours per week are spent with an affeercianado instructor who can help students better understand the material, grade homework and quizzes, conduct labs, and give a final exam. Students view the lectures on their own time. Night courses consolidate all three hours of instruction into a single day of the week probably from 6PM through 9PM. Non-residents of Prosperity pay $250 per quarter for the same course. Table 6.3 assumes a state grant of $5000 per full-year student (minimum 45 units). In 2011, the vast majority of states contributed more than this per student[FTN6.01]. Failure to receive any state or federal grants could result in higher tuition for residents and non-residents alike.

At the end of Phase-I (Year 21), tuition for residents will increase to the non-resident rate of $250 per 5 units per quarter, while entitled citizens will pay $35 copay/quarter regardless of units taken.

Transportation Depot

At the end of Year 6, in the virtual NE quadrant, not far from downtown, we will be building a prefabricated transportation depot. In the following 10 years, this will become the central hub of all Prosperity transportation. In Year 14, the prefabricated depot will be replaced by a magnificent structure.

The depot will be the starting and ending point for free city buses to downtown and the campus, the free luxury buses to Old Metropolis, private bus routes, interstate carriers, jitney cabs, jitney distant ride sharing, hotel shuttles, rent-a-car shuttles, airport limousines, auto pickup and drop-off , and most importantly, municipal parking.

Every year from Year 7 through Year 14, a 3000 car garage will be built. Each will be 10 stories and take up about an acre. These 8 garages will surround the depot at sufficient distance for the traffic lanes and stations. Protected bridges from the depot will allow travelers to cross from the depot to the garages, with no danger from the traffic.

The new depot built in Year 14 will have underground moving walkways to what will ultimately be 40 garages allowing 120,000 cars to park.

Municipal Parking will be a subsidiary of Prosperity's roads and infrastructure team. A smartcard should be required for all municipal parking. Without a smartcard, garage parking might be $20/day in advance, although if a smartcard is obtained on that day, the $20 could be credited to the smartcard minus normal fees.

Municipal Parking Fees		Table 6.4
Street – Campus and near downtown	Hour	.25
	Day	.75
	Month	10.00
	Annual	50.00
Lower level downtown	Hour	2.00
	Day	7.00
	Month	80.00

Remote – At depot	Hour	.25
	Day	.75
	Month	20.00

Beginning in Year 7, free buses (or perhaps a people mover or monorail) will run continuously between lower level downtown and the transportation depot. These buses and their operation are expensed to municipal parking.

Municipal parking and utility delivery charges make roads and infrastructure the largest source of municipal revenue outside of the ground rents.

Years 7-8

Grant to Municipality

The city of Prosperity will have a huge bill in paying every citizen's medical premium. The affeercianados, expected to be minting money, will donate the funds to make this possible. Paid only $25/week in cash, a citizens' dividend enhances affeercianado spendable income, and only a prosperous Prosperity can issue the CD. However, this will be the last grant for 7 years. During these next 7 years, all affeercianado profits will be used to buy land.

Affeercianados Table 7.1	Debit	Credit	Balance
Year 7	$0	$0	$276,028,099
Grant to Municipality	$400,000,000	$0	($123,971,901)
Hospital	$0	$77,448,878	($46,523,022)
Accommodations	$0	$1,150,675	($45,372,347)
Supply Depot	$0	$2,510,249	($42,862,099)
Surplus Labor	$0	$153,349,940	$110,487,841
AMS Software	$0	$30,000,000	$140,487,841
Metro Bus Service	$0	$651,200	$141,139,041
Downtown excavation	$0	($3,400,960)	$137,738,081
Rent Dividend	$0	$6,319,355	$144,057,436
Pay Unauctioned land Rent	$0	($2,155,200)	$141,902,236
Repay land trust	$0	$0	$141,902,236
Rent Owed	$385,600	$385,600	$141,902,236

The $400 million grant to the city leaves a lower balance at the end of the year than the start.

AMS

Year 7 marks the first time AMS generates revenue. With expected interest in smartcard software by other cities, AMS sells the package to a software marketing firm for $30 million. Every year thereafter, AMS will earn royalties for sales and payments for maintenance and support. This will also give AMS more time to concentrate on transitioning from the smartcard to the VIP.

Of course, there is no way of saying if, when, or how much AMS will earn on their software packages, or even if those packages will be smartcard related, or related to other municipal software. So the $30 million in Year 7 is just a wild guess that could be way low or way high. At $30 million, the revenue is not critical to the outcome. We have fixed their employees at 42 affeercianados, although there is also a team at the ABC headquarters, not shown.

In Year 7, it is time for AMS to begin perfecting the protocols for an inter-business production control system. Although the actual nature of this project could be quite different, the production control system fits in well with an economic goal of import replacement, discussed later. This so-called "internet of things" allows for the rapid and automated routing of parts and merchandise from business to business and business to consumer. Our lower downtown is a good fit for the hardware.

Library

In Year 7, the library shared by the municipality, the college, and ultimately the medical school is completed and stocked.

Higher Education – Library Expenses Table 7.1		Debit	Credit	Balance
Library computers, supplies (6)	6	$600,000		$4,431,800
Library Books and periodical subscriptions (8)	8	$12,000,000		($7,568,200)
Library furnishings (10)	10	$800,000		($8,368,200)

Notice that a full $12 million dollars is spent on books and periodicals depreciated over a short 8 years. This means that over the course of every 8 years, the depreciation fund will gain another $12 million for replacements or new additions. Every year, in perpetuity, the librarians will be able to spend $1.5 million on new and replacement books and periodicals. Jane Jacobs University could convert the second floor of the chancellery into a special library for the building trades, with the majority of the collection moved to the new library. The medical school can have their collections built before they even open for business. The doctors at Thomas Paine will appreciate this resource from the start.

Depreciation

You might have noticed in the tables that a depreciation expense is taken every year. Taking a wider view of the tables shows other columns that control depreciation. Here is "Affeercianado accommodations" for Year 8.

Accommodations Table 8.1	Debit	Credit	Balance	Depr.	Cum Depr.	Assets	Depr. fund
Year 8	0	$0	$0	0	$0	$10,487,375	$0	$47,154,750
Number of kitchens	21			0	$0	$10,487,375		$47,154,750
Number of buildings to maintain	31			0	$0	$10,487,375		$47,154,750
Rent		$393,600	$0	(393,600)	$0	$10,487,375		$47,154,750
Number of prefab rooms	3600			(393,600)	$0	$10,487,375		$47,154,750
Prefab rooms for affeercianados	1800			(393,600)	$0	$10,487,375		$47,154,750
Number of dorm rooms	4200			(393,600)	$0	$10,487,375		$47,154,750
Number of trailer park slots	1000			(393,600)	$0	$10,487,375		$47,154,750
Number of affeercianados in prefab	5400			(393,600)	$0	$10,487,375		$47,154,750
Number of affeercianados in dorms	8400			(393,600)	$0	$10,487,375		$47,154,750
Number of affeercianados in trailer park	0			(393,600)	$0	$10,487,375		$47,154,750
Prefab rooms to let	1800			(393,600)	$0	$10,487,375		$47,154,750
Prefab rentals @45 a night	180	$788,400	$2,956,500	1,774,500	$0	$10,487,375		$47,154,750
Prefab rentals @195 a week	1080	$2,246,400	$10,951,200	10,479,300	$0	$10,487,375		$47,154,750
Prefab rentals @700 a month	540	$648,000	$4,536,000	14,367,300	$0	$10,487,375		$47,154,750
Trailer site rentals @18 a day	1000	$3,650,000	$6,570,000	17,287,300	$0	$10,487,375		$47,154,750
AFFEERCE a'Cookin @22 a day	1180	$3,230,250	$9,475,400	23,532,450	$0	$10,487,375		$47,154,750
AFFEERCE a'Cookin @140 a week	1080	$2,808,000	$7,862,400	28,586,850	$0	$10,487,375		$47,154,750
AFFEERCE a'Cookin @560 a month	2540	$6,705,600	$17,068,800	38,950,050	$0	$10,487,375		$47,154,750
Affeercianados working at accommodations	910			38,950,050	$0	$10,487,375		$47,154,750
Maintenance cost		$1,860,000		37,090,050	$0	$10,487,375		$47,154,750
Supply cost		$930,000		36,160,050	$0	$10,487,375		$47,154,750
Purchase 60 washes/dryers (6)	6	$40,000		36,120,050	$6,667	$10,494,042	$40,000	$47,154,750
Purchase kitchen equipment (8)	8	$70,000		36,050,050	$8,750	$10,502,792	$70,000	$47,154,750
Dorm furnishings (10)	10	$600,000		35,450,050	$60,000	$10,562,792	$600,000	$47,154,750
Materials for 2 Dorms (20)	20	$24,000,000		11,450,050	$1,200,000	$11,762,792	$24,000,000	$47,154,750
Depreciation		$11,762,792		(312,742)	$0	$11,762,792		$58,917,542
Revenue		($312,742)		0		$11,762,792		$58,917,542

When an item is to be depreciated, it will have a number in parenthesis after the item. For instance "Purchase kitchen equipment (8)" means that the $70,000 worth of kitchen equipment is depreciated over 8 years. This means that every year we put aside $8,750 for replacement. That number appears in the depreciation column. This number is added to the Cumulative depreciation column, which is the total amount that must be put aside every year. Finally, on the Depreciation line at the bottom, we put aside the $11,762,792, adding it to the depreciation fund in the very last column.

On these spreadsheets, we never bother to subtract from the depreciation fund for replacement purchases, so the fund is smaller than what is shown. However, it is not much smaller. Most of the depreciation fund comes from buildings, like the two dorms being built with $24 million of materials. These are depreciated over 20 years, so none are replaced over the course of Phase-I. By the end of Phase-I, several of these funds are in the hundreds of millions of dollars. In the business plan, no interest is ever taken on the depreciation fund, and we never borrow against it. Furthermore, most cities today do not maintain depreciation funds. No provision is made in these cities for the replacement of capital goods, particularly buildings. When a building needs to be replaced, cities often go to the bond market, or hunt for grants rather than withdraw from the depreciation fund like we would.

For Prosperity this is added insurance against the unexpected. Not only will we earn interest on the balance, but in an emergency, we can borrow from the depreciation fund. The municipality, affeercianados, and educational district will each earn interest on their own depreciation funds. In Phase-II, these can be comingled with citizen investor funds.

New Community Center

In Year 8, we should reach a population of 46,800 residents plus 14,342 affeercianados. Work will begin on a second community center with an adjacent high school to be built in Year 9.

Higher Education

By Year 8, we will know whether or not chancelleries are a valuable way of financing education and healthcare. If they are, we will move ahead with a Vice-Chancellery of Urban Studies. If the interest is high, we can subsequently implement a Vice-Chancellery of Engineering and then a Vice Chancellery of Liberal Arts and Sciences. Even if chancelleries are unpopular, we still need to build additional classrooms, labs, and offices for urban studies. To that end, the business plan will include a new school building with classrooms, lecture halls, laboratories, and offices at a material cost of $25 million with 200 affeercianado construction workers. There will be unaccounted benefit to the extent it is a vice-chancellery and built by students of Jane Jacobs University.

Year 9

Affeercianado Land Purchase

This $700 million contribution to the land trust along with an additional $120 million provided by the trust itself is used to purchase 60,000 acres at $15,333 per acre. The total purchase likely consisted of many small purchases by various land brokers. The 80,000 acres of Prosperity in Year 9, might have a funny shape. Of those 80,000 acres, about 16,000 are developed. The remainder hopefully forms a speculative ring of undeveloped land.

Affeercianados Table 9.1	Debit	Credit	Balance
Year 9	$0	$0	$410,052,113
Donate to land trust	$700,000,000	$0	($289,947,887)
Hospital	$0	$125,102,402	($164,845,485)
Accommodations	$0	($1,776,158)	($166,621,644)
Supply Depot	$0	$2,781,723	($163,839,920)
Surplus Labor	$0	$174,821,440	$10,981,520
AMS Software	$0	$2,000,000	$12,981,520
Metro Bus Service	$0	$651,200	$13,632,720
Downtown excavation	$0	($3,400,960)	$10,231,760
Rent Dividend	$0	$14,247,935	$24,479,695
Pay Unauctioned land Rent	$0	($19,754,853)	$4,724,841
Repay land trust	$0	$0	$4,724,841
Rent Owed	$401,600	$401,600	$4,724,841

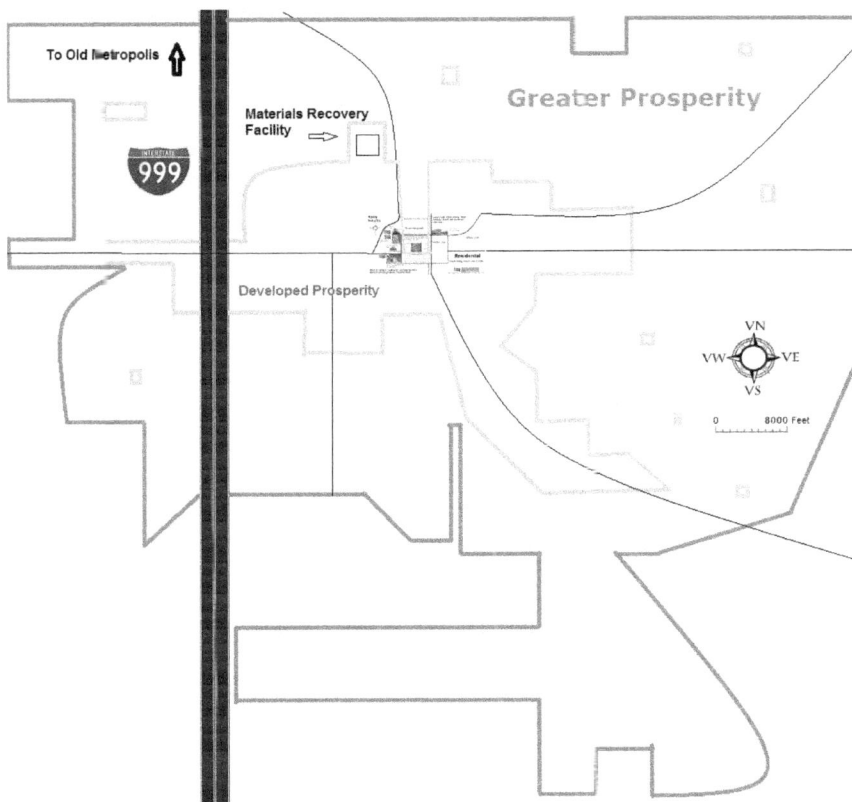

Developed Prosperity is shown in blue. Downtown, city hall, Thomas Paine Hospital and the Jane Jacobs campus are shown in blurred detail at the center. Notice that developed Prosperity does not include much of downtown, the central park, and the area directly virtual north of downtown. This is not completely true. The prefabs and trailer park are there. However, these will be torn down and the land first auctioned in Phase-II. This speculative holding is meant to significantly increase affeercianado and investor pensions.

The location of the material recovery facility in the north industrial area is shown. Jitney service is available along the roads shown, within the blue zone developed areas. Jitneys leave from the transportation depot and will drop-off within 1/2 mile of their route, covering the entire developed area except some of the industrial north-west, and isolated developments.

Supply Depot

We now take a close look at the affeercianado Supply Depot, import/export operation. It holds key information for a new stage in Prosperity growth.

Supply Depot Table 9.2		Debit	Credit	Balance
Year 9	0	$0	$0	$0
Number of rigs and flatbeds	93			$0
Distance to major city in miles	120			$0
Number of refrigerated food trucks	3			$0
Estimate number of trips needed	48926			$0
Number of trips	67890			$0
Miles per gallon rigs and flatbeds	4			$0
Miles per gallon food trucks	5			$0
Fuel cost @$3 per gallon	3	$6,215,220		($6,215,220)
Affeercianado Workers	196	$2,224,992	$2,224,992	($6,215,220)
Maintenance parts/utilities		$100,000		($6,315,220)
Cost of trips at 10% profit	48		$4,688,262	($1,626,958)
Cost of trips at 15% profit	46		$4,492,918	$2,865,959
Profit on 10% trips	10		$468,826	$3,334,785
Profit on 15% trips	15		$673,938	$4,008,723
Depreciation		$1,227,000		$2,781,723
Revenue		$2,781,723		$0

In Year 9, there are 196 workers at the supply depot. Most of them are rig and flatbed drivers serving Prosperity, the affeercianados, the educational district, and predominantly private industry. During the year they made about 68,000 trips to Old Metropolis, ports, rail yards, and wholesalers. That is 164 trips a day, a steady stream of trucks coming into the supply depot with cargo, or delivering it directly to site.

We are interested in the content of those loads. What is being imported? This knowledge will help drive the import replacement process described shortly.

By Year 9, we should have plenty of restaurants, grocery stores, a movie complex, and even a department store or two, plus many specialty shops. There will be no more reason to allocate special slots in the land auction for missing retail. As far as retail goes, at this point the free market can do its thing.

But what about those imports, traveling hundreds or even thousands of miles to Prosperity? If we could eliminate some of this long distance shipping, certainly Prosperity would be more prosperous.

Import replacement is part of a strategy called entrepreneurial mercantilism and it will serve us well from Year 9 through capitulation.

Entrepreneurial Mercantilism

Entrepreneurial mercantilism describes a local economy based on Jane Jacobs' ideal of a highly diversified set of small businesses. These businesses make the local economy highly resilient and dynamic in the face of technological and economic change. It is both self-sustaining and self-renewing. It is a complex network of economic interrelationships in which a web of producers and suppliers, wholesalers, retailers, and consumers are joined. [FTN9.10]

Each actor fulfills a particular niche and strengthens the economy as a whole. This model is also the ecologist's dream of constructing a society based on the principle of local self-reliance. Use local resource basins as the chief means of satisfying local needs. Achieving local self-reliance requires ecological loops where the waste of one production system is the raw material of another. [FTN9.10]

Self-reliance creates the walled cities of old. According to sociologist Norman Long, un-walled cities have no significant real boundaries and are vulnerable to social and economic buffeting by forces beyond their control. [FTN9.10]

According to Jacobs, urban economic vitality results, when there is a physical, social and financial climate favorable to small-scale entrepreneurs. This environment promotes what she calls "two master processes:" innovation and import replacement. As stated earlier, import replacement occurs when entrepreneurs produce goods and services locally that were previously imported. [FTN9.10] Innovation occurs when entrepreneurs learn to add new forms of work to established types of labor. Small businesses are more flexible in this regard. Such innovation leads to increasing import replacement. [FTN9.10]

In the entrepreneurial mercantilist strategy, the city is an independent economic system. It conceives of itself as a nation and evaluates its balance of payments. Since most things are produced locally, exports exceed imports. [FTN9.11]

It might seem odd for mercantilism and self-reliance to be treated positively in building a Georgist society. Rather Georgism demands free trade and encourages comparative advantage. Our mercantilism is not based on tariff, but innovation, cheap labor, and an immaterial subsidy. Furthermore, our goal is to rapidly increase land value, partly through land speculation, to reward our investors and landlord-working class, the affeercianados. This short-term goal is clearly non-Georgist and perhaps similar to naming a missile "The Peacekeeper." As more non-Georgist economies fall, however, mercantilism disappears to be replaced by free trade and comparative advantage.

There are two guiding principles for a city to implement this strategy. In Prosperity, both principles are implemented through the Mercantile Letter (an online interactive publication described below), auction slots, and inter-business production control.

1. Pursuit of indigenous economic development.
2. Focus on resource flows.

An export multiplier is defined in entrepreneurial mercantilism. Assume that the exporter is supplied by two local importers. Every additional export provides sales for three businesses, not just one. The export multiplier is said to be 3. The effect of this multiplier is less than linear. Otherwise the existence of cycles (discussed below) would create an export multiplier of infinity. Jacobs defines the export multiplier less quantitatively. "The larger a city's own collection of various local industries that supply goods and services to producers of export work, the larger will be the total multiplier effect from increases in export work[FTN9.12].

According to Jacobs, there are three processes by which organizations can first become exporters[FTN9.13]:

1. They can add the export work to other people's local work.
2. They can add the export work to different local work of their own.
3. They can export their own local work.

More powerful than the export multiplier is the import-replacement multiplier. For every import that is replaced, the following is true:

1. Every additional export provides sales for the import replacer and all of its local suppliers.
2. A balance of trade surplus is created making "room" for new local enterprises.

Here is Jacobs' complete prescription for building up a new city: [FTN9.14]

1. The city finds in an older city or cities an expanding market for its initial export work, and it builds up a collection of numerous local businesses to supply producer's goods and services to the initial export work.
2. Some of the local suppliers of producer's goods and services export their own work. The city builds up an additional collection of local businesses to supply producer goods and services to the new export work. Some of these new local suppliers will take to exporting their own work, and so on.
3. Many of the imports the city has been earning are replaced by goods and services produced locally, a process that causes explosive city growth. The city, at the same time, shifts the composition of its imports. Its local economy grows large (and diverse) in proportion to the volume of the cities exports and imports. Owning to the powerful multiplier effect of the replacement process, the local economy contains room for entirely new kinds of goods and services, that is goods and services formerly neither imported nor produced locally. Among these can be unprecedented goods and services. The replacement of imports causes total economic activity to expand rapidly.
4. The cities greatly enlarged and greatly diversified local economy becomes a potential source of numerous and diversified exports, including many consumer goods and services as well as producer goods and services, and still other exports built upon local goods and services. Many of the new exports replace exports now obsolete or transplanted into the rural world.

There is a fine line between productive import-replacement and non-productive restraint of free trade and a planned economy. The ABC Board, city council, and Affeercianado Guild would be wise to follow the suggestions of the experts at the Jane Jacobs College of Urban Studies over the proposals in this book. As always, the proposals are intended to facilitate discussion and put hard numbers on the business plan.

Before describing these proposals, let me discuss some key concepts in import, export, and free trade. This is especially important since AFFEERCE and traditional Georgism differ on some of these.

Trade and the Seller Advantage

It is a common knowledge and basic economics that when buyer and seller engage in a trade, the buyer values the product more than the money and the seller values the money more than the product. In a fair trade, both sides win, each having gained something of greater personal value.

However, if we add the element of time going forward what seems a fair trade becomes fundamentally more lopsided. The buyer's product begins to wear out, become obsolete, or depreciate, while the seller's money begins to grow, earning interest. Often, the buyer loses interest in the product after the initial excitement wears off. Should the buyer try to sell the product, they likely will receive only a fraction of the original cost. This is the quantitative seller advantage. This quantitative advantage increases with time until the purchased product breaks and is thrown away, or is consumed and excreted as waste. After that the quantitative advantage is a function of the interest rate alone.

The qualitative seller advantage is more interesting. The money earned by the seller has the power to purchase any product in the world, at any time now, or in the future. The seller is free to choose between an infinite number of future times and places to satisfy their wants and needs. The buyer has already chosen a single product at a single time in the past. The have given up the freedom to choose.

While we consider selling a cup of water for one thousand dollars to a man dying of thirst as onerous, it is actually a metaphor for every trade where the buyer is unable to behave as a rational, disinterested party and thus loses interest in the product shortly after purchase. Since we are human, we are driven to purchases by impulse, addictions, fears, and fleeting desires, more often than not. (This was covered under the AFFEERCE theory of value in *Volume I*.) As mentioned above, even a rational purchase wears out and becomes obsolete, while the money spent grows in the seller's bank account.

In a fair trade, the seller always wins over time.

The most rational purchases are for capital goods. Although they become obsolete, wear out, or are exhausted, they generate other products to be sold, resulting in more wins than loses.

There is nothing morally wrong with indulging in products that meet our fleeting desires. That is part of what it means to be human. Recognize though, that such indulgences represent big wins for the seller.

Consider Prosperity as though it were an individual. If we want our city to be a winner, it had better be a net seller of goods. When a city sells goods, it is exporting. When a city buys goods, it is importing. The "city" referred to is not just the municipal government, but also the collective group of businesses, and individuals that make up the city. We want our city to be a net exporter of goods; to export more goods than it imports. That is, we want money to flow into the city and product to flow out. Such a city is said to have a balance of trade surplus.

Earning Imports

What does it mean to earn imports? It means that all imports are paid for with exports. Cities that use other funds to import goods will either soon run out of money or be dependent on a third party, usually the government, for funds. For instance, a city of retirees might depend on Social Security to fund imports.

A tiny agricultural community, using old farming methods, might still be able to provide enough food for its citizens. However, since it cannot economically export its grain, it has no money for imports. All of its clothing, tools, and homes must be locally produced. As long as the townsfolk spend money amongst themselves, the money will stick around. Any time a product is imported, money becomes scarcer. Nothing brings it back and soon there is no more money in town. All trade must be done with barter or some local scrip. Further imports are impossible without outside charity or government assistance.

Simply earning imports is not sufficient for continued prosperity. A town that earns its imports from the exports of a single factory will stagnate and die if the factory closes or the exported goods become obsolete or are produced cheaper elsewhere.

The goal of a vital city is to earn imports with a diverse and growing collection of exports. There is a virtuous cycle as it is the natural tendency for earned imports to generate new exports. Consider that earned imports are some combination of consumer goods and capital goods. Capital imports are used to produce a greater value of product than the imported capital. Otherwise, the company producing the product would go out of business. This means more exports are produced from imported capital than the exports that paid for those imports in the first place. Or the new product is used locally reducing imports to the same effect.

Unless all of the earned imports are used for consumer goods, earned imports lead to a growing set of exports. Pumping up exports is not always a good idea. Overproduce, and the exports will not sell. If the collection of exports is sufficiently diverse, there will be more opportunities for pumping up exports in one industry or another. But unless the whole world has a vibrant economy, in a vital city earning its imports, money will grow faster than markets.

If the city is a net exporter of goods, and has a balance of trade surplus, it is a winner. But what is to become of this extra money? Suppose it is used to pay bonus wages for a job well done and extra dividends to the owners of these wealth machines. After all, they deserve it. A side effect of this largess is that people around the world hear of this land of milk and honey, pack up, and head for Prosperity. Land values, and therefore rents, are pushed sky high, and all of that extra money ends up in the landlord's pocket (the affeercianados and investors in our case). This is a consequence of Ricardo's law of rent. Anytime people are paid more than they could earn elsewhere, others will move in, land value will increase, and all of that extra money will go for rent.

Alternatively, the extra money can be used to increase production. But this has exactly the same effect. New workers are needed, increasing the density, increasing land value, and increasing rents. Of course, increasing land value is our objective. The very same force that causes poverty will be used to eradicate it.

Prosperity will follow the path of earned imports and a diverse and ever growing set of exports. The affeercianados will live sparsely, even as the wealth machine delivers tremendous bounty to the citizens. Land values and rents should skyrocket. In most explosively growing cities this would spell doom. But in Prosperity, existing tenants are protected by a long-term lease, so they remain hyper-competitive. Higher rents from new tenants are reinvested in more land, used to fund cheaper labor for business, used to replace imports and thereby grow export diversity, and distributed to the citizens. This causes land values to rise even faster, and makes newer tenants, with fixed leases, more competitive. Older tenants become even more hyper-competitive.

There is a flavor of Ponzi to all this. Were it not for Phase-II and the monetization of land, the affeercianados would never indenture themselves. Nor would investors provide the free land to industry without the promise of explosive growth from affeercianado labor and Phase-II monetization of their own investment. Belief in the dream of ending poverty and bringing about world peace and freedom through common ownership of the land might also be necessary, but it is hardly sufficient. Affeercianado land ownership is.

This, of course, is the entire philosophy behind Phase-I; a landlord-working class creates wealth, and becomes wealthier inversely proportional to their consumption, provided consumption does not fall below an optimal minimum, below which less wealth is created due to poor nutrition and mental health. Abundant nutritious meals, warm, safe shelter in the luxury dorms that provide many physical and mental activity options, and political power through the Affeercianado Guild, keep the optimal minimum truly optimal.

By Year 9, it is predicted we have generated enough wealth from exports to earn imports needed for a virtuous cycle that will enhance the wealth effect of the affeercianados. The earned imports are naturally used to generate import replacement and business object creation, simultaneous outcomes of promoting the need within the business community and inter-business production control. The serendipity of import replacement and the diversity of business objects create new exports, thereby continuing the cycle.

In the next section, we examine the kinds of business objects we intend to create in Prosperity.

Modular versus Object Oriented Design

In a Rube Goldberg contraption, every piece fits just perfectly, so that a ball dropped at one end, after wending its way through an amazing obstacle course, causes the baby to put the bottle in its mouth at the other. Cool as they are to watch, change just one thing and the entire system fails. The same can be said for large, efficient, industry. It doesn't respond well to change. Everything is clockwork, a ballet of efficiency. Put in raw materials at one end and out pops a finished product at the other. The dance of people and machines in the middle, perfected over decades, produces the product with optimal efficiency.

We call these industries, dinosaurs; large, and hopefully soon to be extinct. Innovation is difficult with dinosaurs. Little can be reused for new ideas. A change might be desirable in and of itself, but not if it causes everything else to break. One solution is to trade off some efficiency for modularity. By converting the elaborate process into a number of distinct and fairly independent processes, change can often be effected by swapping out one module and leaving the others intact. But one of the problems of modular design is that the partial product that comes out of the new module, never quite fits into the modules that follow. Change is easier than with dinosaurs, but still quite painful.

The most flexible way to produce a new product is by adopting an object orientation. Objects perform an operation on their input and pass it along. Ideally, the nature of the input is unimportant. For instance, a polisher polishes its input, whether a mirror, silverware, rare coins, or furniture, before passing it along. All of these items might require different polishes and different techniques, but this object has the expertise to know which method to use.

The old modular polisher polished the glass input. When an earlier module changed the product to half glass and half metal, the polisher module had to be upgraded to polish the glass and metal parts independently. If that earlier module again changed the product to be two thirds metal and one third glass, the old polisher module would once again have to be upgraded.

The polisher object has no such problems. It understands the difference between glass and metal or even pewter. Whatever the input, it has the knowledge to know how to polish it. No matter what changes are made to the earlier module even if a wide variety of compositions are output, the polisher rarely needs to be changed. And if it does, it gains increased versatility in other processes as well. Clearly efficiency has been sacrificed. The polisher must devise a strategy every time something new is input.

Each object is a combination of machines and people that ideally work together to perform a specific function on arbitrary input.

There are many costs associated with object oriented design. For one, the business is paying for machines and knowledge that will never be used. If the only thing coming down the assembly line is glass, why should the polisher have machines and knowledge to polish rare coins and furniture? In addition to paying for these unused resources (and many objects could be predominantly unused resources) the assembly line goes much slower as each object strategizes how to deal with its input.[FTN9.15]

More realistic than polishers are flexible manufacturing systems (FMS). Each machine in an FMS can do hundreds of thousands of jobs by changing the program. Because of their versatility, they are much slower than fixed hardware counterparts.

Every business strives for maximum efficiency and object oriented design is without a doubt contrary to that goal. Business will never institute object oriented design, because if they do, they will be out of business.

So we have a conundrum. Object orientation is essential to support innovation and rapid product change. Business must strive for maximum efficiency to stay in business. Can you solve this conundrum?

The solution involves spinning off the object. Suppose the polisher is its own enterprise. Its polishing business is designed as efficiently as possible, modular with no object orientation at all. It follows a set of rules to maximize efficiency, such as: [IF IT COMES FROM COMPANY X, SEND TO PEWTER MODULE WITHOUT INSPECTION]. No machines and knowledge are superfluous, because the polisher works with all businesses that need polishing. And the polisher is so good at what it does, that transporting product to be polished is paid for by the efficiency of the polisher.

It is not possible for a city to be highly efficient and for the city to excel at the development of new goods and services. No it seems not. The conditions that promote development and the conditions that promote efficient production and distribution of already existing goods and services are not only different, in most ways they are diametrically opposed –Jane Jacobs.[FTN9.16]

There is a new concept, "distance" that enters the equation. If the polisher is next door, then the above set-up sounds pretty good. If the polisher is 20 miles away, then it simply doesn't pay. If we substitute for polisher a far more sophisticated function, then a distance of 20 miles might be reasonable, while several hundred miles would be out of the question.

Both Henry George and Jane Jacobs were fascinated by this idea of distance between efficient enterprises, and used it to frame their respective theories. A diverse collection of efficient enterprises, reduced to their essence, as close together as possible, can adapt almost instantly to innovation and can produce the greatest variety of products. George said if this were done, the value of the land would rise exponentially. Jacobs showed us how to do it.

Density and division of labor are keys to the discussion. In the abstract, we want many objects tightly packed. In Prosperity, we want a cornucopia of small businesses. Those businesses that do not add much value, like the polisher, need to be densely packed in the downtown area. Those that add more value to the end product can be farther out in the industrial area. Yet the more value a business adds to a product, the more likely it can be broken down into smaller objects (enterprises) whose efficiency is enhanced by moving closer to the downtown and taking on the knowledge and machinery to deal with any input.

Topology prevents all businesses from being next to all other businesses, but I propose that Prosperity be designed for the next best thing, inter-business production control.

We add a new concept called an agent. An agent asks questions and makes requests of business objects. Agents also talk with each other. Agents are robotic programs associated with transportation that automatically moves objects on special roads in the industrial sector, through lower-lower downtown, and up and down elevators to retail, industry, and homes. Agents also oversee the transfer of goods from vehicle to vehicle and the loading and unloading of goods. Agents communicate with business objects to cost jobs based on price, distance, time constraints, number of stops, and availability. They schedule jobs, and reschedule in the event of breakdowns.

There is some additional terminology. A business object is usually a small business. Each object implements one or more methods. A method performs an action and has a name that begins with a verb, like "polish," "attach," or "convert." The method has an interface which describes the range of inputs, when they are needed, and in what quantity, along with the composition and amount of the outputs. A single method often supports multiple interfaces. These interfaces are queried by agents who can plan and implement an entire production run. Methods are connected together in a flow. A flow begins as a tree with many branches. The outputs from methods on several branches converge as input to a method on a single branch. Inputs to the final method produce the output product at the root. Higher level agents (programs, but not robots) oversee the merging of branches.

Sophisticated flows are designed by innovators and engineers. Simple flows (e.g. pickup ingredients at various stores, bring them along with recipe to a chef business object that exposes a "prepare your dinner" method, with an interface that requires ingredients and a set of recipes or dish titles, and bring the hot meal to the dining room at exactly 6:00 PM) can be created by less savvy users.

Each business object is the brainchild of an entrepreneur, established to fill a need. But that doesn't mean that Prosperity can do nothing to help it along. We can promote a culture that encourages object orientation in enterprise design. The best way to do that is through an interactive online publication for businesses and future entrepreneurs called the Mercantile Letter that attempts to achieve import replacement through business objects by coordinating competing and cooperating object designers.

Jacobs talks about import replacement: replacing imports with locally produced products. For locally produced import replacements, I am going to use the term "input" in keeping with the object oriented paradigm. Import replacement will be defined as replacing imports with inputs.

It remains suppositional that the promotion of needs within the business community through the Mercantile Letter can induce the formation of business objects, but it is certainly true that any time an entrepreneur responds to the promotion with "I can do that," their enterprise is closer to be being a business object than it was before.

In the next section, Import Replacement, we examine how the Prosperity achieves earned imports implemented through business objects and an ever growing set of exports

Import Replacement

The benefits of import-replacement:

1. Decreases imports.
2. Increases import diversity.
3. Increases exports.
4. Increases export diversity.
5. Builds local economy including cycles.
6. Increases the value of land.

The first step in creating an import replacement strategy is to do an analysis of Prosperity businesses, in terms of their import and export activity. We are concerned with how much money is staying in Prosperity and how much is being drained from the economy. Although we can't know all of this for certain, we have a complete understanding of affeercianado, municipal, and educational imports and exports. There are also business exports and imports coming through the supply depot which can tell us a great deal about the exports and imports of private industry, without revealing confidences.

The primary export of Prosperity is medical care. Because medicine is a government protected monopoly, there is fat at every layer. Replacing staff with affeercianados allows us to undercut every other hospital in the nation, and still make a handsome profit. Therefore, the hospital exports far more in services than it imports in material and services.

Prosperity imports far more than hospital supplies. The affeercianados import food, perhaps electricity, and cable TV. The city imports building supplies. The hospital imports all of these plus bandages, medicine, testing equipment, hospital furniture. Are all the imports, including affeercianado and municipal imports, earned? Certainly if the hospital is able to generate $32 million in profits after its second year they would be.

What about the private industries that won the bid for land at auction? If they are headquartered in Prosperity, privately owned, and making a profit their imports are earned by definition. However, if export profits are delivered to a far off corporate headquarters, or distributed amongst shareholders, they might not be contributing to our trade surplus.

If a business pays their workers more than the cost of imports, great, they are contributing to the surplus. But what if they use cheap affeercianado labor? If the money saved from cheap affeercianado labor leaves Prosperity, how effective is it in increasing the value of land?

A retail outlet that is part of a large chain with corporate headquarters elsewhere, is selling more product than money distributed to workers and paid as rent, otherwise they would go out of business. The retail outlet is thus a net importer. These are unearned imports that drain the local economy.

For a retail outlet headquartered in Prosperity, the outlook is a little better. Purchases by city residents are neither imports, nor exports; however, purchases from those out of town are exports. On the other hand, purchases of inventory from out of town are imports. Only if out of town purchases exceeded purchases of inventory from out of town, would the locally headquartered retail outlet be a net exporter. Even if this is unlikely, that doesn't make the locally headquartered retail outlet a net negative. The outlet purchases the inventory from out of town at wholesale. Without the outlet, individual residents would travel farther to purchase the same inventory at retail. Thus the retail outlet reduces the import of this product from retail to wholesale.

The chief benefit of pumping up exports and reducing imports is to make way for more diverse and exotic imports, including capital imports for growth and consumer imports for residential wealth. The more we succeed at doing this, the faster Prosperity grows, the wealthier our residents become, and the more land values increase.

By their very nature, business objects are privately owned and locally headquartered. When used for import replacement, they maximize the benefits of import replacement.

Our municipal hospital imports bandages. Suppose two methods are exposed: one for turning cotton into cloth and the other for turning cloth into bandages. Instead of importing bandages, the hospital inputs bandages from the "Make bandages from cloth" method. The only import is to the first method, and it is the much cheaper cotton. In addition to supplying our hospital, the bandages can be exported.

In exposing these two methods, we generated interest in an entrepreneur who created a business object with three methods, one to turn cloth into underwear, another to turn rubber into an elastic band, and the third to attach the elastic band to material. The business object hosting the method to turn cotton into cloth has a new market. Prosperity no longer needs to import underwear or bandages, instead importing cotton and rubber. The underwear not only replaces an import, but can be exported in its own right. The underwear maker exposes the method for attaching an elastic band to material and gets a new market from a hairnet maker.

The FMS (flexible manufacturing system) plays an important role in the creation of business objects, particularly for innovators. FMS includes such things as 3D printing, and generic cutting and hole punching. Exposed home 3D printers will be useful for early prototypes. Early flow trees that are FMS rich, highlight areas where specialized business objects could increase the efficiency of the process. Proximity is critical for business objects whose exposed methods are easily accessed from one another in a densely packed downtown.

The manufacturer need not have a large factory, just a single business object to assemble the final inputs from a collection of business objects.

It is the job of AMS to develop the protocols for agent to agent and agent to business object communication.

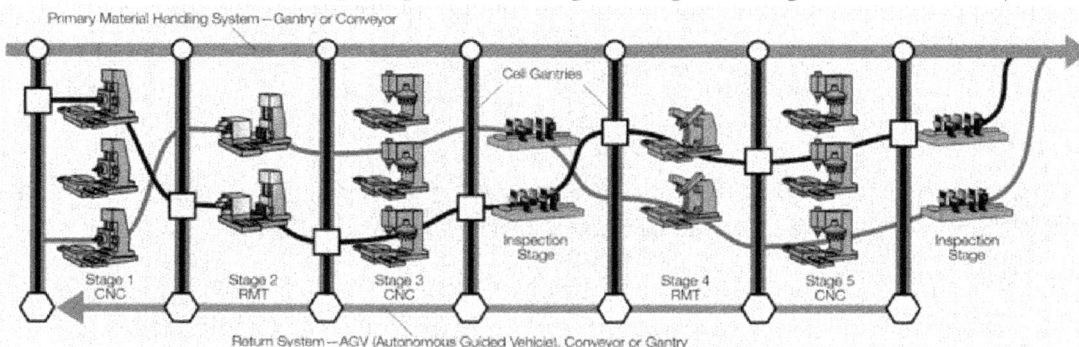

The autonomous guided vehicles take the product along a flow from FMS to FMS to inspection. The Prosperity model assumes more efficent business objects separated by larger distances. [FTN9.80]

Each new method increases land value downtown, and throughout Prosperity. Methods spawn new business objects which spawn new methods. When a new need is created, the diversity of methods makes Prosperity the number one choice as a city to fulfill that need because so much of the manufacturing is already complete. Even if the goal of universal manufacture remains science fiction, the attempt to reach it will drive up land values and bring greater prosperity to Prosperity.

The analysis will help us determine if a company is open to import replacement. Franchises are almost never open to import replacement. Companies with distant headquarters are also unlikely to switch import suppliers, even if they save a few cents. Companies that have a relationship with a single importer are also less likely to switch import suppliers for a few items. Affeercianados can talk to purchasing managers at these companies in confidence to see if they are open to switching suppliers of an import to save money on transportation cost. Using data from the supply depot and interviews with purchasing managers, a list is created of the top 10 imports by cost that are candidates for replacement.

These top 10 imports are then featured in the online AFFEERCE Mercantile Letter, perhaps run by a class at Jane Jacobs. Business experts, students, and qualified affeercianados discuss resources needed and possible flows between methods. Discussions and proposals are published for input from business and citizens. Local businesses can expose methods in any of the various flows and these are freely published in the Mercantile Letter once they have been verified as legitimate. Businesses can also propose alternate methods in alternate flows, and experiments with FMS can be tried. As more methods are exposed, various flows for an import replacement are taking shape. Ultimately, perhaps a single missing method is all that remains for an import replacement in one of the flows.

At this point, one of the non-FMS business objects in the nearly complete flow will offer to implement the missing method, or there might be competition among several small businesses. Once a single flow is actually in production, and the quality and price acceptable to the importer, the import will be considered replaced, and dropped from the top 10, to be replaced in that list by a new import.

Flows in the Mercantile Letter will incorporate any of the various materials recovered by waste management, if possible.

The Mercantile Letter will highlight missing methods that no business has volunteered to expose, and discuss how to attract businesses that will expose these methods. In an effort to attract businesses that implement those methods the affeercianados will create auction slots for businesses that promise to meet an interface and implement the method, just as they once created auction slots for grocery stores and gas stations in the earliest auctions.

By participating in Mercantile Letter discussions, businesses will generate new services, new interfaces, and new customers. Discussions will stimulate innovation. Members of the general public will figure out ways to become entrepreneurs, expose interfaces and implement methods so they too might become part of the Prosperity symphony of business objects.

By replacing imports through object-oriented businesses connected by automated agents in an inter-business production control flow, the value of the land will skyrocket along with the hyper-competitiveness of Prosperity business. Balance of trade surpluses will feed the virtuous cycle: new imports, new import-replacement, new exports, new imports… The process is unstoppable because while the value of land is skyrocketing, rents for existing businesses are frozen for another 10 years.

Cycles

In addition to feeding the virtuous cycle, import replacement through business objects produces another kind of cycle in the local economy. If business object A inputs from business object B and business object B inputs from business object C and business object C inputs from business object A; A, B, and C form a cycle. Currency spins in one direction, and product spins in the other.

In the unrealistic case that the price of each product output were the same, at the end of one complete cycle, the currency would all be back to where it started, but each company would have created additional product. The currency would have been unnecessary except for accounting purposes. Monopoly money would have sufficed.

Since inputs rarely equal outputs, the cycle currency is equal to the smallest output in the cycle. If a business is a participant in multiple cycles, the total cycle currency is the sum of the currency in the individual cycles. High cycle currency moves money to where it can optimally be used for imports, without forcing the business to take out a loan.

The ratio of cycle currency to exports is a good measure of the independence of the local economy. In an economic downturn, local cycle cash flow can buffer the effects of falling exports. The irrelevance of absolute currency value in a cycle makes it easier to lower the cost of exports before a corresponding drop in the price of imports. This can turn external economic dislocation into opportunity by increasing market share.

Given sufficient cycle density, export money enters the local economy and cannot escape. Regardless of whether this generates even more growth, or is paid in wages or basic income from the distributions, the value of land goes up accordingly.

I propose that import replacement with business objects is the fastest way to grow cycles in the local economy, and that such cycles produce the most wealth with the least amount of currency, by trapping currency, and reusing it over and over again.

In addition to cycle benefits in Phase-I Prosperity, there is an added benefit in Phase-II, when we convert to the VIP$. Cycles add to the convenience and acceptance of a local currency. Our goal in Phase-II is for export money to enter the Central Bank where it will sit forever.

Current Thought on Entrepreneurial Mercantilism

Goals of Entrepreneurial Mercantilism [FTN9.18] and Prosperity Implementation	Table 9.3
Stimulating small business	Financial/technical assistance including help locating new markets, seed capital, incubators. A freeze on the rent provides financial assistance. An educated affeercianado labor force provides technical assistance that is financially beneficial. The Mercantile Letter helps locate new markets.
Promoting local ownership	Prosperity amenities including a citizens' dividend, free medical care, Phase-II auction eligibility, and the Metrobus, encourage local ownership. The Mercantile Letter creates locally owned business objects which should gain a competitive edge over foreign owned dinosaurs.
Increasing import substitution	Identifying imports to replace, notify small businesses of needs, and report on businesses that will satisfy those needs. This is actively done through the Mercantile Letter and supported with land auction slots for businesses supporting specific interfaces and methods.
Conserving resources	One way to limit capital outflow is to conserve resources and recycle local waste. Waste management recovers many different materials at the MRF. These can be incorporated into flows at the Mercantile Letter.

Strengthening Local Multipliers	These cause a small increase in local productivity to have a larger positive impact on the community. Manufacturing has been found to have the highest multiplier effect. While manufacturing will not be specifically targeted, business objects exposing methods have the highest multiplier of all.
Innovative local finance schemes	Affeercianado and entitled labor in Phase-II will save businesses considerable money on labor. Free medical care will be a huge financial incentive. The supply depot will save businesses money on import/export and building materials. In Phase-II and beyond, citizen investors will compete with banks to provide low interest financing.
Localizing employment policy	Free medical care and other city perks, as well as rural densities in the surrounding area, will make it unlikely employees won't be residents.

Some economists object to mercantilism in that it is protectionist and stifles free trade. Yet by earning more imports, we insure free trade. If there are any economic costs, there are more distinct advantages: not using local resources entails substantial opportunity costs (local employment, more money circulating locally), secondly, the local economy is more stable and immune to shocks, and thirdly, local actors maintain more control over their economic destiny.[FTN9.19]

There are also legal objections to mercantilism. The municipality cannot use its regulatory power from blocking non-local business from doing business in the city, nor would we want to. However, the judicial system has ruled that cities are free to procure goods locally, even at a higher price. Because of affeercianado labor, goods produced locally would be cheaper, so this would not be an issue. Landlords certainly have the right to be of service to their tenants, and not to others, so affeercianado labor cannot be found illegal. Rules requiring private companies that receive city funds to hire locally have also been upheld judicially, although no such rules are anticipated.

Many studies have shown that small businesses disproportionately create jobs. All studies show that small businesses create more jobs than their share of total employment[FTN9.19].

Adaptability and flexibility are more favored over mass production assembly line operations in a highly competitive environment. Vertical disintegration encourages commerce and allows vertically disintegrated companies to be more flexible, as well as creating market opportunities for other small businesses[FTN9.20].

According to research in 170 large metropolitan areas, between 1956 and 1987 those areas with highly diverse industrial bases (having only 20% of jobs supplied by the top four industries) grew considerably during the period, while those with highly concentrated bases (having 60% of the jobs supplied by the top four industries) declined. Even the large industries in towns with diverse industrial bases thrived over their siblings in towns dominated by that industry. The benefits of a diverse industrial base are universal and favorable to Jacob's entrepreneurial-mercantilist model[FTN9.21].

Entrepreneurial mercantilism has met with considerable success when used as a strategy, although failures were reported in Latin America in the 1950s and 1960s. These stemmed from local price gouging and the use of inferior local products[FTN9.22]. By favoring business objects for import replacement, the problem of inferior local products is almost completely eliminated. A single bad method in a flow can be replaced.

According to Jane Jacobs in *Cities and the Wealth of Nations*, for new cities to arise and flourish, they must find solvent markets for their initial work in already existing cities[FTN9.23]. Yet it is fatal if backward cities confine themselves to that kind of trade, for such trade is only a springboard for embarking on a different kind of intercity trade; trade with cities in much the same circumstances and stage of development as themselves. Otherwise the gulf between what they export and what imports they can replace locally becomes too great[FTN9.23].

In *The Economy of Cities*, Jane Jacobs discusses many of the internal dynamics of entrepreneurial mercantilism, often with case histories. In particular, the division of labor often leads to a new activity that spawns an indeterminate number of new divisions of labor[FTN9.24].

To take advantage of these divisions of labor requires the opportunity to radically change ones work, class, and place in society. Freedom is a prerequisite for taking advantage of innovation[FTN9.25].

Jacobs notes that a balance of trade surplus is also required to take advantage of these divisions of labor. Otherwise there are insufficient funds to pay for the new enterprise's required imports. She uses the metaphor of room, in that room must be made for these new divisions of labor before they appear. Only the generation of new exports can provide this room[FTN9.26].

Prosperity, by concentrating on medical care as its chief export, puts itself on par with the largest cities in the world. Medical care, because of violent protectionism by the United States government can be optimally exploited for export by a new city. Like effective self-defense, this technique uses the enemy's own strength as a weapon.

Currency

We have seen above that where import replacement creates currency cycles in the local economy the value of currency is unimportant; bars of gold and play money that cannot be counterfeited have equal utility. The value of the currency is only important for import and export, and only then if they are out of balance. If imports equal exports, external demand for the currency will exactly equal local demand for the currency as payment for exports. The demands cancel each other and the intrinsic value of the currency is again unimportant. If exports exceed imports, the relative value of the currency strengthens and if imports exceed exports the relative value of the currency weakens.

For this reason, Jacobs points out that relative currency value serves as a good feedback mechanism for not only measuring balance of trade but fixing it. Since the city and its region is where we live, work, and play, according to Jacobs, each city should have its own currency. That way, a weakened currency is a signal to increase exports through diversification, however, the weakened currency, in and of itself, will increase exports through lower prices, and decrease imports through higher prices[FTN9.27].

This is a built-in design advantage that many cities of the past had, but which almost none have now. Singapore and Hong Kong, which are oddities today, have their own currencies, so they have this built-in advantage. They have no need of tariffs or export subsidies. Their currencies serve those functions when needed, but only as long as needed[FTN9.28].

Thriving rural exports raise the value of a currency and make imports too cheap for cities to engage in import-replacement. Adding a tariff can work to increase import-replacement in the cities, but hurts agricultural areas. This was one cause of the American Civil War [FTN9.28]. Of course, Prosperity has no need for tariffs and other obstacles to free trade. Our cheap affeercianado labor is all the protection we need.

Prosperity would be crippled by its own currency at this stage. By using the currency of our primary market, the U.S. dollar, we can maintain a trade surplus, making our exports the cheapest in the land. Our primary export, medical care, will draw people from around the country for inexpensive procedures. If we had our own currency, it would rise in value relative to the dollar making our medical care only competitive, not hyper-competitive.

In Phase-II, our own currency is a necessity. However, to maintain the balance of trade surplus, we peg it to the dollar. Our Central Bank will issue 2 VIP$ for every U.S. dollar, regardless of the markets. As our currency becomes stronger people will overwhelm the figurative "VIP window" at the Central Bank, trading in their U.S. dollars. This is jokingly called the "dollarnado," where U.S. dollars are sucked into the AFFEERCE Central Bank and can't get out (crossing a bad movie and a bad commercial). In the final years before capitulation we will agree to limit access to the VIP window in exchange for an IRS peg of 2 VIP$ for every U.S. dollar.

It is clear that national currencies help maintain a balance of trade between nations. Without them, great disparities would emerge. As Jacobs says, "We must be grateful that world government and world currency are still only a dream[FTN9.29]." In a Georgist world, one country or many countries is a matter of cultural preference. All that matters is that the collection and distribution of rents be in the same currency, and that conditions of collection and distribution be universal to the currency's domain. Multiple governments and alternative currencies can exist comfortably within this framework. This is called the panarchy. Movement of people between AFFEERCE nations is a balance of trade event. A high level currency will maximize freedom of movement.

Liberation through Mercantilism

Prosperity does not need or want currency as a feedback mechanism. We do not want any feedback mechanism save for rapidly increasing land values, which forces density and further increases land values. Our cheap affeercianado labor and cheap rents relative to land value will force a strong balance of trade surplus.

Interestingly, mercantilism will be our strategy from the first land purchase by the ABC until the very last country in the world becomes Georgist. After capitulation, universal distribution will allow enterprises to be hyper-competitive. We might even peg our currency to the strongest non-AFFEERCE nation, thereby sucking it dry. All other countries need do is become one of us by implementing the collection and distribution of rents separately, or joining our panarchy, and our advantage disappears. I know it sounds like one of those bad sci-fi vampire movies, but that is how the workers of the world will be liberated.

Year 10

Year 10 will be the first full year of entrepreneurial mercantilism and the Mercantile Letter. But if you look on the spreadsheets, you won't find the Mercantile Letter or import/export analysis anywhere. So how are these paid for and who does the work?

ABC Admin

Here is a look of the major ground rent distribution in the first 10 years, excluding the 60% that goes to the land trust and the capped 1% to the land broker.

The city and county share 30% of the rent on developed land based on a negotiated formula. Prosperity, with all its services, receives 65% of that 30%, or $73 million in Year 10, while the county receive $39 million. The investors and affeercianados share 5% of the rent on developed land as a dividend. With the affeercianados recent $700 million donation to the land trust, in Year 10, they own 90% of the 80,000 acres of developed and undeveloped land. Smack in the middle of Table 10.1 is ABC administration which gets 4% of the rent, or $16,836,560.

Year Table 10.1	% City	ALR	City	County	ABC Admin	Investor Dividend	Affeercianado Dividend
1	15%	50%	$313,380	$1,775,820	$415,936	$233,500	$233,500
2	20%	50%	$768,480	$3,268,920	$675,872	$397,550	$397,550
3	20%	50%	$1,807,470	$5,474,880	$1,115,008	$674,763	$674,763
4	60%	50%	$7,650,180	$5,685,120	$1,926,944	$1,185,575	$1,185,575
5	60%	74%	$15,211,380	$10,075,920	$3,711,424	$1,128,333	$3,259,217
6	65%	74%	$24,187,800	$13,024,200	$5,284,160	$1,648,954	$4,763,046
7	65%	74%	$32,292,390	$17,388,210	$6,958,128	$2,187,745	$6,319,355
8	65%	74%	$41,226,900	$22,199,100	$8,767,920	$2,778,637	$8,026,163
9	65%	90%	$61,033,271	$32,864,069	$13,931,433	$1,654,621	$14,247,935
10	65%	90%	$72,845,175	$39,224,325	$16,338,560	$1,973,391	$16,992,859

ABC administration began the journey paying out in scrip. In the 10th year of Prosperity, they have rent revenue of $16.3 million. The ABC board and other affeercianado staff at the ABC are paid from this fund at the same rate as all affeercianados. The payout at the end of Year 20 for affeercianados on staff at ABC headquarters will be financed by the $125 million ground rents in Year 20 and the ABC growing balance sheet. As such, ABC affeercianados will be of little, if any, liability to the regular affeercianados. It is extremely likely that ABC headquarters will move to Prosperity early on, resulting in considerable overlap.

The Mercantile Letter and object oriented business expertise, coordination of VIP and online land system development, smartcard oversight, marketing, public relations, lobbying, coordinating Affeercianado Guild meetings and political conventions, oversight of affeercianado businesses, especially the hospital, and update of the business plan will be done from ABC headquarters and financed with the ground rent dividend. Some of these projects might be done in coordination with departments and classes at Jane Jacobs University. Because of the large rent revenue that easily supports a staff of 100 affeercianados, there is also money available starting in Year 10 for low-interest loans to businesses that expose valuable methods for import replacement.

Roads and Infrastructure

Roads and infrastructure brings great profits to the city of Prosperity. Here is the Year 10 spreadsheet.

Roads and Infrastructure	Table 10.2		Debit	Credit	Balance	
Year 10		0	$0	$0	$0	
Road Miles		105			$0	
Road acres @1 mile = 5 acres		525			$0	
Rent = $2000/acre*.10			$105,000	$0	($105,000)	
Affeercianados working at infrastructure		300	$3,120,000		($3,225,000)	
Maintenance cost			$157,500		($3,382,500)	
Gas tax revenue sharing			$0	$4,263,000	$880,500	
Municipal parking subsidiary			$0	$2,108,527	$2,989,027	
Utility delivery charge and taxes			$0	$36,604,800	$39,593,827	
Office supplies			$20,000		$39,573,827	
Utility infrastructure materials (16)		16	$3,000,000		$36,573,827	
Road infrastructure materials (10)		10	$3,000,000		$33,573,827	
Road signs and signals (12)		12	$3,000,000		$30,573,827	
Depreciation			$6,180,556		$24,393,271	
Revenue			$24,393,271		$0	

In Year 10, roads and infrastructure has 300 affeercianados extending utilities, building roads and putting up traffic signals and signs. Their material budget is $9 million with over $6 million of annual depreciation. Yet they manage to bring in $24 million in net revenue for Prosperity By and large this is done through utility delivery charges and utility taxes. These delivery charges and taxes are competitive with major cities and far better than the charges in small towns and rural areas.

Not shown are charges for utility supply, since this is highly region dependent. However, the affeercianados along with individual households and businesses can recoup much of the utility delivery charges by supplying solar electricity to the grid. With all dormitories, and prefabs having solar panels integrated into the architecture, affeercianados will have a great deal of expertise in installation and maintenance of solar panels. This knowledge base will increase lease demand for affeercianados and attract private enterprise, making Prosperity a solar center. I imagine that solar panels will be a good candidate for import replacement.

Citizens' Dividend

In Year 10, every registered Prosperity voter will receive a citizens' dividend of $310. This will likely be much more appreciated by the affeercianados than the generally well-to-do residents of Prosperity. However, a couple with two children age 18 or older living at home, will receive $1,240. This might easily pay the ground rent on 1/8 acre of land bought in the first few years, making that land completely free to that family for the next 10 years, since the CD is slated to rise every year.

Student Union

With an increasing number of non-affeercianados, a growing number of colleges and, in preparation for the medical school, a student union will be constructed in Year 10 on the Jane Jacobs campus.

Higher Education Table 10.3		Debit	Credit	Balance
Year 10	0	$0	$0	$0
Affeercianados enrolled full time at Jane Jacobs/quarter	2040	$0	$0	$0
Prosperity resident students enrolled full time/quarter	200	$0	$128,000	$128,000
In-state nonresident students enrolled full time/quarter	100	$0	$400,000	$528,000
Medical school students	0	$0	$0	$528,000
Medical student lab costs	0	$0	$0	$528,000
Jane Jacobs affeercianado instructors	150	$0	$0	$528,000
Jane Jacobs affeercianado non-dorm staff	195	$0	$0	$528,000
State grant @5000 per full time college year	0	$0	$11,700,000	$12,228,000
Paid university professors/Department heads	11	$1,100,000	$0	$11,128,000
Med school affeercianado instructors not hospital affiliated	0	$0	$0	$11,128,000
Hospital affiliated med school instructors	0	$0	$0	$11,128,000
Paid med school instructors not hospital affiliated	0	$0	$0	$11,128,000
Med school affeercianado non-dorm staff	0	$0	$0	$11,128,000
Total affeercianado educators and staff	345	$3,588,000	$0	$7,540,000
Number of student dorms of 250 rooms for 2 + paid room debits/credits	7	$9,792,000	$15,024,000	$12,772,000
Rent Owed	0	$326,000	$0	$12,446,000
Dorm Staff	315	$3,276,000	$0	$9,170,000
Construction workers	400	$4,160,000	$0	$5,010,000
Materials for 2 Student Dorms (20)	20	$24,000,000		($18,990,000)
Purchase 60 washes/dryers (6)	6	$40,000		($19,030,000)
Purchase kitchen equipment (8)	8	$70,000		($19,100,000)
Dorm furnishings (10)	10	$600,000		($19,700,000)
Materials for student union/activities (30)	30	$65,000,000		($84,700,000)
Depreciation		$13,237,292		($97,937,292)
Revenue		($97,937,292)		$0

A landmark student union will cost $65 million for materials. In addition, 2 more student dorms are being built for $24 million to add to the 7 already in operation. In Year 10, the 7 student dorms house 660 affeercianados, 1,260 migrant workers and only 200 other students.

There are 345 affeercianado educators and staff, with 11 paid professors or department heads. 400 affeercianado construction workers are needed for the student union and the two dorms. If chancelleries prove to be popular, the student union can be made a vice-chancellery with unaccounted for benefits.

Because of the construction, there is a $98 million deficit for the higher education group. If we look at education as a whole, the deficit for Year 10 is much lower at $18 million and is easily borrowed from the land trust. Based on local politics, it might not be possible to group higher and lower education on a single balance sheet. This is more an accounting issue than a practical one.

Education	Table 10.4	Debit	Credit	Balance
Year 10		$0	$0	$21,063,147
Lower Education		$0	$59,367,200	$80,430,347
Higher Education		$0	($97,937,292)	($17,506,945)
Rent Dividend		$0	$0	($17,506,945)
Rent Owed		$524,000	$0	($18,030,945)
Borrow from land trust		$0	$0	$0

Lower education's surplus is all a function of cheap affeercianado labor. Lower education (K-12) receives large state revenue sharing grants relative to the pay for affeercianado teachers, administrators and staff. This produces a net profit of $59 million, which is being used to build the university. In addition, the affeercianado grant of $140 million to higher education in Year 6, has kept the balance workable despite the massive amount of building.

Year 11

Municipal Parking

Municipal parking is a subsidiary of roads and infrastructure, which is building up the transportation depot for its grand opening in Year 15.

There are 4 remote garages at the transportation depot in Year 11, each allowing 3000 cars to park. During much of the day, there are 2 free buses on each of 2 routes to different parts of lower downtown. Buses leave the depot and lower downtown ever 7 to 8 minutes. There is very late night bus service every 15 minutes with online bus locators.

Lower downtown has 12,000 parking spaces in use with annual revenue of over $11 million. The 4 remote garages, also hosting 12,000 spaces, bring in over $5 million. Street parking brings in $3 million with an estimated $750,000 charge for metering machines and enforcement in excess of fines.

Three more buses are purchased for the downtown/depot shuttle that will be relatively continuous by Year 15.

R&I – Municipal Parking Table 11.1		Debit	Credit	Balance
Year 11	0	$0	$0	$0
Number of remote garages	4	$52,000		($52,000)
Number of buses	12			($52,000)
Bus drivers	12	$12,000	$0	($64,000)
Bus maintenance	3	$30,000		($94,000)
Depot security	0	$3,600		($97,600)
Depot janitorial and maintenance	0	$0	$0	($97,600)
Construction workers	50	$0	$0	($97,600)
Total affeercianados	65	$676,000		($773,600)
Fuel	4	$105,120	$0	($878,720)
Depot utilities	0	$5,000	$0	($883,720)
Revenue from lower downtown parking	12000	$0	$11,520,000	$10,636,280
Revenue from remote parking	0	$0	$5,760,000	$16,396,280
Revenue from hospital/university parking	0	$750,000	$3,000,000	$18,646,280
3000 car garage (30)	30	$12,000,000		$6,646,280
3 buses (6)	6	$600,000		$6,046,280
Depreciation		$833,333		$5,212,947
Revenue		$5,212,947		$0

Highlights of Year 11

- 2,900 acres auctioned off at an average rent of $21,000/acre. A total of over 19,000 acres developed.
- 5 acres of downtown auctioned off for a rent of $500,000/acre. To date, a total of 37 acres of downtown developed.
- The affeercianados purchase another 40,000 acres at $30,000/acre. Most of the undeveloped land will be withheld from market until developed by settlers of the AFFEERCE territories in Phase-II.
- Thomas Paine Hospital brings in $182 million in revenue. Construction begins on another 160 bed wing including two surgeries with student galleries.
- Affeercianado leasing brings in $215 million in revenue.
- The resident population of Prosperity, excluding affeercianados, is 85,050.
- There are 22 elementary schools, and 3 high schools.
- A third community center is built for $18 million.
- There are 3 police and fire stations, with a fourth under construction. The police department has a total of 134 vehicles, mostly squad cars. The fire department has 19 engines and ambulances. This is in addition to the fleet of ambulances maintained by the hospital.

Year 12

Thomas Paine and Metrobus

Year 12 completes the purchase of Thomas Paine Hospital's ambulance network. The hospital will have extended its coverage to include Old Metropolis. With a fleet of 5 ambulances at scattered sites throughout the major city, one is always within a few minutes of any home or accident site. Once a single ambulance is dispatched, restoration of the complete ambulance network is possible within 30 minutes. The same is true for two ambulances. Three ambulances dispatched might require just under an hour before the network is restored.

Even if accident victims are missing they're smartcard, ambulance EMT's can use biometrics to pull up the patient's entire medical history to insure proper first-aid and facilitate phoned orders from physicians.

Because Old Metropolis is in the HMO coverage zone, the number of premium payers is assumed to be 1.8 times the total population of Prosperity. This will increase to 2.6 over the next 8 years.

The new 160 bed wing that has two surgeries with student galleries opens in Year 12, although the average beds used per night is still well below half the beds available. To increase efficiency the hospital might consider self-admission nursing services for those with the flu or other conditions where they don't feel comfortable alone at home, but hospital admission is not warranted. For $120 a day, the price of an average hotel, the patient can be served 3 meals, have their doctor visit them on rounds, and in case of a turn for the worse, be already at the hospital for regular admission. One affeercianado aide can easily handle 4 ambulatory patients, making the venture profitable. Usually there will also be $35 doctor and lab test copays.

To accommodate those people in Old Metropolis who need to come to Prosperity for doctor's appointments, tests, procedures, and surgery, 6 more luxury buses will be added in Year 12 to the free service. By this time, it is assumed that total trips will exceed the demand for shipping, cargo, and U.S. mail contracts, causing the service to operate at breakeven or a small loss going forward.

Metrobus Table 12.1		Debit	Credit	Balance
Year 12	0	$0	$0	$0
Total trips	8760	$0		$0
Passenger's cargo-Suitcases assume 200 lbs./trip	20	$0	$350,400	$350,400
U.S. Mail cargo contract	30	$0	$525,600	$876,000
Shipping company cargo contracts	40	$0	$700,800	$1,576,800
Business cargo @$1 for 10 lbs., assume 1000 lbs./trip	100	$0	$1,752,000	$3,328,800
Messenger service average 2/trip (costs extra)	40	$0	$700,800	$4,029,600
Maintenance Cost @$20/trip	20	$175,200		$3,854,400
Tolls/access @$20/trip	20	$175,200		$3,679,200
Fuel cost Total trips * distance*2/4 MPG*$3/gal	4	$1,576,800		$2,102,400
6 luxury buses (6)	6	$2,400,000		($297,600)
Depreciation		$800,000		($1,097,600)
Revenue		($1,097,600)		$0

Jane Jacobs University

Despite a university dedicated to boosting city construction, partially financed with the innovation of chancelleries, sharing resources with a hospital, and a city, hosting a world class library, and with a landmark student union, the campus has no athletic facilities.

The only athletic facilities beyond dormitory fitness centers are those that are shared with a community center on the campus next to Henry George High. These are shared with the high school as well as the community. To rectify the situation, $75 million is being spent in Year 12 on top notch athletic facilities for the university, including fields and gymnasiums for all sports.

The athletic facilities will be coming at a time when students are replacing affeercianados in the dorms. The affeercianado population will be under slight pressure until Year 14 when the prefabs and trailer park will no longer be open to migrant workers, allowing new affeercianados to take their place.

Higher Education Table 12.2		Debit	Credit	Balance
Year 12	0	$0	$0	$0
Affeercianados enrolled full time at Jane Jacobs/quarter	3144	$0	$0	$0
Prosperity resident students enrolled full time/quarter	300	$0	$192,000	$192,000
In-state nonresident students enrolled full time/quarter	300	$0	$1,200,000	$1,392,000
Medical school students	0	$0	$0	$1,392,000
Medical student lab costs	0	$0	$0	$1,392,000
Jane Jacobs affeercianado instructors	240	$0	$0	$1,392,000
Jane Jacobs affeercianado non-dorm staff	272	$0	$0	$1,392,000
State grant @5000 per full time college year	0	$0	$18,720,000	$20,112,000
Paid university professors/Department heads	25	$2,500,000	$0	$17,612,000
Med school affeercianado instructors not hospital affiliated	0	$0	$0	$17,612,000
Hospital affiliated med school instructors	0	$0	$0	$17,612,000
Paid med school instructors not hospital affiliated	0	$0	$0	$17,612,000
Med school affeercianado non-dorm staff	0	$0	$0	$17,612,000
Total affeercianado educators and staff	512	$5,324,800	$0	$12,287,200
Number of student dorms of 250 rooms for 2 + paid room debits/credits	11	$15,343,200	$23,770,800	$20,714,800
Rent Owed	0	$398,000	$0	$20,316,800
Dorm Staff	495	$5,148,000	$0	$15,168,800
Construction workers	400	$4,160,000	$0	$11,008,800
Materials for 2 Student Dorms (20)	20	$24,000,000		($12,991,200)
Purchase 60 washes/dryers (6)	6	$40,000		($13,031,200)
Purchase kitchen equipment (8)	8	$70,000		($13,101,200)
Dorm furnishings (10)	10	$600,000		($13,701,200)
Athletic field/gyms/track/pool (10)	20	$75,000,000		($88,701,200)
Depreciation		$21,004,792		($109,705,992)
Revenue		($109,705,992)		$0

Years 13 – 14 – 15

Obviously, as the years go by, the business plan becomes more uncertain. Not only errors, but new innovations and ideas can lead to significant changes in direction. I am but one person while the Affeercianado Guild will have tens of thousands with their feet on the ground and intimate knowledge on how to create new efficiencies.

Of course, the reason this business plan will succeed has little to do with my crafting of the years. It is due to the fundamental nature of the landlord-working class. But, a summary of viral community theory would hardly encourage investors or affeercianados, so a business plan is needed to anchor us in reality. Nevertheless, it hardly seems worthwhile to go into too much detail in the final years of Phase-I considering the inevitability of changes to the plan.

Jane Jacobs University

In Year 13, an additional hall with new classrooms and labs is built. Liberal arts, pre-med, and community college curriculums are established, if those have not already happened years earlier. Two new mixed use student dorms are built every year with additional classrooms and a lecture hall in each. In Year 15, we take a giant leap forward for Prosperity tourism, Jane Jacobs' prestige, and land value with the building of a football stadium worthy of the Big 10, for $170 million in materials.

Mercantilism

We built the entire university with no debt. All needed funds supplied by the affeercianados, inexpensive tuition, and state revenue sharing. Of course, without cheap affeercianado labor, it would have been impossible. With no debt to repay and depreciation funds for all capital assets, we have created a hyper-competitive hospital and university. Absolutely nobody can compete with us.

Our private industry meanwhile is also benefitting from cheap affeercianado labor, frozen rents, citizens' dividends, imports at wholesale pricing, free medical care and very inexpensive courses at the community college and university. They too, with any kind of decent management, are becoming hyper-competitive.

Furthermore, the pump is being constantly primed with new business objects created for import replacement. By Year 15, Prosperity should be turning into a mercantile powerhouse, unseen since the days of empire. Of course, our population is still low, albeit highly efficient, at 158,350 or about 193,000 including affeercianados.

By Year 15, the affeercianados own 94% of 200,000 acres. Investors own the other 6%. However, less than 40,000 acres are developed. The other 160,000+ acres are being held speculatively so that growth can be controlled, additional land can be purchased cheaply, and rents maximized.

Total ground rent on developed land is $672 million, with 60% going back into the land trust. As the margin gets farther away from the center of Prosperity due to increased speculative holdings, price increases for the purchase of new land will be subdued. Still, the spreadsheets push prices to $40,000/acre for undeveloped land as a maximum; though it is expected land brokers will be able to negotiate far better deals. As the margin increases, so does our choice of property. Sellers have more competition and uncooperative sellers can easily be ignored. Purchasing land at cheaper prices than planned is the biggest ace in the hole for countering unexpected expenses.

In Year 15, the citizens' dividend is $581 for every registered voter of Prosperity. The assumption used in the calculation is that the number of children and non-registered voters is equal to the number of affeercianados.

Affeercianados

Accommodations

In Year 13, the migrant workers are phased out from the prefabs and trailer park virtual north of downtown. By Year 14, they are all gone. So is AFFEERCE A'Cookin, as a public accommodation. The accommodations department shows a $50 million deficit from new dorm construction and a large depreciation on all the dorms built to date.

In Year 14, a summer intern program for potential affeercianados is opened with the trailer park. Students on summer break who want to get in a few months of affeercianado service to enhance their retirement can use the trailer park for their RV's, trailers, and other mobile homes. They get free dining at AFFEERCE A'Cookin (only for affeercianados), standard affeercianado medical policy and pay. Based on their skills, they will be assigned to teams. Most likely, they will be given the least desirable work. All occupants of any mobile home must be affeercianados. Termination for cause during the 6 month probationary period will automatically invoke "take the money and run."

At this point, the waiting list to be an affeercianado should be huge due to the obvious success of the plan. Summer internship will be a good way to break in for those far down on the waiting list and whose skills are marginal. (There will never be a waiting list for affeercianado doctors.) If an intern has performed well and is approved by the Guild's human resources, they can continue the probationary period for the full six months, and if there are no problems, be admitted to the Guild. If they wish, they will be given housing in the prefabs or the dorms as soon as room is available.

Balance Sheet
The affeercianado balance sheet in Year 15 is interesting. We see the $49.9 million deficit for Accommodations.

Affeercianados Table 15.1	Debit	Credit	Balance
Year 15	$0	$0	($246,280,262)
Donate to land trust	$1,000,000,000	$0	($1,246,280,262)
Hospital	$0	$512,915,765	($733,364,497)
Accommodations	$0	($49,900,308)	($783,264,805)
Supply Depot	$0	$2,781,723	($780,483,082)
Surplus Labor	$0	$410,630,036	($369,853,046)
AMS Software	$0	$2,000,000	($367,853,046)
Metro Bus Service	$0	$382,600	($367,470,446)
Downtown excavation	$0	($3,400,960)	($370,871,406)
Rent Dividend	$0	$47,768,911	($323,102,495)
Pay Unauctioned land Rent	$0	($99,558,000)	($422,660,495)
Borrow from land trust	$0	$0	$77,339,505
Rent Owed	$449,600	$449,600	$77,339,505

One billion dollars is donated to the land trust, even though this requires that the affeercianados borrow $500 million from the land trust (column not shown) to keep a positive balance at year end. It isn't a big deal. With Thomas Paine Hospital bringing in $513 million in revenue, while the surplus labor of affeercianados brings in $410 million, the interest free loan will be paid back in Year 16. The affeercianado land speculation charge of $99.5 million is half covered by the ground rent dividend of $47.8 million.

Downtown
For the first time, ground rent on downtown land has reached $1 million/acre. This corresponds to net rents (profits) of $3 million/acre which on 21-story mixed use buildings, is quite reasonable.

Out of the 140 downtown acres to be auctioned, 117 have been auctioned as of Year 15. There are several downtown milestone events that will occur this year. The first involves the central park. I hesitate to call it Central Park since Manhattan seems to have an unofficial trademark on the name, but that is likely what it will be called.

Central Park
In Year 15, all of the dirt taken from the excavation of downtown will be returned to create a hilly 40 acre central park in the very middle of downtown. The entire lower level beneath the park will be dedicated to parking. Natural geological and botanical artifacts will be used to maintain the integrity of the terrain. Well placed drainage into lower level sewers will prevent flooding and further insure the integrity of the park during heavy rains. We do not want a mudslide onto our beautiful downtown thoroughfares.

A run for skiing and sledding will have a side tow rope that will be operated in the winter by parks and recreation. Users must sign a waiver that will be stored on the smartcard.

Dry Sewer
The second major milestone in Year 15 is activation of the dry sewer. Prior to this year, all garbage for downtown buildings will have been dropped from chutes into receptacles collected regularly by the waste management department and brought to the MRF (materials recovery facility).

In Year 15, the receptacles will be removed and garbage will fall into the lower-lower level dry sewer. This will be a conveyor belt system that moves the garbage to a single egress point, and then on to waiting trucks which take the garbage to the MRF. Because the garbage will move frequently, and secondary conveyors will be completely sealed from lower level public walkways, the smell of garbage in the lower level will be minimal, and downtown will be completely garbage free.

Installation of the dry sewer will be done as part of the excavation/foundation project from the very beginning; however, Year 15 is the first time it is complete enough to actually use.

Production Control
The third milestone, also on the lower-lower level is the extension of automated production control into downtown. Residents can use the system for shopping while businesses use it for innovation and import replacement.

Transportation Depot
Year 15 will mark the grand opening of Prosperity's transportation depot. At that time, there will be 8 remote garages surrounding the depot. Underground moving walkways will take travelers to the garages.

The depot will be built like Los Angeles International Airport with an interior circle for shuttles, free buses to downtown, drop-offs and pickups, jitneys and cabs, including scheduled buses and jitneys waiting for a regular slot to open on the exterior circle. The exterior circle is for scheduled buses, public and private, and scheduled jitneys. Jitneys that fail to meet their schedule will lose their slot on the exterior circle.

Besides restaurants, shops, and waiting areas for scheduled departures, the interior will contain the largest smartcard facility in Prosperity, much larger than at the city clerk's office. Why is this? Twelve free luxury buses make 2 trips every day to and from Old Metropolis. Tourists and conventioneers will park in the remote garages and catch a free bus to downtown. Private interstate carriers and limousines from the airport will enter Prosperity through the transportation depot. The smartcard is the ticket to Prosperity. It is needed for parking; hotels can use it for a door key, it is a debit card, and can be used as a credit card if hooked up to the appropriate credit account. If you are treated at Thomas Paine hospital, your medical records are placed on the card. Jitneys require a smart-card to insure payment and record identity for safety. City passes placed on the card are good for discounts at retail and free admissions to clubs. There is no charge for the smartcard and money placed on the smartcard will never go away until spent.

Large Smartcard Facility
Can we require a smartcard for admission to Prosperity? It is the age-old debate between "Big Brother" and freedom from crime and convenience. Once Prosperity is incorporated in Year 4, its streets and sidewalks will no longer be considered private property. However, nothing can stop us from charging a much higher usage fee for parking, transportation, and other services for those without the card. Without the card, it will cost $20 to park in remote parking, and admission to lower downtown is simply prohibited by auto unless the card is used for entrance. Beginning in Year 15, free luxury buses leaving the city will require the smartcard or $25. Free buses to and from lower downtown require the smart-card or $5. Treatment at Thomas Paine Hospital requires a smart-card or cash for copays. Merchants pay nothing for smart-card debit transactions so many merchants will take only the smart-card. For Prosperity residents, the smartcard is a driver's license, state ID, medical insurance card, and voter registration card.

The smartcard contains biometric information, as well as a face shot. Identity theft is thwarted by those merchants with biometric smartcard readers, or those merchants who simply check the picture. A lost card can easily be replaced for a nominal fee and the old card disabled, with no loss of money or information. If your wallet is stolen and you have no identification at all, there will be no problem getting another smartcard once biometric readings verify your identity.

List of allergies and other life-saving information are on the smart-card for EMT's to use with an unconscious patient. Of course EMT's don't need the card at all. They just use the biometrics. In Year 16, the same technology will be tried in merchant establishments.

Year 16

Smartcard Optional – The VIP is born

In Year 16, implemented biometric search algorithms and hardware will be sufficiently powerful and accurate to handle real time biometric identification, versus the simpler identity verification. Such systems are already in use today, so the feasibility is not in doubt.

Those merchants who have smartcard readers that verify biometric identity (unobtrusive iris scan keyed on facial recognition) will hopefully not need to change hardware. The smartcard will simply be optional.

It is impossible to accurately plan a role for Prosperity in the development of this hardware and software. The state of the art might be past this point before we even get to Year 1. Certainly as of this writing, business objects that produced biometric components such as facial recognition, iris scan, palm reading, and voice recognition, would be useful in building readers with varying degrees of sophistication. The degree that AMS (Affeercianado Municipal Software) builds the smartcard/VIP infrastructure, or simply builds applications will be determined by the future of technology.

Land

Year 16 sees "marginal" land on the inner speculative ring auctioned for an average rent of $23,500 an acre, with downtown land auctioned for a rent of $1,100,000/acre.

Most single family home owners are not bidding to pay $23,500 every year for an acre of land. This would be rather pricey even for a home on a quarter of an acre. Instead, there is a wide variance. Land for apartment buildings and retail very close to downtown likely will see rents from $50,000 to $500,000 per acre. Land for single family homes in average communities will go for reasonable bids, perhaps as low as $10,000/acre, even as late as Year 16.

Medical School

In Year 15, $150 million will be spent on materials and 400 affeercianado construction workers will be used to build the medical school on campus. It will be the unifying element between Jane Jacobs University and Thomas Paine Hospital and should reflect that unity architecturally.

Years 17 – 18 – 19

Here are the highlights for the final years of Phase-I:

- The population of Prosperity goes from 198,250 in Year 17 to 235,050 in Year 19. Beginning in Year 13, population growth will be stable at 18,000 to 20,000 new residents a year. Including affeercianados, the population in Year 19 is about 280,000. By Year 20, the population goal of 300,000 will be exceeded making Prosperity bigger than Akron Ohio, and smaller than Atlanta Georgia.

- Average rent bid for land at auction will go from $24,000 in Year 17 to $27,000 in Year 19. Downtown land will go from $1,200,000 to $1,400,000 in the same period. As expected, these bids are closing-in on a treble-safe bid.

- By Year 19, Thomas Paine Hospital will collect 695,465 annual premiums, which is 2.5 times the population of residents and affeercianados. With 42 highly paid medical specialists, 1,291 affeercianado workers and an unknown number of interns/students from the medical college and volunteers, the hospital will have a 24/7 ambulance network with a radius of 120 miles, 434 beds, use state of the art VIP technology, have the best medical value in the nation, and bring in a profit of $894 million.

- Affeercianado leasing in Year 19 will bring in $513 million net profit, with 30,980 affeercianados available for lease. Of the 43,136 affeercianados, 3,006 work in education K-12, and 1,997 work in higher education including dormitory maintenance workers and kitchen staff, 1,862 work in the affeercianado dorms and prefabs, and over 3,000 work for the city of Prosperity with about half, 1,518, in police and public safety.

- In Year 19, there will be 54 elementary schools and 7 high schools. There will be 6 community centers, each sharing resources with a high school and each with an affeercianado dormitory on campus.

- In Year 19 there will be over 6,800 university and full-time community college students plus the set limit of 3,000 medical school students. Medical school has a projected cost of $5,000 per year for residents and non-residents alike. If accepted, a student loan would actually be a good investment. When Phase-I ends, prices will go up for non-entitled citizens and down to a $35 copay per quarter for entitled ones.

- The city of Prosperity in Year 19 pays over $282 million in hospital premiums for citizens. It collects $192 million from roads and infrastructure which includes municipal parking as well as utility delivery. From the ground rents, Prosperity collects $325 million. The recovery of materials by waste management brings in $28 million, while city hall brings in $7.8 million, mostly through the gift shop. Every registered voter receives a CD of $689.

Year 20 – Let the Trebling Begin

For many of Prosperity's citizens, Year 20 will be the first downer in a long stretch of prosperity. Free land does not last forever and the landlords want their due. By this time, 94.5% of the land will be owned by the affeercianados, even more with donations. It is reasonable to assume that a large percentage of the population will be former affeercianados who could only take the slave wages and hard labor for so long before they opted for a nice paying job in town. With the rent freeze lifted, they also await the coming large payout for their 2 or 3 years of service. Newer residents will have bid a rent close to the treble-safe amount anyway which is estimated to be an average of $28,000/acre and equal to the amount bid at auction in Year 20. The grumblers will be the ones still paying an average of under $10,000/acre for valuable land near downtown, or downtown office building owners still paying less than $200,000/acre. They shouldn't grumble. If they were smart, they spent those years, turning that gift of land into a small fortune.

A treble-safe rent is about 33% of the net rent the most efficient building could earn on the same land. Of course, this is very difficult to know by all but the most skilled players. How can an ordinary person set a treble-safe rent?

The most efficient thing to do is nothing. Wait for the trebler to come for your land and pay low rents until that happens. When the treble comes, match it. This will allow you to pay the lowest possible rent for the longest possible time. There are a few drawbacks. You must have the liquidity to match the treble in three business days. Rent is paid a year in advance. If the current rent on your single acre is $4,000/acre and you are trebled to $12,000/acre, then you must come up with the $8,000 difference in 3 business days. Secondly, the trebler must at least triple the rent, but they can go higher. If you are paying $4,000/acre on land near downtown, they might treble you 8X to $32,000/acre. You would then need to come up with $28,000 for the advance payment. Another tactic of the trebler is the re-treble. Suppose they treble you from $4,000/acre to $12,000/acre. After you come up with the $8,000 they re-treble to $36,000/acre. Now you need to come up with another $24,000 or surrender.

Trebling appeals to the age's old lust for land in conjunction with modern online gaming. With aristocratic title, societal recognition and privilege accompanying the largest land holdings some will be willing to pay several times the market price for land.

It is not all grim, surrender can be sweet. Most importantly, the trebler must give you 150% on the objective depreciated value of the improvements on your home or business. This includes any furniture or machinery you leave behind, although the trebler can decide whether to pay 150% on these pieces or whether to pay for storage and shipping once you relocate. Anything attached to the land that you leave behind the trebler must pay for. Suppose you bought a Picasso sculpture for $1 million and installed it out on the lawn. The trebler has no choice but to pay you $1.5 million for the sculpture, should you leave it behind (assuming experts agree $1 million is a fair market value). Anything of value attached to the land that you plan on taking must be noted in the online land system. Anything of value, unattached, that you plan on leaving behind, must also be noted online, although the trebler has the option of shipping that to you, instead. Getting 150% on the value of your property is rather sweet. Having the trebler pay a premium for your junk or pay to ship it to you is also sweet. Your full year advance payment of rent is also refunded. Use it for the advance payment on another property, or any way you please.

If the place has priceless sentimental value, just be sure you can match the trebler when he comes.

If you have treblephobia, fear of treblers, and don't want to ever see, hear, or be bothered by a trebler then you must set your rent high enough to be ignored. That isn't too difficult. Just set it higher than your neighbor who has similar or better property. Of course, if your neighbor retaliates by setting his rent higher than yours, this is not a good strategy. If you keep on one-upping each other soon they will crown you land baron of the district. It is far better to become a land baron by renting a lot of land than by bidding up your tiny quarter acre in a trebler war with your neighbor.

You can look at the latest bid price at auction, although this land tends to be much further out than the land you bought years earlier. Still it might help you set a treble-safe and efficient rent.

Here is an option people might demand. If you are willing to pay a premium you can be treble-safe. City assessors will create a contour map of treble-safe rents each year, beginning in Year 20. If you pay this premium rent, your land cannot be touched by a trebler and it will say so in the online land system. Rents are based on an estimate of the best possible use of the land. Only homeowners, without mixed-use business, would be eligible. It won't be the best rent, but can give peace of mind.

In the spreadsheets it is assumed that rents are raised such that the average rent is equal to the average rent bid at auction in Year 20. That is $28,000/acre for land and $1,400,000/acre for downtown land. This is bound to be conservative as newly bid land is closer to the margin.

The City

Prosperity began the year with $823 million and ended with almost a billion. Even paying hospital premiums of $304 million and a citizens' dividend of $750 to every registered voter, it still manages a profit. That is due primarily to the ground rents. They went from $325 million in Year 19 to $501 million in Year 20 with the end of the rent freeze. While the CD could have been much higher, Prosperity must save the money for a very special CD in Year 21.

Prosperity Table 20.1	Debit	Credit	Balance
Year 20	$0	$0	$823,275,716
Roads and infrastructure	$0	$205,055,111	$1,028,330,827
City Hall	$0	$7,881,153	$1,036,211,980
Parks and Recreation	$0	($29,528,258)	$1,006,683,721
Police	$0	($37,065,451)	$969,618,270
Fire	$0	($12,161,783)	$957,456,487
Waste Management	$0	$28,666,728	$986,123,215
Hospital Premiums	$304,140,000	$0	$681,983,215
Rent Dividend	$0	$501,415,200	$1,183,398,415
Rent Owed (10% only)	$106,000	$106,000	$1,183,398,415
Payment for affeercianado labor	$29,556,355	$29,556,355	$1,183,398,415
CD issued for $750 to each citizen.	$190,000,000	$0	$993,398,415

The Affeercianados

The affeercianados began Year 20 with a balance of over $974 million. Expenses include $331 million in ground rent for undeveloped land, although over 1/3 of that is returned to them with their regular rent dividend. Thomas Paine Hospital brings in over $1 billion and the surplus labor of affeercianados brings in $551 million. The $241 million balance at the end of the year can be used very profitably for affeercianado trebling. In fact, if the trebling opportunities are abundant, they are likely to use much of that $2 billion for trebling, rather than land purchases.

Affeercianados Table 20.2	Debit	Credit	Balance
Year 20	$0	$0	$974,168,634
Donate to land trust	$2,000,000,000	$0	($1,025,831,366)
Hospital	$0	$1,003,751,198	($22,080,167)
Accommodations	$0	($84,363,792)	($106,443,959)
Supply Depot	$0	$2,781,723	($103,662,236)
Surplus Labor	$0	$551,772,748	$448,110,512
AMS Software	$0	$2,000,000	$450,110,512
Metro Bus Service	$0	$382,600	$450,493,112
Downtown excavation	$0	$0	$450,493,112
Rent Dividend	$0	$122,488,739	$572,981,851
Pay Unauctioned land Rent	$0	($331,080,000)	$241,901,851
Repay land trust	$0	$0	$241,901,851
Rent Owed	$2,436,000	$2,436,000	$241,901,851

Affeercianado Trebling

It might seem unfair that the Affeercianado Guild can treble as an organization. They have a balance sheet of over $241 million, and up to $2 billion optional dollars that can be used for land purchases or trebling. The affeercianados have a material advantage. They profit in the coming payoff if the treble is matched, and profit by seizing the land if the treble is not.

The truth is they would suffer financially like anyone else if they overbid on ground rent. There is no right to free land. If you pay your fair share of the rent, neither the affeercianados nor anyone else is going to treble you. Nor is it likely the affeercianados will go after small inefficiencies. If you built an 8 story complex and could have built a 21 story complex, but are paying fair rent for that 8 story complex, somebody might treble you, but it won't be the affeercianados. The goal of this exercise is not to tear down buildings and build more efficient ones (unless the inefficiency is egregious), but to create new easy revenue streams from those who refuse to pay a fair rent.

Let's take a simple example. Suppose there is a 12-story building downtown on ½ acre downtown land that is bid in year 10 for a rent of $500,000/acre. The landlord is paying $250,000 each year for the land. In Year 20, the landlord decides not to raise the rent under the faulty reasoning that 3 x $500,000 is equal to $1,500,000 which is the highest rent bid at auction, so trebling would be unlikely after factoring in paying 150% of the objective depreciated value of the 12-story building.

1/2 Acre 12 - Story Downtown Building	Area sq. ft.	Net rent/sq. ft./Mo.	Monthly Total	Annual Total
1st Floor Retail Showroom	20,000	$5.80	$116,000.00	$1,392,000
2nd Floor Restaurant	20,000	$2.20	$44,000.00	$528,000
10 floors of apartments	180,000	$1.25	$225,000.00	$2,700,000
Total Net Rent				$4,620,000
		Cost/sq. ft.		Total cost
Original Building cost	230,000	$150.00		$34,500,000
Depreciated value - 30 years		$22,000,000.00 x 150% =		$33,000,000
Cost of building loan at 5%				$1,650,000
Annual depreciation on building - 30 years				$1,100,000
Trebler net rent (total net rent - building loan - depreciation)				$1,870,000
Fair LVT at 33% net rent				$617,100
Note: net rents do not include depreciation and taxes				

This table, even using a higher than expected building cost of $150/sq. ft., shows that the landlord should be paying at least $617,100 for this ½ acre. Because the landlord is paying less than half of the fair rent, the affeercianados are likely to treble to $750,000. If the landlord matches, he ends up paying over $130,000 more per year than he could have paid to be treble-safe. If the affeercianados win the treble, they get a free $1,870,000-$750,000=$1,120,000 every full vacancy year thereafter, assuming net rents include building management fees. Nor does that include the obvious benefit that as low-paid affeercianados, they can run the building for less. Because $750,000 exceeds an efficient treble-safe rent, freezing the rent at $750,000 will likely be treble safe for many years to come. And after the loan is paid-off, the depreciation fund will finance the building in perpetuity, more than doubling revenue.

Land at the End of Phase-I

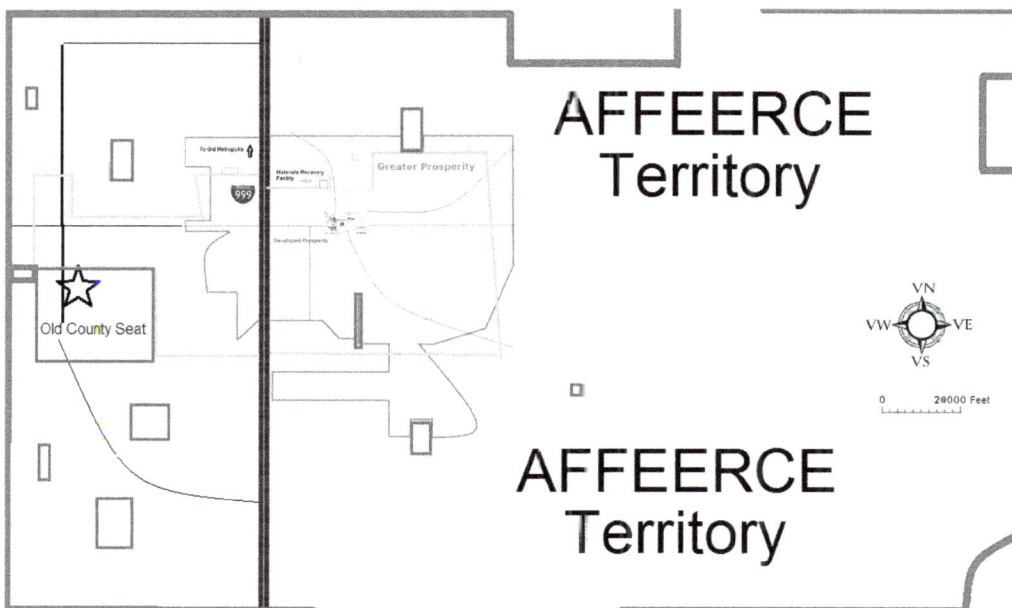

Red squares within the 645,000 acres of land are privately held properties. Developed property is outlined in blue. Some of the AFFEERCE territory extends beyond the map on the south, east, and north. Not all jitney roads are shown. The radius of the speculative ring is much too small on the virtual west side, although the need for a speculative ring ends with Phase-I

Phase-II

Year 21

Blessed are the meek, for they shall inherit the Earth.

Expected Outcome	Table 21.1
Total Acreage	465,000
Affeercianado acreage	435,576
Developed Acres	48,096
Post treble rent/year	$1,629,970,000
Latest average rent per acr	$33,890
Land value per acre	$677,799
Imputed Land Value	$30,536,615,098
Affeercianado Years	445200
Value of Year	**$68,591**
Investor return	**$2,062,784,902**

This is where the affeercianados having labored long hours, with time spent in the sewers and material recovery facility, time exposed to the wind in cold winters, and time pampering our most finicky residents, get their just reward. For some, 21 years will have been spent without a paid vacation, earning only $25/week plus room and board. As Phase-II begins, the affeercianados are about to inherit the earth. Those that toiled the longest will rise from slavery into that fabled 1%. Furthermore, the opportunity for affeercianado wealth is just beginning.

There are 48,096 developed acres in Prosperity. The total rent on these acres is $1.63 billion. Based on an historical 5% discount rate, the value of the land is $32.6 billion ($30.5 billion is affeercianado land as shown in table 2.1). This $32.6 billion is going to get distributed to the affeercianados and the investors. The investors will get $2.06 billion back from their $65 million investment 21 years earlier. Including the large dividends, the annualized return is about 20%. The other $30.5 billion will go to the affeercianados. And this is just the beginning of the large payouts. Both investors and affeercianados will receive large payments every year for the rest of their lives, or up until one huge payment at capitulation.

Affeercianados receive $68,591 for each year of service, or $27.43 for each hour of service. An affeercianado who put in 21 years of service at the hourly average will receive a payment in Year 21 of $1,440,411. In subsequent years, affeercianados will receive a minimum of $3,565 each year for every year of service, as new land is developed. For affeercianados who put in the full 21 years of service, they will receive a minimum annual pension of $74,865. A single investor will receive a minimum annual pension of $107 million.

Where does all this money come from? Why, we create it.

So now the other shoe drops. You think, "I've read this far and he plans on paying us off in funny money?" But hold on. I'll show you how serious this money really is.

The VIP$ is pegged to the U.S. dollar at 2:1. A 21 year service affeercianado in Year 21 will not receive $1.44 million in U.S. dollars, but V$2.88 million, 2.88 million VIP dollars, which is equivalent to $1.44 million. But why is it equivalent? Not just because I say so.

Here is why. The ground rent can be paid in VIP$ as well as U.S. dollars. If your monthly rent is $8,000, it can just as easily be paid with V$16,000, or some combination of the 2 currencies. If you are petrified that your big payoff is worthless, find a land rights owner and offer then $V2.20 for $1.00. They will snatch it up since you are giving them a free 10 cents on the dollar for their next ground rent payment. If you are panicking, desperate to get rid of your "funny money," a new service of the Phase-II merged Affeercianado Guild and ABC, called the AFFEERCE Central Bank, will be happy to redeem $V3.00 for $1.00, but then you are really being taken to the cleaners.

In addition to the rent, all Prosperity municipal services must take VIP$. In fact, any money in a VIP debit account, that was previously denominated in U.S. dollars will be denominated in VIP$ at 2:1. But it goes beyond Prosperity municipal services. It includes Jane Jacobs University and the medical school. All affeercianado businesses, including Thomas Paine Hospital must take the VIP$ at 2:1. The leasing of affeercianado labor can be paid in VIP$. This is built into the city charter and the charter of the Affeercianado Guild. PPO patients not covered by a Thomas Paine premium will be more than happy to take your VIP$ for their large out of pocket deductible. So will medical school students for their tuition, room and board.

Everyone can trust VIP$ because they are backed by developed land whose value is denominated in U.S. dollars, or simply U.S. dollars themselves. Anybody can exchange a U.S. dollar for 2 VIP dollars at the Central Bank for no fee. Going in the other direction, the fee is expensive, so it is better to do it in a private transaction.

In fact, success in reaching Year 21 will have earned AFFEERCE a good deal of confidence and trust. It is such confidence and trust that will cause many people not to redeem VIP$, or even to spend them, but to hoard them. The day will come when those VIP$ will have parity with U.S. dollars. That is, they will double in value.

We are about to embark on a mercantile adventure that will not end until there is peace and prosperity throughout the world.

Why will the Wealthy Affeercianados Continue their Slave Labor?

Obviously, most of the long timers will retire and enjoy their new found wealth. They will become entitled citizens (discussed below) and take advantage of the many business opportunities that entails. The most enterprising will turn a million into a hundred million or more.

Most of the affeercianados are late to the game. But this is certainly a case of better late than never. If they started in Year 17, they would receive $274,364 or V$548,728 in Year 21. (I'll use equivalent U.S. dollar amounts from this point forward in the examples unless the example explicitly calls for the VIP$.) Every year thereafter they will receive a minimum of $14,260. This might provide a modest retirement, but these guys are in their early or mid-20s. Why should they stop when each year of additional service will dramatically increase their share of the pie? The clock for computing years of services does not stop at Year 21. Their pension will grow by at least $3,565 with every additional year of service.

Beginning in Year 21, affeercianado wealth is no longer used to buy land. The approximately 400,000 acres of undeveloped land still owned by the affeercianados and investors is all the land they will ever own. The $3,565 yearly pension is based on the development and monetization of 6,000 acres/year at half current ground rents. The AFFEERCE territories, as undeveloped land will be called, will be settled by entitled citizens trebling land for their own industries, cities, and cultures (See, below). With one year of treble-safety, pensions on developed territory land are delayed a year to achieve the greatest possible ground rent for computing pensions. A final significant land auction for land on the virtual north side of downtown in Year 21 pays the pension that first year of Phase-II. If capitulation does not occur in 66 years, the pensions will stop, although considering that most affeercianados would be in their 90s or 100s, the final pensions for the last survivors are apt to be in the billions of dollars.

Because the affeercianados are no longer buying land, the business profits can be distributed. In order to encourage people to remain affeercianados or become affeercianados, the business profits are only distributed to active, working, affeercianados, but distributed based on years of service.

The actual salary for affeercianados drops to zero in Year 21. Instead, they must pay $220 a month for food, $370 a month for housing, and $100 a month for medical insurance. These fees are paid automatically for those affeercianados who choose to become entitled citizens by taking advantage of selective distribution (more on that later). Those that choose to live outside the dorms must be entitled citizens. Those that live outside the dorms are still responsible for the full workload, and must attend Guild meetings, or they will be terminated by a 2/3 vote of the Guild.

Despite the costs and lack of salary, it is expected that the demand to be an affeercianado in Year 21 will be overwhelming and only the most qualified will be accepted. Affeercianados are treated as partners in the enterprises, with ownership based on years of service.

Let us look at the Affeercianado balance sheet in Year 21.

Affeercianados Table 21.2	Debit	Credit	Balance
Year 21	$0	$0	$241,901,851
Hospital	$0	$1,067,613,970	$1,309,515,821
Accommodations	$0	$41,251,554	$1,350,767,375
Supply Depot	$0	$2,933,996	$1,353,701,371
Surplus Labor	$0	$882,000,000	$2,235,701,371
AMS Software	$0	$50,000,000	$2,285,701,371
Metro Bus Service	$0	($2,000,000)	$2,283,701,371
Rent Owed	$16,635,237	$16,635,237	$2,283,701,371
Distribution of $11,328 per year of service	$2,283,701,371	$0	$0

The hospital is bringing in a profit of over $1 billion. There is no more dorm building and affeercianados are now paying for their housing, yielding a conservative $41 million in accommodations profits. Since affeercianados are no longer paid, profit from surplus labor is at 100%, a full $882 million, and this is assuming the average affeercianado is bid out for $7/hour including overtime! The minimum bid of $5/hour is intended to create an explosion in land value that will greatly benefit the affeercianados in their pensions. The increase in land value will also counter any inflationary pressures from the payouts. AMS is bringing in profit on sale of its agent and VIP technology as well as any other municipal software developed. The portfolio does not show any office buildings, apartment buildings or retail trebled in Year 20. If affeercianado trebling occurred, the initial balance and total land holdings would be less, but the annual profits greater.

The affeercianados no longer receive a portion of the ground rent, but neither do they have to pay the rent for unauctioned land. Dormitories and the Thomas Paine Hospital can be trebled like any other land, so they pay a treble-safe $16.6 million rent on their property. Jane Jacobs University, however, is under jurisdictional covenant.

During the year, the over $2.28 billion in profits is distributed to the active affeercianados based on years and months of service. Over the course of the year, each affeercianado would receive $11,328 for every year of service. The calculation is based on the assumption that the 50,000 affeercianados working have an average of 4 years of service each. This will be less if more of the old-timers decide not to retire. Unless profits increase accordingly, distributions per year will tend to drop with more career affeercianados. However, total distributions should always increase with each additional year of service. These distributions are independent of the pensions each year for newly developed land.

An active affeercianado with 4 years of service will earn a minimum $14,260 for land monetization and $45,312 in distributed profits, or $59,572 in Year 21. A retired affeercianado with 4 years' service would only receive $14,260 for the land monetization. A 22-year old-timer who decided not to retire would receive total annual compensation of $327,646 – a salary that easily places them in the elite 1%.

Apprentice Affeercianados

During Phase-II and Phase-III, there should be a way for unskilled workers to become affeercianados without waiting years on a waiting list. For many around the country who have given up, Prosperity reaching Phase-II will bring new hope. It would be tragic if those young idealists had to wait 30 or 40 years until capitulation before they could share in the dream. The apprentice affeercianados program allows those without special skills, but with sufficient dedication to bypass the waiting list and enter the program.

It is unlikely that more dormitories will be built beyond the 40 built during Phase-I. The dorms can hold only 48,000 affeercianados. However, all of the affeercianados with at least two years' service will have sufficient income to live in nearby homes and apartments. Thus it is expected that even with 50,000 affeercianados, many of the dorm rooms will be available.

Unlike the affeercianado who must pay for room and board (but has a large income to do so), the affeercianado apprentice gets free room, board, and medical in the dorms. However, the first six months are probationary. They get neither land credits nor proceeds from affeercianado businesses. They are still expected to work a minimum of 50 hours/week. After the probationary 6 months is up, they get land credits at 50% for the next 4 years, or until they can maintain an above average lease rate consistently for 6 months, or until they are called-up from the waiting list, whichever comes first. Only then do they become full affeercianados receiving all land credits and business income, and rights to unlimited free education on the campus.

Even with these limitations, demand might exceed supply of beds. If so, newbie apprentices will have to sleep on a cot brought in as a third bed per dorm room. Our goal is to drive down the bid rate of unskilled labor to $5/hour, pushing undeveloped land values sky high as manufacturers from around the United States and abroad, rush in to take advantage of this cheap labor. There will be a net benefit to the affeercianados as annual pension income rises faster than business income falls. Some might argue that the affeercianados in Phase-II are wealthy enough to support a bid rate as low as $3/hour for unskilled labor which would likely create the most valuable land in the world, jacking pensions well above the $10,000 per year served. $3/hour unskilled labor bids for 12,000 affeercianado apprentices would cost only $100 million or less of Thomas Paine Hospital's billion dollar plus profit. The growth in the community from the cheap labor would probably lead to new profits at the hospital that meet or exceed the losses.

Prosperity in Year 21

Starting in Year 21, 5% of rent proceeds will be split between Prosperity, the county and the school district. The other 95% of rent will be used to award entitled citizenship. The received ground rent of $507 million in Year 20 has dropped to $43 million in Year 21. But there is a new category, called the distribution package. In Year 21, it brings in over $48 million. Each entitled citizen, who is also a resident of Prosperity, is entitled to certain municipal services, and this is the money to pay for those services. The more entitled citizens living in Prosperity, the greater this revenue. If entitled citizens leave Prosperity for the AFFEERCE territories, it will be a loss for Prosperity and a gain for the territorial communities.

Prosperity Table 21.3	Debit	Credit	Balance
Year 21	$0	$0	$983,617,688
Roads and infrastructure	$0	$212,309,718	$1,195,927,406
City Hall	$0	$22,793,119	$1,218,720,525
Parks and Recreation	$0	($32,008,008)	$1,186,712,517
Police	$0	($39,010,190)	$1,147,702,327
Fire	$0	($12,024,337)	$1,135,677,990
Waste Management	$0	$33,658,333	$1,169,336,323
Rent Dividend	$0	$43,307,440	$1,212,643,763
Distribution Package	$0	$48,247,998	$1,260,891,761
Rent Owed (10% only)	$2,472,000	$2,472,000	$1,260,891,761
CD issued for $14,525 to entitled citizens.	$800,000,000	$0	$460,891,761

There are many changes to benefits in Phase-II that are meant to encourage residents to become entitled citizens. Most noticeably, medical premiums for citizens will no longer be paid by the city.

Looking at Table 21.3, we see a rather prosperous Prosperity in Year 21. Roads and infrastructure, which includes municipal parking and utility distribution, is the biggest source of city revenue. In and of itself, it is enough to cover police, fire, and parks and recreation. That is why far more than the proceeds from the rent and distribution package can be used for a citizens' dividend.

The question is, which citizens? It is in the interest of Prosperity and the Affeercianado Guild to promote selective distribution, creating, what I am calling entitled citizens. There are many reasons to become an entitled citizen that will be discussed later. This is another. Only those who have won a bid at auction for entitled citizenship, or who buy it outright are entitled to the citizens' dividend. If only 1,000 people become entitled citizens, they will each receive $800,000 as a CD. If 10,000 become entitled citizens, they will each receive $80,000. Table 21.3 assumes 55,078 will become entitled citizens in Year 21, giving each of them a CD of $14,525.

For each entitled citizen the following monthly payments will be made to local government.

Public Distribution Table 21.4	City	County	Education
Fire Protection	$5	0	0
Law Enforcement	$20	$10	0
Judiciary and Public Defense	$1	$8	0
Social Worker	$10	0	0
Education	0	0	$50
Transportation and Sanitation	$22	$10	0
Total Monthly Public Distribution	$58	$28	$50

Annually, the municipality will receive $696 for each entitled citizen. Parks and recreation are expected to be paid out of municipal profit centers such as parking, utility delivery, inspections, city store, licenses and fees, and waste management.

If all 300,000 residents of Prosperity were entitled citizens, the city would receive $208 million. By the same token, the $100 million to the county and the $180 million to education will create massive surpluses. In fact, the $180 million to education is slightly greater than all state and federal revenue sharing combined. Going into Year 21 with no debt, a $260 million credit balance, and for the first time, a significant profit from higher education due to dormitory profits, state grants, and medical school tuition, education does not need the money at all.

So what should we do? Eliminate the $50 per month and lower the cost of selective distribution? Return the revenue sharing back to the state? Phase the affeercianados out of education? We are in a very favorable negotiating position with the host-state having a massive educational surplus. The money should be used primarily to make our campus the best in the nation, but secondarily, to win important concessions from the host-state in the event of unexpected issues that might arise, particularly during Phase-II. Returning over $100 million in revenue sharing back to the state can probably work wonders.

Not shown is a $3/month intellectual property distribution. It has its own method of distribution, unique to the embryonic nation and discussed later.

The AFFEERCE Central Bank and Mercantilism

The AFFEERCE Central Bank maintains accounts. This function will be taken over by the U.S. Treasury following capitulation. Most of its accounts are denominated in VIP$ or enterprise scrip (See *Volume I - Scrip*), but it maintains 2 U.S. dollar accounts, one for U.S. dollars backing VIP$ and the other for U.S. dollars that are not. At the start of Phase-II, all smartcard/VIP balances will be redenominated in VIP$. Those accounts will no longer be maintained by the Prosperity city clerk, but at the central bank.

In the days of old, mercantilism, competitive advantage through trade surpluses, was accomplished through destructive protective tariffs, harsh laws, and other unfair trading practices. In Phase-I, we engaged in a new kind of mercantilism, predominantly through utilization of a new economic class, the landlord-working class, or affeercianados. Where low wages lead to low spirit, low output, and the failure to utilize capital, they do not help a trade surplus. To the extent they do, profit ends up in the hands of landlords.

In the previously unheard of case where low wages increase spirit, output, and the utilization of capital, the effect on the trade surplus is predicted to be explosive. Much of the profits do end up in the hands of the landlords, but the reason the spirit of these low-paid workers is so high, is that they are also the landlords. In addition, Phase-I emphasizes the entrepreneurial mercantilism of Jane Jacobs with the Mercantile Letter encouraging import replacement. The results will be dollars coming into Prosperity faster than they can leave. We will be given great freedom in when and what to import.

In Phase-II, the entitled workers of Prosperity join the mercantile explosion. Because of their basic income, they too can afford to choose jobs that better suite them, even though the pay might be less. With higher worker satisfaction, there is considerably less sabotage and shrinkage. Worker productivity is also increased.

The VIP – It's not for U.S. dollars anymore

Although the smartcard will be a debit card, it is likely people will use it that way only after a new citizens' dividend is distributed. People would then spend down their smartcard like a gift card. For the rest of the year, the smartcard would be treated more like a credit card, with parking and transportation fees, copays, fines, and other municipal charges accumulating until paid off. Although actual credit cards could be attached to the smartcard for shopping versatility with a single card, most people probably will prefer carrying multiple cards.

When the VIP replaces the smartcard near the end of Phase-I, the attitude toward using the VIP should also change. It will no longer be a case of one card or another but card versus no card. The wallet becomes optional as driver's license, ID, credit and debit cards, become a single card that is the iris of one's eyes.

Even then, the VIP will more often than not be a conduit to credit cards and debit cards associated with the customer's bank, rather than an account set up at the Prosperity city clerk's office. However, merchants will discover that there is no transaction fee associated with debits from the customer's city hall account. They will encourage using the VIP in that way.

In Year 21, the start of Phase-II, those accounts will be denominated in VIP$ and moved to the AFFEERCE Central Bank. The VIP will no longer transfer U.S. dollars in response to a debit or credit request. VIP$ from central bank accounts will be used in all transactions.

The merchant will never pay a penny in transaction costs for VIP customers

---

No transaction fees are a merchant benefit that is paid from the VIP and infrastructure distribution and subsidized early on by the Affeercianado Guild.

The mercantile advantage of no VIP$ transaction costs are astonishing. The workings of the free market suggest that a U.S. dollar counterpart would quickly arise to neutralize the VIP advantage. But that is impossible. It is a matter of trust. People who moved or visited Prosperity did so with the understanding that we would maintain a biometric identity for each of them. Many potential residents probably turned away when they realized they would be VIP identified. Our honesty and transparency, along with a multi-year record of using the information to liberate and not oppress builds trust. We are a like a private enterprise maintaining identities for free. Who else could do this but a government? Would the U.S. population allow their government with its NSA, CIA, and DIA, to maintain biometric identities on each of them? That would never happen. Which private agency would do it and what would be their reward? They have no distributions. Despite the involvement of ANSI (American National Standards Institute) and ISO (International Standards Organization) committees, and a public specification, the AFFEERCE monopoly on biometric identity is safe.

The Dollarnado

As mentioned earlier, beginning with Phase-II, rent can be paid in either U.S. dollars or VIP$. The VIP$ is pegged to the U.S. dollar at 2:1. That means if the ground rent is $1000 U.S., it can be paid as well with 2,000 VIP$. The Central Bank will issue 2 VIP$ dollars for every U.S. dollar. However, the bank will only redeem a U.S. dollar for 3 VIP$, forcing these transactions into the open market. It is far better to use the VIP$ to pay rent, medical copays, premiums, and tuition than to redeem for U.S. dollars at a high premium.

The Dollarnado: Dollars sucked in and they can't get out

Redemption of tourist VIP$ at 2.10 VIP$ for $1 U.S. is encouraged and profitable. In the case above, where the rent on a property is $1000 U.S., 2000 VIP$, a departing tourist will exchange with a Prosperity resident 2100 VIP$ for that U.S. $1000 allowing the resident to pay the ground rent with a 100 VIP$ profit. The tourist saves over exchanging 3 VIP$ for $1 U.S. at the central bank. However, the VIP$ lasts forever, and soon the smart tourist will save their VIP$ for the future.

While it might seem that the expense of converting the VIP$ to a U.S. dollar would damage the VIP$, the benefits are predicted to far outweigh the damage.

The Dollarnado – A list of Phase-II Mercantile Advantages

1. Import replacement
2. Business objects

3. Landlord-worker class: the affeercianados
4. Common owners of the land: entitled citizens
5. Favorable AFFEERCE Central Bank exchange rate
6. No VIP$ transaction fees
7. No monetization of land value increases after move to commons
8. Effective monopoly on biometric identity

The dollarnado is critical to the success of Phase-II. It literally sucks U.S dollars into the AFFEERCE Central Bank. These U.S. dollars, which along with land provide the backing for the VIP$, are invested in U.S. treasuries, while the VIP$ are invested in entitled enterprise. (See *Citizen Investors* below).

> **As Prosperity attracts tourists and investors, U.S. dollars come in, but they can't get out.**

It isn't a complete one-way street. The central bank must release U.S. dollars for payment of federal/state income tax and sales taxes must be paid back to the state in U.S. dollars.

Capital expenditures in VIP$ are exempt from consumption tax. That also applies to outside firms purchasing capital goods in Prosperity, so these firms have every incentive to exchange $1 U.S. for 2 VIP$ at the figurative VIP window of the central bank. In this way, exports feed the dollarnado.

Entitled Citizens

Phase-II has arrived. With it, the most important task of Prosperity and our embryonic nation: the creation of entitled citizenship. If such citizenship were universal, as it will be after capitulation, poverty, homelessness, and extreme inequality would be eradicated. There are so many advantages to society from universal distribution, most of them discussed in *Volume I*, that we literally enter a new epoch of mankind through its adoption.

Unfortunately, the transition to universal distribution is a bootstrapping operation that requires several decades and a good business plan – this business plan. In Phase-II, that transition continues with what will be called "selective distribution." Indeed, that is every bit as elitist as it sounds. The only ones who can afford selective distribution are the ones who don't need the distribution in the first place. Our wealthy residents and nouveau riche affeercianados will invest in entitled citizenship, but the homeless person who desperately needs the distribution will still be excluded. The desperately poor in the host-state, however, will find their salvation in Phase-III.

The implementation of selective distribution is slightly different in Phase-II and Phase-III than universal distribution will be after U.S. capitulation, but basically the same. The following benefits are provided by Prosperity to entitled citizens. The table also shows what non-entitled citizens must pay. The old categories of resident and non-resident are replaced by the new categories entitled and non-entitled citizen. However, even non-entitled citizens, by virtue of living in or near Prosperity, will have advantages citizens of other cities do not.

Benefits of Entitled Citizenship Table 21.5	Cost of Same Services for Non-Entitled Citizens
$220 every month for food	--
$370 every month for housing	--
$35 cash (universal copay) every month	--

100% free coverage at Thomas Paine Hospital with a universal $35 copay that covers all services for a month. Free emergency PPO coverage and Medevac for out-of-state-travel. Seniors receive free supplemental insurance with all deductibles paid beyond $35 copay. Daily draw on food distribution.	$110/month HMO premium for full coverage at Thomas Paine Hospital. Multiple $35 copays, for doctor, ambulance, testing, hospital admission, drugs. Premium includes free emergency PPO coverage and Medevac for out-of-state travel.
Long term care for 90% of SS, SSDI, or SSI after Medicare period. All Medicare deductibles covered. Food, housing, and cash distributions must be surrendered.	$4000/month for long term care with HMO policy.
Free drug and alcohol rehab and psychiatric hospitalizations. Food, housing, and cash distributions must be surrendered.	$200/day with HMO policy.
All pharmaceuticals from Thomas Paine Pharmacy for $35 copay.	Standard generic, non-generic, specialty drug copays with HMO policy. (See Table 1.6)
Free tuition and fees at the community college, Jane Jacobs University or, the medical school if accepted, with $35 universal copay per quarter regardless of number of credit hours. Free dormitory living in exchange for food and housing distributions.	Fees: $250/quarter, Tuition: $250/quarter per 5 credit hours, Medical School: $10,000/year, Dormitory: $700/month
Free homeschool teacher registration and certification. Receive pay for each entitled student. Receive future annuities. (See *Volume I* for details)	$500 for homeschool teacher registration and certification. Receive pay for each entitled student. Receive future annuities.
Free day care at a community center if both parent and child are entitled. $8/day if either parent or child is entitled. $35 copay once per year for community center pass.	$16/day with community center pass.
Right to a family social worker for counseling, family creation, character witness, navigation through potential benefits, domestic and child abuse management, business opportunities, and wellness checkups, etc.	$10/visit with community center pass.
Minimum eligibility of $600/year paid to the U.S. IRS in your name for wages and profits earned in VIP$. Free income tax preparation if 100% of wages, profits, and revenue is in VIP$, otherwise 1099 for VIP$ income	1099 for VIP$ income
Free remote garage and street parking. Reduced rate for lower level downtown parking. Free municipal transportation.	Street parking: $10/month, Remote garage parking: $20/month, Lower level downtown parking: $80/month. See table 6.4 for daily, hourly rates. Transit pass: $15/month

Limited membership in the Affeercianado Guild, including the right to run for office on the AFFEERCE party and vote in the AFFEERCE party primary and contribute to the discussion on the future of Prosperity and AFFEERCE. If desired, move to the front of the waiting list to become a full working affeercianado with financial benefits.	--
The right to be seriously considered for billions of dollars in venture capital.	--
Free music, e-book, movie, software downloads from artists, innovators and other intellectual property owners who sign up for our very lucrative distribution-based intellectual property royalties. Might expand to include patent drugs and machinery.	Standard pricing.
The right to treble up to 10 acres of undeveloped land per year. The land will be treble-safe for 1 years' time. Base price of $2,000 x 3 = $6,000/acre for 1 year. Property must border utility grid for free hookup, post inspection.	Large auction of virtual north land in Year 21. Subsequent smaller auctions will be held if maximum of 6,000 acres are not trebled by entitled citizens.
The right to be sentenced for crimes in facilities that provide nutritious meals, quality medical care, online education, rehab, and counseling. Requires judicial approval and payment of $600/month security fee from state. Requires surrender of food, housing distributions.	Judges can sentence non-entitled citizens to our facilities. Cost to state is $700/month food and housing, $300/month medical, counseling, and education, $600/month security fee, $30/month victim fee, $70/month clothing fee, $400/month annuity fee,
The right to form cellular democracies and rogue states in the AFFEERCE territories and receive funds for education, health care, police, fire, transportation, and sanitation. Financing based on distribution tranches. (See *Volume I* and discussion below.)	--

Cost of Entitlements   Table 21.6

Food	$220
Housing	$370
Cash	$35
Education	$50
Medical	$100
Non-Universal disability	$45
Social Worker	$10
Fire Protection	$5
Law Enforcement	$30
Judiciary and Public Defense	$9
Transportation and sanitation	$32
Infrastructure and VIP	$7
Defense/taxes	$50
Intellectual property	$3
Monthly Total	$966

These benefits of entitled citizenship last until capitulation. Subsequent modifications last a lifetime. They will never be taken away.

The food and housing distributions are stored in VIP$ in special accounts at the central bank. Every month on the citizen's birthday, they are replenished. Merchants register to accept these distributions. For various reasons, it is expected that all Prosperity grocery store merchants will accept the VIP$ food distribution. However, in the unlikely event there is a shortage of such establishments, the affeercianados will start a competing chain of grocery stores that accept the VIP$.

The housing distribution can be used to pay ground rent on the main family residence, but not on business properties, unless they are the same, encouraging mixed use. It is expected that landlords and mortgage lenders will come to accept the VIP$. If too many landlords are hesitant to rent to entitled citizens, the affeercianados will build competing apartments that accept the VIP$. If there are not enough competing mortgage lenders that accept payment in VIP$, or the interest rate is more than 1/4 point higher than U.S. dollar loans, the citizen investors will make a small number of mortgage loans, as will the affeercianados. Individual long time affeercianados who are receiving $200,000/year can make one mortgage loan a year to enhance their income. Repayment is assured by the distributions. Monthly mortgage payments automatically go directly from the borrower's account at the central bank to the lenders account.

Here is an example of the housing distribution in action. A family of four entitled citizens, living on 1/5 acre of residential land with a rent of $18,000/acre will pay an annual rent of $3600, $300 monthly. A $160,000 home (they are not paying for land) at 5% with $16,000 down has a monthly payment of $1,030 on a 30 year mortgage. The family of 4 has a monthly housing distribution of $1,480. After mortgage and ground rent, they have $150/month left over for utilities. (More details about the housing distribution can be found in *Volume I*.)

The cash distribution of $35 is the universal copay. If an entitled citizen visits the doctor, attends a class at the community college, university, or medical school, trebles a property, takes a matter to family court, or takes advantage of various uncommon benefits, the copay for the following month will be surrendered. However, once it is moved to an entitled citizen's spending account at the central bank, it can be spent however they wish.

Medical care is free. The $100 a month premium is sent to the participating hospital chosen by the entitled citizen. At the very least, this will include Thomas Paine Hospital, and auxiliary hospitals around the state, established by the affeercianados. The hospital provides all inpatient, and outpatient medical care including routine visits to a doctor. The hospital must have an emergency PPO coverage and medevac policy for all insured. The $35 universal copay is automatically charged from the next month's distribution. It is divided equally between claims if there is more than one claimant. The hospital receives an additional $300/month for each inpatient from the disability distribution, and a $25 wellness annuity every month thereafter. The hospital also receives a daily draw on the food distribution for inpatients.

Hospitals must fill prescriptions for the universal co-pay. For most generics, this is profitable, although patients are apt to fill them elsewhere if the copay is unused. If a non-generic or specialty drug is required, the doctor must explain in a report to the hospital administration.

Long term care is funded by the $220 food distribution, $370 housing distribution, $35 cash distribution, $300 disability distribution, and 90% of the patient's social security, or social security disability receipts, as well as charges to Medicare.

Psychiatric hospitalization and rehab require surrender of both food and housing distributions ($370/month from the patient if housing cannot be surrendered). Both also receive $300/month from the disability distribution. Judicial sentencing of entitled patients to these facilities requires a $600/month security fee from the state. In addition, medical staff is paid by the affiliated hospital. Both receive a $25 annuity after the patient is released, however, it can be a different annuity depending on circumstance of admission. The psychiatric hospital and rehabilitation facility receive the wellness annuity for voluntary admission. For judicial admission, they receive the non-recidivism annuity. Like the wellness annuity, the $25 non-recidivism annuity continues for the rest of the life of the formerly incarcerated, until they are resentenced to a different facility. Facilities can be owned and staffed independently of the affiliated hospital, but they should be located on the hospital campus. It is the self-insured hospital that pays for contracted services to the facility.

Entitled citizens can enroll in up to 5 community college or Jane Jacobs University courses each quarter for the $35 universal copay. The same is true for post-graduate work and medical school tuition, if accepted. The AFFEERCE theory of grading is based on C being an average grade, with as many D's as B's, and less A's than B's. However, entitled citizens can repeat classes as often as they wish, and only the highest grade will appear on the transcript. Payments to teachers and schools from the distribution package will be handled as described in *Volume I – The Vision*, or as modified by the Affeercianado Guild. It is even possible we can replace state revenue sharing with academic and school annuities from the consumption tax, if the state legislature approves.

Any community college, university, or medical school entitled student can choose to live in the dorms by surrendering the food and housing distributions. Because the housing distribution is more than sufficient to pay dorm depreciation, maintenance, utilities, and services, the Affeercianado Guild can allow dormitories to issue monthly vouchers for school supplies and hard-copy textbooks, in order to remain competitive with other housing choices.

Many of the other benefits listed are either self-explanatory or will be discussed in greater detail below.

Trebling in the AFFEERCE Territories

Land auctions will continue for the high-priced land just virtual north of downtown. The prefabs and trailer park will have been cleared away. However, the majority of the 6,000 acres developed each year will be claimed by entitled citizens. Each entitled citizen can treble up to 10 acres of undeveloped land a year. The spreadsheets predict an AFFEERCE territories land value of $40,000/acre and a rent of $2,000/acre/year. Trebling the land produces a rent of $6,000/acre. As a benefit to entitled citizens, it is marked as treble-safe in the land system for an entire year. However, once the year is up, anyone can treble the land. There is no telling what a treble-safe rent might be at that point. It might be $12,000/acre or as high as $38,000/acre. There is no way to predict "hot" areas or disputed land that leads to trebler wars. The rise of towns in the territories, especially profitable ones, can bring the rent up to $60,000 or $70,000/acre near newly developed downtowns.

The land is not formally monetized until the year has passed, and treble-safety is lifted. A land auction for far more than 40 acres north of downtown in Year 21, allows the pension to begin in Year 22. A minimum distribution of $3,565 per year served is assumed, although the chart below shows a pension per year served of $3,302 to $10,848 based on a probable range in land valuation. If annuities exceed $10,848 per year of service, additional funds for both affeercianados and investors will be carried over to later years.

		Acres or Years	Rent/acre	Land value/acre	Total land value
LOW	AFFEERCE Territory	5960	$12,000	$240,000	$1,430,400,000
	North Downtown	40	$50,000	$1,000,000	$40,000,000
	Affeercianado Years	445200			$1,470,400,000
	Per Year of Service				$3,302.79
HIGH	AFFEERCE Territory	5960	$38,000	$760,000	$4,529,600,000
	North Downtown	40	$375,000	$7,500,000	$300,000,000
	Affeercianado Years	445200			$4,829,600,000
	Per Year of Service				$10,848.16

Trebled land by individual citizens can be consolidated into a single property if the citizens VIP register as a family. Married couples and their live-at-home children are automatically registered. Family members are expected to live behind a common lockable entrance and share a kitchen and dining area. A gated community with a common dining area, a dormitory, or a mansion would all qualify as large family domiciles. Intention to live as a family after building is complete will suffice. Modifications to the default family charter must be VIP registered as well. Family is not required for communes, collectives, and other group enterprises, however, the family charter allows for rules and hierarchies that would otherwise not be possible without violating natural rights. Under U.S. law, a 5/6 super-duper plurality might not be sufficient to allow rights violations that would be allowed within a family. This will change after capitulation lessening the difference between family and collective.

Humane Incarceration

Entitled citizens have the right to be humanely incarcerated, although this is in the hands of the state judiciary in Phase-II. Nutritious meals, warm and safe shelter, medical care and online education, as well as job training courses in the penitentiary, will not be denied even if liberty is. These are all paid for by the distributions. It is also a requirement that $30 of the $35 cash distribution be sent to the victim every month. The other $5 can be used for commissary or the universal deductible for education and medical care. Able inmates are required to labor 3 days a week, or 2 days a week at hard labor, for commissary money and possible additional victim compensation.

It is very likely judges will sentence entitled citizens to these facilities, as the cost to the state is only a $600/month security fee. The rest of the expense is covered by the distributions. However, because of the savings from affeercianado labor and the protectionism of selective distribution, it is possible these facilities will be competitive with other state prisons, and judges will also sentence non-entitled citizens, particularly first-offenders, to these facilities. These inmates will have the same rights as entitled citizens, although the state will pay $2,100/month.

Intellectual Property

The amount of this distribution will vary with its success, but it begins at $3/month. It is predicted to generate higher auction bids (see below) than its cost. The Affeercianado Guild will attempt to sign deals with book and music publishers, individual authors and artists, journal publishers, streaming video distributers, popular software vendors, and others to compensate them from a pool of funds for every item downloaded by an entitled citizen. This is the Netflix or Amazon Prime model applied to all intellectual property with free membership for all entitled citizens. VIP biometric identity would restrict downloading to entitled citizens, and credit only a single download of the same item. This will give us needed technical experience for proper handling of intellectual property, post capitulation.

To gain an idea on distribution size, consider that 100,000 entitled citizens will generate $300,000 each month to be distributed to musicians, publishers, filmmakers, software vendors, and authors.

There is a dynamic that will tend to assure the success of the program. If there are few takers, the size of the pool will be very large, attracting people into the program. On the other hand, as the number of participants increases, publishers will be compelled to take part in the program to be competitive. It is also the dream of every author and artist to be paid by the number of people who freely download their work. Like trebling itself, the intellectual property distribution is win-win-win.

On This Land I Plant My Flag

Entitled citizens not only have the right to treble undeveloped land, but the right to build cells and districts, the equivalent of towns, cities and counties on that land. They can even build rogue states provided they can shoe horn their system into the private property rights allowed by the U.S. constitution, and AFFEERCE exit rights.

Outside of Prosperity which formed during Phase-I, the primary political organization in Phase-II and beyond is the cell. A full discussion of the cell and cellular democracy can be found in *Volume-I*.

To establish a town, 621 entitled citizens must organize into a level-1 cell; 9 groups of 69. This single level-1 cell can call itself a governing district. Cells in Phase-II are orphaned. Prosperity is their direct ancestor at level-5. The governing district will receive all distribution tranches for missing levels. This level-1 cell of 621 entitled citizens will get funds for police protection, fire protection, and other municipal services.

By a 2/3 majority, they can override the already loose spending requirements and use these funds however they please. A consensus group of settlers, or a 5/6 plurality with the treble option, can store the distributions in an import/ground rent account and create their own currency. If an entitled citizen living in the AFFEERCE territories objects to a super-majority decision of their tribe to, for instance, distribute police protection funds as cash, they can return to Prosperity or another tribe, where the money is used for its intended purpose of police protection.

Orphaned cells that do not wish the responsibility of providing municipal services can return those funds to Prosperity in exchange for services. Once responsibility for a distribution is assumed by a governing district, it is solely responsible. For instance, a level-1 district cannot take 10% of the law enforcement distribution and then pass the rest up to a responsible law enforcement disbursement district at level-2. If the level-1 district refuses to take complete responsibility, 100% of the disbursement goes to the level-2 disbursement district, which can then choose to distribute 10% to level-1 for community policing. If there is no level-2, the responsibility and disbursement would go to Prosperity at level-5.

These governments will not be recognized by the host-state in Phase-II. From the point of view of the state legislature, they are private property under the jurisdiction of the giant city of Prosperity. All monies received by these disbursement districts come from the AFFEERCE Central Bank, and not state coffers.

Because distribution is not yet universal, non-entitled citizens living within the town, contribute nothing to town services. Since this is private property they can be excluded to the extent allowed by federal and state civil and equal rights legislation. Means testing is considered valid for renting.

There are several sources of revenue for a cell beyond the distributions. The council of a governing district can propose a fully budgeted project and place it before the citizens within the cells. The tax must have a sunset provision of no more than 2 years. All project contracts must be public. The tax must be approved by a 2/3 plurality of the citizens within the governing district. Once approved, an account is established at the central bank, and automatically funded by a consumption tax for district members.

The councils are elected and responsible only to the entitled citizens within their dominion and not area businesses unless those businesses are integrated with residences. Business/residence integration is an important AFFEERCE goal, and is supported by everything from mixed-use buildings, large family businesses, and mutual organizations of every kind.

Such integration provides the basis for the cellular aristocracy, another source of revenue. Aristocracy can be obtained by sufficiently raising one's own rent, purchasing or trebling other properties within the dominion, or by trebling properties that border the dominion. The quest for aristocracy can extend the borders of a cell or district. For instance, a level-3 cell might form in the AFFEERCE territories and conquer parts of Prosperity or territory held by another cell as it expanded. Following capitulation, the quest for aristocracy can change mega-state (level 5) boundaries as well. In this way, the most innovative governments will grow and prosper as the poorly managed dominions disappear. For more details, consult *Volume I*.

A source of revenue at cellular levels 1 through 6 is utility delivery and supply. Delivery includes water, electric, gas, cable, sewer, and drainage, while supply can be electric or water. To earn supply revenue, the city must add electricity or fresh water to the supply channels. To earn delivery revenue, the cell must build and maintain the supply channels within its dominion. Otherwise the responsibility and the revenue will be kicked up to a higher level dominion. Homeowners can pay their utility delivery and supply charges from the housing distribution.

Cities will form around particular themes and missions. They can use top-down or bottom-up development, employ covenant patterns, and settle conflicts in natural rights with a 2/3 vote of the citizenry. With a 5/6 vote of the citizenry, natural rights can be restricted to the same extent they can be restricted in a family. Possible financial consequences of such votes are discussed in Volume-I.

Two or more cities can merge into a county at level 4, provided they have at least 69,000 entitled citizens. However, any number less than 100,000 entitled citizens is difficult, as it requires significant reorganization of lower level cells. Because ground rent does not constantly decrease as it will in the latter stages of Phase-III, dominion trebling will be rare, except for land where the rent is not very high to begin with.

The bulk of the judiciary and public defense distribution is disbursed at level 4, although 20% is disbursed at level 3 for municipal and family court. Following capitulation, members of the judiciary are chosen by law schools, are independent of the councils, and can be removed by a 2/3 majority of the next higher level council or a 2/3 plurality of the citizenry in their dominion. Prior to capitulation, the judiciary is selected according to state law.

The Cost of Entitled Citizenship

The Phase-II cost of distributions is $966/month/person.

The rent in Year 21, if completely distributed to all 300,000 citizens would pay $461/month. That is almost half of the $966 distribution cost. However, by the end of the period, projected increases in ground rent, on the same developed land area, distributed to 300,000 citizens would pay $1,389/month. Ground rent will exceed distribution cost. As long as this is true once we have completed using ground rents for other purposes, the present value of these distributions need not account for any longer time than that. We will also assume an ambitious 4% real rate of return on citizen investing (see below), as this will still beat the prime rate. Our present rate calculations will be based on the 40 years until the end of Phase-III. Every year during Phase-II, the actual term drops by a year, but to err conservatively, costs will not be adjusted for shorter terms.

Based on all of these factors, we show the cost of entitled citizenship for selected ages.

The full cost of entitled citizenship pro-rated by age	Table 21.8
Age	Approximate Cost
0	$230,000
10	$220,000
20	$210,000
30	$200,000
40	$185,000
50	$168,000
60	$145,000
65+	$125,000

Because these are lifetime benefits only costed at 40 years, the prices are competitive with other investment vehicles for the benefits outlined, although other annuities don't usually pay for government services in their distributions. Still, those who wish to treble undeveloped land will be quick to take advantage of the opportunity. However, the average person doesn't have this kind of money, and would be leery of putting their life savings into a vehicle that carries the risk of unchartered waters. Annuities, in general, are not the best investments.

Buying full-price entitled citizenship is a risk best taken by the wealthy (who don't need the distributions to begin with). The goal in Phase-II is to create as many citizens as possible from those who would never dream of paying full price. We wish to reward those who supported Prosperity from the beginning: the investors, donors, affeercianados, and homesteaders. Secondly, we want to attract the best, the brightest, and those with needed skills to Prosperity.

The ground rents as they stand at the start of Year 21 can pay the full cost of 7,408 entitled citizenships for 30 year olds. However, if the ground rents are used instead to subsidize at auction the purchase of distributions, we can entitle many more citizens. With the subsidies, a weak investment becomes a killer investment. The rent is used as a subsidy in "Dutch" auctions. The following table shows sample rent allocations to the different groups we want to reward or attract. The auctions are repeated every year until all residents who want to be entitled citizens become entitled citizens. Less wealthy residents will have a longer wait, but can still become entitled citizens at the price they are willing to pay. The minimum bid is 1%, so if a 20 year old will not pay $2,300 for a lifetime of distributions that will pay back that much in food, housing and cash alone in fewer than 4 months, it is clear they are not interested.

Distribution of Rent Subsidies in Distribution Auction for Year 22		Table 21.9
Affeercianados	26%	
Homesteaders	41%	$2,000 subtracted for each year in residence
Donors	18%	Donation x (20 – Year of donation)/20 subtracted from bid
Family of entitled citizens	8%	$2,000 subtracted for each year in residence.
Outreach/special skills, talents based on comprehensive testing	7%	Must score in top 12% to bid. 2% subtracted for each percentile over 90.

The actual categories and breakdown will be set by the Affeercianado Guild. It is assumed that interested investors will simply buy their distributions outright, as a gesture of support; otherwise they can bid with donors. Based on the determination of the Guild, multiple special skills auctions can be held to maximize Prosperity diversity. As needs change, categories will be added and deleted and percentages modified. Once all interested affeercianados and donors have become citizens, previously allotted funds will be merged into the homesteaders and "family of entitled citizens" categories. Those citizens that fall into multiple categories can participate in multiple auctions every year until they are successful. In Year 21, there is no "Family of entitled citizens" auction by definition. Here is the breakdown*.

Auctions Table 21.10	# of Distrib.	Avg Age	Distrib Cost	%Paid	Credit Unused Rent	Credit Active Fund	Active Fund
Year 21			0		$1,645,682,730		$0
Affeercianado Auction	32,097	38	$188,000	97%	($181,025,100)	$6,034,170,008	$6,034,170,008
Homesteader Auction	8,815	45	$178,000	57%	($674,729,919)	$1,569,139,347	$7,603,309,355
Donator/Investor Auction	4,087	47	$174,000	19%	($575,988,955)	$711,097,476	$8,314,406,831
Skills Auction	1,147	26	$205,000	9%	($213,938,755)	$235,097,533	$8,549,504,363
Paid in full entitled citizenship	8,932	53	$162,000	100%	$0	$1,446,984,000	$9,996,488,363
Total	55,078		$0		$0	$0	$9,996,488,363
Cost of Distributions			$0		$0	($638,459,805)	$9,358,028,559
Interest at 4%			$0		$0	$374,321,142	$9,732,349,701

The 95% of ground rent for distributions is expected to be $1.646 billion dollars. All of it will be used for auction subsidies with 11% or $181,025,100 subsidizing the first auction for current or former affeercianados. With their new found wealth of $32 billion dollars, or 64 billion VIP$, purchasing entitled citizenship will be well within budget. Many affeercianados will have dreamed of this day when the opportunity of financed enterprise, or new worlds in the AFFEERCE territories beckoned. In the projection, the average age of affeercianados winning this auction is 38. Many will be old-timers who started in the first few years. The average full cost of distribution for a 38 year old is $188,000. It is predicted that 32,097 affeercianados will pay 97% of the full amount to become entitled citizens, with only 3% of each distribution paid by the subsidy.

The average age of citizens winning the homesteader auction is projected to be 45, making the average full cost of distribution $178,000. It is further projected that homesteaders will not be willing to pay the same high percentage of full cost as affeercianados, but rather bid 57% of the full cost. At least that is what is shown in table 21.10. Consider that this percentage is reduced from the percentage bid, as many of the homesteaders have been residents for 10 or even 20 years. $2,000 is deducted from the final bid for each year in residence. Table 21.10 shows the effective bid without accounting for discounts. Of course, the effective bid is highly speculative anyway. Note that although the homesteaders received a much higher subsidy than the affeercianados, $647 million versus $181 million, the revenue contributed by the homesteaders is so much lower that only 8,815 will win entitled citizenship versus 32,097 affeercianados.

The column that reads Active Fund shows the total funds available for distribution. From the active fund comes $966 a month for each entitled citizen. Some of the money goes to individual food, housing, and cash accounts. The rest is allocated to accounts at cellular levels 1, 2, 3, 4 and 5. As each auction is held, the full cost of distribution (the rent subsidy + money bid at auction) is added to the active fund. Thus the fund always contains the full present value for every entitled citizen, regardless of how much is bid.

In the projection, only 4,087 distributions will be issued at an effective 19% in the donator auction. That is because homesteaders who donated at least $1,000 will be able to deduct their donations in the homesteader auction as well, further complicating the predicted effective return of 57%. Although not shown, the affeercianados will be expected to pick up part of the cost of donations. The donors' auction will likely have a low turnout because a $1,000 threshold is required to qualify for the auction. These will be donors who did not move to Prosperity and donated some twenty odd years earlier. Only large donors probably kept track. With an average age of 47, the full cost of the distributions is only $174,000 on average. Suppose the actual bid is 50%, meaning each donor would pay $87,000. However, if a donor had an effective donation of $100,000, they would actually get $13,000 back from the auction if they were exactly 47 years old and if that is the way the prospectus is written. The worst case for such a donor would be free distribution for any bid under 57%. It is easy to see how the effective bid in the donors' auction will be 19%.

Donations made in the early years are far more effective in increasing affeercianado ownership of the land than later ones. Thus the effective donation is found by multiplying the donation by 20 minus the year of donation divided by 20. The setup year is considered Year 0, so a donation made in or before the setup year is fully effective. A $2,000 donation made in Year 10 would be an effective donation of $2,000 x (20 – 10)/20 = $1,000.

The skills auction has an effective bid of 9%. The goal is to attract the best and brightest to Prosperity without having them pay very much for entitled citizenship. After comprehensive testing, 2% is subtracted from the final bid for each percentile over 90%. Only those in the 88th percentile or above are eligible to bid. If you scored 93% on the exams, you would get a 6% discount at auction. If you scored 100%, you would get a 20% discount at auction. The auction is designed so everyone in the top 12% would be admitted with a final bid of 21%. This is also the most expensive case for the bidders. The top percentile would pay 1%, the next percentile 3%, and so on, with the 88th, 89th, and 90th percentile paying the full 21%. In Table 21.10, the final bid is 18%. The top two percentiles will be admitted free, and those admitted in the lowest three percentile will pay the full 18%. The effective bid will be 9%.

We can assume that skills' testing will be closely coordinated with domestic needs expressed in the Mercantile Letter. The skills that we want are those that will allow the creation of business objects to further import replacement.

In order to qualify for the homesteaders' auction, one must be a registered voter for at least a year in Prosperity or the AFFEERCE territories. It is predicted that at the start of Year 21, a large number of people who do not qualify for any auction will, for various reasons, simply buy entitled citizenship. These will be mostly well-to-do entrepreneurs who plan on trebling land, or starting a business and obtaining funding. We see from Table 21.10 that 8,932 people are projected to buy entitled citizenship outright, paying 100% of full cost. This number should drop rapidly each year as entrepreneurs have time to move to Prosperity and qualify for the homesteaders' auction.

On the line Cost of Distributions in Table 21.1, we see the Active Fund dropping from $9.99 billion to $9.38 billion. This line accounts for the actual payment of the distributions to individuals and their public services. We see a total of 55,078 distributions costing $638,459,805. We know that the remaining $9.38 billion isn't going to be needed this year, and we correctly expect that as long as the auctions are being held, it will never be needed. The money is invested with our entitled citizens by citizen investors at an average yield of 4%. In Year 21, this earns $374 million, over half the cost of distribution. Unfortunately, as less people pay full cost or 97% of full cost like the first affeercianados, the interest earned will decrease as a proportion of the distribution cost, even as ground rent increases by an ultra-conservative 5% annually. This will not reverse until Phase-III is complete and in the unlikely event of gross miscalculation, could force the pace of Phase-II or Phase-III to be slowed.

How the Auction Works
To bid for entitled citizenship, funds are deposited in a bidding account at the central bank. Based on money deposited and age, along with such factors as years as a Prosperity voter, effective donations, and test scores for the skills auction, a highest permissible bid and an effectively free opening bid will be generated. The bidder is not forced to bid at this level, or at any level. But they cannot bid at a level higher than the highest permissible bid.

The pot used for subsidies is a certain percentage of the ground rent proceeds allocated for that auction. $181 million of the $1.6 billion (11%) is used for the affeercianado auction in Table 21.10. If a bidder bids 67%, it means that after subtracting $2,000 for each year in residence or 2% for each percentile over 90%, the bidder is willing to pay that percentage of the full cost of entitled citizenship for their age discounted by their effective donations. The remainder of what is needed to pay the full cost of entitled citizenship for a particular age is taken from the pot. A program continuously updates the results of the auction and the status of the pot.

The bid starts at 99%. If there are no takers, it drops to 98%, then 97%, and so on. Bidders use a VIP reader to record their bid. If 10 bidders bid at 96%, the new value of the pot is calculated and the bid drops to 95% if the pot is not for all practical purposes empty. If 30 more bidders bid at 95%, all 40 bidders are computed at 95%. If the pot is not exhausted, bidding drops to 94%. This continues until the pot is exhausted or a drop in bid will automatically exhaust the pot with no new bidders. All successful bidders pay the lowest bidding percentage, regardless of their opening bid.

When the auction is complete, money from successful bidding accounts will be moved to the active fund, and the excess returned to individual accounts. Money from the rent pot will also be moved to the active fund. Food, housing, and cash distributions, pro-rated to the next monthly birthday of the successful bidder will be moved into those accounts. Every month at 12:01 AM on the bidder's birthday, those accounts will be restocked. There is immediate full medical coverage at Thomas Paine Hospital or other affiliated HMO's of the citizen's choice. Premiums are paid to the local affiliated HMO of the bidder's choice, if a choice exists. The $300/month disability payment and $25/month wellness annuity in addition to the $100/month premium are likely to bring other hospitals on board that are not staffed with affeercianados.

Other payments for municipal and educational services do not begin until the bidder's monthly birthday and current month amounts are used to help fund orientation.

Citizen Investors
In Year 21, there is predicted to be $9.3 billion in the distribution package that will not be used to pay distributions. These billions will be used to fund enterprises started by entitled citizens.

The person dispensing these funds is the citizen investor who is given custody of a small portion of the active fund based on past results. The training required to be a citizen investor is discussed in *Volume-I*.

In Phase-II, the requirements to receive the money and the compensation of the citizen investor are more constrained than in a post-capitulation society.

In Phase-II, the money is loaned at 5% and the citizen investor retains 1% as a salary and returns the other 4% to the active fund. If the investment goes bad and fails to produce at least 2% for the active fund, the citizen investor must either make up the difference from personal funds, or be barred from the program until they do so, if ever. Fraudulent loans will be vigorously prosecuted.

To obtain these funds, an entrepreneur must present a rigorous business plan to a citizen investor. If the investor is not interested in making the loan under any circumstances, they are required by the covenants of their trade to give a list of reasons why not in a reasonably short period of time. Since the citizen investors are in the business to make these loans and are competing with one another, most will try to develop a more positive relationship with an entrepreneur if the business plan has any chance of being salvaged. They will suggest modifications to the plan, courses, training, or certification that needs to be met, regular meetings, and the addition of new talent to the team.

There are stringent requirements for eligibility that supersede the judgment of the citizen investor.

- The one most contrasted with business today, is that nobody in the company can receive a salary from the business itself, until the loan is repaid. If applicable, scrip held in a personal account at the central bank and tied to the enterprise must be used instead. Therefore, all employees must be either entitled citizens, of independent means, or with an otherwise employed family member. Generally, this is a partnership or collective, where the old distinction between employer and employee is gone.
- The loan cannot be used to pay for services, except those whose independence is required by law, such as an accounting service. Other service providers, if used at all, must be paid in scrip which pays no interest and carries the major risk of enterprise failure. It is far better that the talent to perform all needed functions be within the enterprise.
- All money must be earmarked for specific capital goods in the business plan. A VIP application associated with the loan account will prohibit spending for any other goods, or over spending for these goods.
- If applicable, a small repayment is made automatically with each sale. Otherwise, a strict repayment plan must be part of the business plan.
- If the plan is underperforming by 5% or more, the citizen investor has the right, but not the obligation to cancel any outstanding lines of credit, and seize all remaining capital goods. Alternatively, the citizen investor has the right to extend a new line of credit to cover the shortfall.

Unlike today, where the chance for an ordinary citizen to obtain millions of dollars to finance a new enterprise is practically zero, it will be the norm for entitled citizens in Phase-II and beyond. Rather than "going it alone," a good manager will assemble a team of entitled talent into collective ownership, perfect the business plan as team members acquire needed skills through free education, obtain whatever is needed in capital funding from citizen investors, and begin business. It is expected that this will often be organized as a large alternative family to maximize economies of scale and division of labor. Uninterested spouses will prepare the common meals, bring in outside income, and maintain the household while their partners create the business.

This one benefit of entitled citizenship could be worth billions to those with business savvy.

Year 22

Thomas Paine Hospital

Let's take a final look at Thomas Paine Hospital in Year 22. The premium for non-entitled citizens has increased to $110, while payment for entitled citizens beyond the $100 monthly premium includes $10/day ($300/month) for each night in the hospital and the likely much coveted $25/month wellness annuity. At the end of Year 22, it is predicted there will be 102,194 entitled citizens.

Thomas Paine Hospital Table 22.1		Debit	Credit	Balance
Year 22				$0
Paid doctors + administrator	30	$6,000,000		($6,000,000)
Total surgery hours	87099.20	$2,177,480		($8,177,480)
Paid staff surgery hours (med school reduced)	21774.80	$6,532,440		($14,709,920)
Medicare/PPO surgery hours	29033.07	.	$20,323,146	$5,613,226
Average beds used per night	238.63	$2,177,480		$3,435,746
Medicare/PPO Beds used per night	79.54		$43,549,598	$46,985,345
Average out patients per day	2386.28	$8,709,920	$27,436,247	$65,711,672
Average daily ER visits	298.28	$1,088,740	$7,621,180	$72,244,112
Average daily generic drugs prescribed	2386.28	$8,709,920	$7,838,928	$71,373,120
Average daily non-generic drugs prescribed	238.63	$8,709,920	$2,743,625	$65,406,825
Medicare/PPO non-generic drugs	79.54		$2,903,307	$68,310,131
Average daily specialty drugs prescribed	23.86	$3,483,968	$1,567,786	$66,393,949
Medicare/PPO specialty drugs	7.95		$1,451,653	$67,845,602
Average tests and procedures per day	1034.05	$3,774,299	$11,889,040	$75,960,344
Medicare/PPO tests and procedures per day	344.68		$25,161,990	$101,122,334
Hospital liability	536.91	$10,690,333		$90,432,002
Lab work per day	1431.77	$10,451,904	$16,461,748	$96,441,846
Disability distribution	29.83		$108,874	$96,550,720
Wellness annuity	9677.69		$2,903,307	$99,454,027
Premiums	870992		$1,097,449,878	$1,196,903,904
Food		$870,992		$1,196,032,912
Bandages and Special Appliances		$3,919,464		$1,192,113,449
Internal and topical medicines		$28,307,239		$1,163,806,210
Prosthesis and Take Home Equipment		$3,483,968		$1,160,322,242
Heat,air,electric,cable		$800,000		$1,159,522,242
Medivac and travel policy		$10,451,904		$1,149,070,338
Miscellaneous and unanticipated		$20,000		$1,149,050,338
Depreciation		$4,126,000		$1,144,924,338
Affeerciarado Workers	1289	$0	$0	$1,144,924,338
Return to Affeercianados		$1,144,924,338		$0

The new disability distribution will never be a big source of revenue, but the wellness annuity, already at $2.91 million in Year 22, with only about 1/8 of the admitted patients in the previous year being entitled, can easily grow by a factor of 50, in 20 years' time when most citizens are entitled and have had the opportunity or misfortune to spend a night in the hospital. By Year 42, the wellness annuity could reach $120 million or more. However, the myriad possibilities of expansion and competition make it futile to carry the hospital tables any further than Year 22, where it is profiting by $1.145 billion.

Prosperity

Prosperity Table 22.2	Debit	Credit	Balance
Year 22	$0	$0	$332,587,665
Roads and infrastructure	$0	$226,096,684	$558,684,349
City Hall	$0	$22,793,119	$581,477,469
Parks and Recreation	$0	($33,352,658)	$548,124,811
Police	$0	($41,660,169)	$506,464,642
Fire	$0	($13,192,528)	$493,272,114
Waste Management	$0	$33,658,333	$526,930,447
Rent Dividend	$0	$46,439,338	$573,369,785
Distribution Package	$0	$89,521,915	$662,891,700
Rent Owed (10% only)	$2,588,000	$2,588,000	$662,891,700
CD issued for $1,468 to entitled citizens.	$150,000,000	$0	$512,891,700

Notice that in Year 22, Prosperity receives almost $89 million from distributions plus $46 million from the 5% of the rents allocated for city, county, and education. These numbers assume all AFFEERCE territory is within Prosperity's bounds. New cellular governments can form in the hinterlands, however, there is no way of predicting how numerous they will be, so for the sake of simplicity, all distribution revenue is shown under Prosperity.

With 102,194 entitled citizens, the CD given out in Year 22 is just $1,468; purposely lowered from the $12,810 given out as an incentive in the previous year. Although flush with cash, by setting the CD to a low $1,468 per entitled citizen in Year 22, it can rise every year thereafter.

Starting in Year 21, and every year thereafter, we are building a community center, high school, police and fire station. Whether these are built in the hinterlands, and whether the affeercianados build an adjoining dorm or allow jobs to be taken by ordinary citizens cannot be predicted at this time. Over Phase-II, the mercantile advantage is being passed from the affeercianados to entitled citizens, who will organize to maximize economies of scale and divisions of labor as they do the jobs they love without worrying about future security.

Entitled Citizens

Auctions Table 22.3	# of Distrib.	Avg Age	Distrib Cost	%Paid	Credit Unused Rent	Credit Active Fund	Active Fund
Year 22			0		$1,764,694,861	$0	$9,996,488,363
Affeercianado Auction	30,028	36	$191,000	92%	($458,820,664)	$5,735,258,300	$15,731,746,663
Homesteader Auction	9,186	44	$179,000	56%	($723,524,893)	$1,644,374,757	$17,376,121,420
Donator/Investor Auction	2,280	48	$172,000	19%	($317,645,075)	$392,154,414	$17,768,275,834
Skills Auction	757	26	$205,000	9%	($141,175,589)	$155,138,010	$17,923,413,844
Family of Citizens	825	19	$214,000	30%	($123,528,640)	$176,469,486	$18,099,883,330
Paid in full entitled citizenship	4,041	51	$166,000	100%	$0	$670,806,000	$18,770,689,330
Total	102,194		$0		$0	$0	$18,770,689,330
Cost of Distributions			$0		$0	($1,184,632,460)	$17,586,056,870
Interest at 4%			$0		$0	$703,442,275	$18,289,499,145

Notice how the active fund has almost doubled in Year 22. There is $18.2 billion available to be invested in new enterprises by entitled citizens. If there is a shortage of enterprises, the money will reluctantly be used for mortgages, but that is certainly not the preference.

The cost of the distributions has gone up to $1.18 billion but the interest earned at 4% has gone up to $703 million. Notice also that the affeercianados bidding in this year's auction are only paying 92% of full cost and the average age has dropped from 38 to 36 as younger affeercianados with fewer resources are able to compete for entitled citizenship. Homesteaders are now bidding 56% of full cost versus 57% in Year 21. This will be the general tendency in years to come as less affluent affeercianados and homesteaders gain the opportunity to become entitled citizens.

Orientation

In Year 22, orientation for newly entitled citizens becomes a major event. After the auctions, winning bidders are invited to various hotels at the downtown convention center for several days of orientation, presentations, lectures, parties, exhibits, and counseling. Those who receive universal distribution at capitulation will not have this luxury.

Those who attend the orientation will be presented with opportunities and adventures that could shape the rest of their lives. There will be lectures on each of the different distributions and how to maximize the advantages they provide. There will be presentations on alternative families, economies of scale, creating cellular democracies in the AFFEERCE territories, freedom and restrictions due to U.S. law, federal tax benefits and more. The great hall will feature booths for diverse families and communities recruiting new members. There is no political correctness, only a chance to join others with whom one truly has synergy. Read family charters. Discuss chores expected, meal options, sleeping accommodations, hobbies, dowries, tithing, allowances, entertainment, and in many cases, most importantly, the family business. Communities, communes, kibbutzim, and tribes in the hinterlands will also be recruiting. Fantasy and reality can merge into a new lifestyle and a new life. I can guess it will be like rushing a frat or sorority times one hundred. More conventionally, there will also be booths for single person studio rentals and one and two bedroom apartments, and others for mortgage bankers and real estate brokers. If Thomas Paine has competition, the HMOs will be here competing for your monthly premium.

If joining a specific community, mutual organization, or large family is not in the cards, orientation will be an excellent place to search for employers. It will be a job fair, but unlike one you have ever seen. Not only do the distributions allow businesses to take you on for a probationary wage, but the education distribution will reimburse them for on-the-job-training, both directly and through long-term annuities. No matter what your qualifications, if you show a keen interest, most Prosperity businesses will give you a chance as an apprentice at a very low wage. It is a chance to embark on a career whose obstacles once seemed insurmountable.

If the newly entitled citizen is overwhelmed, there will be plenty of social workers at orientation to help allay fears, and special concerns, as well as help with life and career planning.

The exhibits will be open to all entitled citizens on an if-room-permits basis. Those who received their entitled citizenship at an earlier auction, tired of living in a studio cubicle or ready for employment or adventure, can treat this as a job, housing, and family fair, or as a gateway to adventure in the territories.

For newly entitled citizens, the meals served at orientation will be exquisite with nightly entertainment. An entitled citizenry is a new concept in human value. Economies of scale turn housing and food distributions into family wealth greater than the sum of its parts. Distribution tranches do the same for community wealth. Every stranger becomes an asset to family and community. Wherever an entitled citizen might go, they will be invited to join families and welcomed into communities.

As far as business is concerned, reimbursement for training entitled citizens is only one benefit. Entitled citizens are not forced to work, and will often take less in wages, carry forth with enthusiastic spirit, and be anxious to become full business partners. They can be paid in scrip as a condition of a business loan, and freely sent to school for specialized knowledge. For a business, an entitled citizen is a cherished commodity.

Similarly, landlords want to rent to newly entitled citizens because the rents are assured.

New towns in the hinterlands view entitled citizens as gold. Each entitled citizen that moves to these towns brings a stronger police force, fire protection, streets, sanitation, and transportation allocations again greater than the sum of its parts due to economies of scale. Entitled citizens increase the size of the cellular structure, possibly causing mitosis, and leading to higher titles for the aristocracy.

It is an equation discussed many times in *Volume-I*: "People=Wealth." Whether it is a family, a business, a landlord, or a town vying for the entitled citizen, orientation with its fine dining and myriad enticements will make the newly entitled citizen feel valuable, possibly for the first time in their lives.

Taxes

Federal Income Tax

The biggest obstacle to the success of the embryonic nation is the double taxation between high ground rents and the U.S. federal income tax. Although the ground rent replaces the property tax and the interest paid on a loan for land, trebling will tend to push values up to 1/3 EBITDA on office buildings, retail, and apartments, and even higher on rich mineral lands. With a corporate income tax of 33% and a rent on the profits of a land-centric business at 33%, double taxation can reduce profits by 50% (the rent is at least deductible from income). Double taxation is countered to some extent by the treble, which is a voluntary bid.

Another insidious form of double taxation, would be a requirement to pay the consumption tax when converting VIP$ to U.S. dollars in order to pay the income tax. That charge is waived. The central bank will make all payments to the IRS directly from its cache of U.S. dollars.

Affeercianado Guild tax lawyers will utilize every loophole, and our congressional representatives will work to make the code as favorable as possible to entitled citizens. However, it is essential we conduct our affairs with absolute honesty and adapt to the financial framework of the nation as it is during Phase-II.

The national defense distribution of $50 a month is used to pay federal income tax.

VIP$ are not U.S. dollars. How do we best calculate the worth of a VIP$ for tax purposes? Are two VIP$ of income really worth a U.S. dollar? Only when paying taxes. Otherwise a citizen might trade 2.1 VIP$ for a U.S. dollar. Although we "hope" that a VIP$ will purchase 50 cents worth of goods, the IRS can't tax us on our hopes. This is where negotiations between our tax attorneys and the IRS can have a big payoff.

Why would they negotiate? Because Prosperity will file the taxes of all citizens who earn all income in VIP$ and provide 1099's for those who earn only part of their income in VIP$. Among our first citizens will be many who consider taxation tyranny, many of whom, in the past, tried to hide as much income from the IRS as possible. Now every Prosperity citizen is earning money in an alternate currency in a corporate account. Not only is it an alternate currency, but it is a virtual currency that exists encrypted in a central computer. Only the individual can make paper records, otherwise no paper records of VIP transactions exist. Adding to the complexity is the consumption tax on money transferred from a corporate account to a spending account. When the distributions are figured in it gets worse.

For citizens who paid for their distributions, the distributions are completely tax free. It is simply a transfer back of already taxed money. Any interest paid will be in a deferred tax vehicle. Distributions for local services such as police, fire, streets and sanitation, are even tax deductible in the year they are paid. Medical insurance purchased can be deducted. Distributions used for education might also be deductible.

For those citizens who gained their distributions through the auctions, or in exchange for selling land, or otherwise as a gift, food, housing, and cash are taxable as income to the extent they were not paid for. The tax attorneys will compute how much of medical insurance purchased or educational distributions used will also count as income.

No individual could possibly be expected to figure out their taxes, and the IRS budget would have to increase ten-fold to handle the audits. I am convinced that if we negotiate in good faith, the IRS will have every reason to do likewise.

Beyond the distributions, all earned VIP$ go into a personal corporate account. Everyone is incorporated. The U.S. tax rate on corporate profits under $50,000 is 15%. However, a single person can pay themselves a salary of over $40,000 and remain in the 15% tax bracket. Since local taxes are deductible from income, the automatic consumption tax paid when moving money from a corporate to a spending account, allows a single person to take $44,440 ($40,000 after consumption taxes) from their corporate account and remain in the 15% federal tax bracket. Assuming the worst case, 2 VIP$ = 1 U.S. dollar, a person can earn $50,000 (corporate profit) + $44,440 (salary + sales tax) or 188,880 VIP$ a year and pay 15% federal taxes[FTN1.01].

Paying 15% of income in taxes is not optimal. Capital expenditures are non-taxable or can be depreciated, although there is a consumption tax on outside (non-VIP$) capital expenditures. In the dual taxation environment of pre-capitulation AFFEERCE, the best use of funds is to start a business. You want to invest in capital, preferably capital purchased with VIP$. These expenditures are not taxed as U.S. income and are not subject to the AFFEERCE consumption tax (although the IRS might require depreciation over several years). To maximize efficiency, establish the business as a family business and grow it during Phase-II. A worthwhile goal is to pay each citizen in the family 7,272 VIP$ a year, and spend the rest on capital goods. This optimal situation assumes distributions were paid in full.

Family Member Income	VIP $7,272
Income in U.S. dollars	$3,636
Social Security (15% as independent)	$545
Medicare	$55
Federal income tax	$0
Total Owed	$600
Federal tax entitlement	$600
Net amount owed	$0

Because entitled citizens receive a federal tax distribution from the distribution package of $600, not one dime, out of pocket, will go to pay federal taxes. With food, shelter, utilities, medical care, and education covered, $3,636 U.S. a year per family member is disposable income sufficient for comfort while building a business empire.

AFFEERCE 401K

Another way to save on federal taxes is to invest in an AFFEERCE 401K. Before capitulation, an AFFEERCE 401K is like any other, tax deductible and tax deferred. However, at capitulation, for reasons of equity, 15% of all regular 401K's, non-Roth IRA's and 30% of other tax deductible pensions will be deducted before the money is moved to a corporate account. Roth IRA's and other tax-deferred but non-deductible plans will be moved without penalty to a corporate account. However, AFFEERCE 401K's will be moved without penalty to a spending account, thus saving the consumption tax on expenditures. At capitulation, all age restrictions are lifted. This benefit, based on trust in our ultimate success, allows pre-capitulation entitled citizens to counter the burden of double taxation.

The maximum contribution, $5,500 can be moved to an AFFEERCE 401K tax free. The employer can contribute 25% of employee compensation. Instead of a 7,272 VIP$ salary, it can be effectively increased to 18,272 VIP$, 7,272 VIP$ after a $5,500 AFFEERCE 401K contribution, with the employer contributing an additional $909.

Consumption Tax

A consumption tax is used to provide achievement annuities for teachers and schools. It funds a discretionary tax that allows citizens to allocate money however they please. Localities can only fund special projects beyond the distributions by approving an earmarked, sunset, increase in the consumption tax by a 2/3 plurality of the citizens. The consumption tax is progressive in that it does not apply to distribution money. It encourages capital expenditures in VIP$. There is no consumption tax on the export of goods, or sales to tourists.

A consumption tax is paid when money is moved from a corporate account to a spending account. That need not be at the point of sale. Unlike a sales tax, the consumption tax is allocated to the consumer's local cell, teachers, schools, and discretionary choices regardless of where a purchase is made. Use of the consumption tax in Phase-II is dependent on state sales taxes and regulations.

Some argue that a sales tax discourages consumption. If so, it has had little effect. Consumption of marginal items, soon tossed in a closet and forgotten, remains a national obsession. Fetishism of commodities has exceeded even the imagination of Karl Marx.

Even Henry George said there should be two taxes, one on land and the other on ostentation. But hasn't so much of our consumption become ostentatious, when even lawn chairs are purchased for the sake of keeping up with the Joneses.

Unlike income taxes which discourage work, and corporate taxes which discourage profit, a consumption tax that actually succeeds in discouraging consumption might be a net positive.

The Government Distribution

Distribution of the government distribution differs from the post-capitulation distribution found in *Volume I*. Primarily this is due to the absence of cellular levels 6 and 7 in the embryonic nation. The distribution also differs from the distribution shown earlier in Prosperity proper.

Government Distribution	Tranche	Average	Monthly Revenue
Level – 1	10%	100	$120
Level – 2	10%	1,400	$1,680
Level – 3	50%	15,400	$92,400
Level – 4	10%	169,400	$203,280
Level – 5	20%	1,863,400	$4,472,160

Orphaned cells in the AFFEERCE territories receive all tranches below their parent cell (usually level-5 Prosperity) prorated for population. For instance, a tribe of 200 (2 level-1 cells) in the AFFEERCE territories would receive a monthly government distribution of $240 for level-1, $240 for level-2, $1,200 for level-3 and $240 for level-4. Prosperity would receive $480/month for the tribe. The tribe would also receive distributions for law enforcement and other municipal services.

High-Rises and High Rents

Collecting ground rent promotes efficient use of the land. Efficient use of the land is reflected in a very large difference between profit from location value and the rent. In the just completed upper and lower downtown, the crown jewel of Prosperity, buildings can be 21 stories high. On the perimeter of downtown, on solid ground, buildings can be much taller, creating a cavern effect, with the hilly central park in the middle.

During Phase-II, most of the newly developed land will be in the hinterlands. Of the 6,000 acres developed each year, as much as 5,960 acres will be trebled by entitled citizens in the hinterlands for a paltry rent of only $6,000 per acre, at least in the first year. Directly to the virtual north of downtown, land that once housed prefabs, the trailer park, and AFFEERCE a'Cookin, is cleared and ready for auction. Except for Year 21, where auctions on this land will be the sole source of the annuity due to the one year delay in monetizing territory lands, it is projected that only 40 acres a year of this highly valuable land will be auctioned. With a 40 story skyscraper of studios, affordable on a single housing distribution, how much ground rent will the land generate? Keep in mind that office, retail, clean industry, larger, and luxury apartments are more efficient, higher paying usages, so the rent we will compute below is a minimum.

With affeercianado and entitled labor, assume that Prosperity building costs in Phase-II are $140 per square foot. A 160 sq. ft. studio, for singles, assuming a hall and common area footprint of 180 sq. ft., would cost $25,200. At 5%, interest would be $1,260/year. Heat, central air, water and electric add another $640, for a total cost of $1900 a year. There is no need to advertise. Newly entitled single citizens are eager for these small but modern 10 x 10 main rooms, 5 x 6 kitchens, and 5 x 6 bathrooms. The cost is $370 a month, a single housing distribution. Annual depreciation over 45 years is $560. Annual onsite maintenance and admin is $340. The annual profit per unit is $4,440 - $1,900 - $900 = $1,640. With a highly efficient building footprint of 180 sq. ft. /unit, or 200 sq. ft. /unit for adjoining land, a wide and thin rectangular building on half an acre would support over 100 units per floor. Assume our 40 story building has 3,800 units plus a swimming pool, gym, game rooms, laundry rooms and other common rooms. Additional costs for the amenities are $200,000 year.

Profit on the building is: $1,640 x 3,800 - $200,000 = $6,032,000.

The trebler must pay 150% of objective depreciated value, so the trebler's interest payments would be $1,890 and the trebler's depreciation would be $840.

Instead of making a profit of $1,640 per unit, the trebler would make $630 + $280 = $910 less or only $730/unit. The trebler's profit would be $730 x 3,800 - $200,000 = $2,772,000. Thus a treble-safe rent for this building would be $924,000. However, rounding up to $1 million would be safer in case the trebler can find an interest rate below 5%.

In this building net rents are $10.25 sq. ft. /year. Gross rents are $30 sq. ft. If there is plenty of retail and office space, and a good supply of luxury apartments for those who can pay more than the housing distribution, the $1 million should be a safe rent. However, retail, office and luxury apartment gross rents are often $100 sq. ft. /year or more. On New York's 5th Avenue, they can go for as high as $2,000 sq. ft. /year. There is also very little difference in maintenance costs in a non-property tax economy, so net rents can easily be 10 times higher or more. So if there is a shortage of such buildings, the trebler will eye this property with thoughts of gentrification and remodeling.

The most efficient ground rent is the lowest ground rent possible. The best strategy is to match the treble when it comes. Unfortunately, most people do not have the liquid assets to match a treble, since rent must be paid one year in advance. The recommended rent for those who can't match a treble is 1/3 net rents. For this building, that would be $2,010,667, leaving an annual profit of $4,021,332.

In the hinterlands, rent for each of 5,960 acres will be $6,000, predicted to rise to $12,000 minimum in a year's time once treble safety is lifted. For the 40 acres auctioned just virtual north of downtown, the average rent is predicted to be $100,000/acre. Once treble safety is lifted, the average rent for the 6,000 acres developed in a Phase-II year is $21,880. This is almost twice the minimum assumed in computing affeercianado and investor Phase-II pensions from land monetization.

Years 23 – 31

Time is speeding up now. There is little to say, except to watch the numbers grow and see how Phase-II is progressing. We do know that by Year 30, all 40 remote parking garages will be complete at the transportation depot. By Year 31, Prosperity probably has an international airport, and a large rail yard. The VIP has spread across the country and the VIP$ is accepted everywhere in the host state and mostly in neighboring states.

Highlights of Year 31

- There are 331,136 entitled citizens. The total population of Prosperity and the AFFEERCE territories is 460,285.
- Homesteaders are paying 47% the full cost of distribution and family members of entitled citizens are paying 30% the full cost of distribution.
- The last affeercianados who wanted to become entitled citizens paid 1% of full cost in Year 30 for the privilege, thus ending the affeercianado entitled citizenship auctions. Newer affeercianados must bid with homesteaders.
- The last donors who wanted to become entitled citizens paid 1% of full cost in Year 24 for the privilege, thus ending the donor citizenship auctions.
- The active fund has $50 billion and earns $1.95 billion in interest. The annual cost of the distributions is $3.8 billion.
- Disregarding any cellular structures, out of the $4.3 billion in distributions, the city is receiving $274 million, the county $108 million, and education $195 million. Intellectual property distributions of $14 million have made most electronic content free to entitled citizens. The entitled citizens are receiving $867 million for food, $1.46 billion for housing and $138 million in cash. Thomas Paine and other affiliated HMOs are receiving $394 million in premiums from entitled citizens and about $71 million in wellness annuities and the disability distribution. Drug companies that provide their drugs at cost in exchange for the intellectual property distribution are making more profit than from monopoly distributions outside of the embryonic nation.
- The ground rent is $3.3 billion, with $3.15 billion going to fund new distributions, $83 million going to the city, $33 million going to the county, and $49 million going to education.
- Prosperity has issued a CD of $1,631 to every entitled citizen. Note that while citizens' dividends are only issued to registered voters in Phase-I, they are issued to every entitled man, woman, and child in Phase-II. This is a significant windfall for large entitled families and will remain so until capitulation.

Years 32-38

The end of Phase-II

In Year 38, the projected number of entitled citizens is 523,705 while the predicted population of Prosperity and the AFFEERCE territories in Year 37 is 577,315. With only 9% of the eligible population still unentitled and the low bid at auction making entitled citizenship free to longtime residents, our mission in giving entitled citizenship to at least 95% of residents who have lived in the territory at the start of Phase-II, and want to take part in the distributions, is complete.

Here are the final auctions for entitled citizenship held at the start of Year 38:

Auctions Table 32.10	# of Distrib.	Avg Age	Distrib Cost	%Paid	Credit Unused Rent	Credit Active Fund	Active Fund
Year 38			0		$4,577,993,451	$0	$57,083,494,659
Affeercianado Auction	0	30	$200,000	0%	$0	$0	$67,083,494,659
Homesteader Auction	16,495	43	$181,000	31%	($2,060,097,053)	$2,985,647,903	$70,069,142,562
Donator Investor Auction	0	0	$0	0%	$0	$0	$70,069,142,562
Skills Auction	2,454	26	$205,000	9%	($457,799,345)	$503,076,203	$70,572,218,765
Family of Citizens	10,963	18	$216,000	13%	($2,060,097,053)	$2,367,927,647	$72,940,146,412
Paid in full entitled citizenship	2	51	$166,000	100%	$0	$332,000	$72,940,478,412
Total	523,705		$0		$0	$0	$72,940,478,412
Cost of Distributions			$0		$0	($6,070,787,570)	$66,869,690,842
Interest at 4%			$0		$0	$2,674,787,634	$69,544,478,476

The homesteader's auction is down to 31% of full cost. These mostly come from the ranks of new citizens with at least one year of residency.

In the auction for family of entitled citizens, only 13% of full cost is paid. Many of the bids are for children with an average age of 18. Consider that entitled citizenship at this level is actually free with a second mortgage. The cost of entitled citizenship for a newborn is $230,000. 13% of this is $29,900. A 15 year loan for $30,000 at 5% has payments of $238/month. Since the housing distribution pays $370/month, the second mortgage payment is assured. A citizen investor will make this loan if all the entrepreneurs they are working with still have business plans in the development stage. However, it might very well be a policy of the citizen investors not to issue a second mortgage if a "baby mill" is suspected. Use of second mortgages and its influence on fertility rate toward the end of Phase-II will provide empirical data for the ongoing discussion of the baby tax as we head toward capitulation.

Looking again at the homesteader's auction, where the average age is 43, the average full cost of entitled citizenship is $181,000. At 31%, the average cost is $56,110. Here too, the monthly P&I on a second mortgage is $343, leaving $27 a month from the $370 for other housing expenses. This loan isn't quite as seductive. We know this is the first member of the family to become entitled; otherwise they would be bidding in the cheaper auction. (This is another good reason to register large alternative families as quickly as possible.) Therefore there is no assurance on the first mortgage, the rent, or the utilities. Since this is a new citizen, there is very little equity in the house. The citizen investors would not make this loan. If the homesteader is employed at a good job, a bank might.

In any case, we are done auctioning off distributions to our citizens. Beginning in Year 39, the start of Phase-III, we will issue a maximum of 20,000 entitled citizenships at 50% of full cost every year. Residents of Prosperity and the AFFEERCE territories will have priority over non-residents.

Phase III

Year 39 – 45

Deluxe Land Expansion

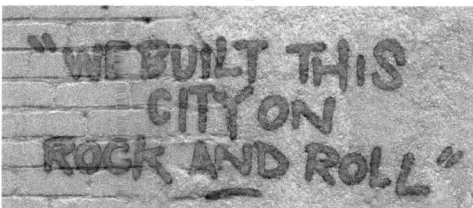

We have built a city, Prosperity, by Year 39, perhaps the biggest city in the state. The value of the land in the heart of downtown is rivaling the most expensive cities in the world. We have our own currency that is accepted throughout the state. Our medical campus is hugely successful and has succeeded in lowering medical costs across the nation. Jane Jacobs

175

University and the medical school are able to maintain highly competitive pricing for non-entitled citizens. Conventions, tourism, medical tourism, and exports are flourishing. Not even assumed in the spreadsheets is the likely monopoly we have on centralized biometric identity. If this monopoly holds, it could mean hundreds of billions of dollars in revenue by Year 39.

This kind of a success is a requirement for Phase-III. Deluxe land expansion is based on the principle that the VIP$ is backed by land. The residents of the host-state must be confident in both our currency and distribution promises. If we have earned that confidence, deluxe land expansion will not be stopped, except by force.

Before starting deluxe land expansion, a new feature must be added to the collection and distribution of rent. It is called a crop surcharge and its need arises from the federal subsidies currently received by farmers. The surcharge and its eventual elimination are discussed in detail in *Volume I*. The Phase-III surcharge is $2,000 and works like this. If a trebler wishes to convert cropland or rangeland to residential, commercial, or industrial land, they must treble the rent and then add the $2,000 surcharge to compute the new ground rent. For instance, if the rent is $500/acre, the trebler must treble to $1,500/acre and then add $2,000 to get a rent of $3,500/acre. Of course, if the trebler wishes to maintain the land as cropland or rangeland, they need only treble to $1,500 acre. If a farmer wishes to develop their own land for residential or industrial use, they must add the $2,000 surcharge.

With this new feature, we are ready to begin conquering land. Here is how it works.

An army of land brokers will move into the countryside surrounding AFFEERCE territories and make the landowners an offer they can't refuse. What landowner would decline to sell us their land for the following bonanza? :

1) The fair value of the land in VIP$.
2) Entitled citizenship for the landowner and resident family.
3) Entitled citizenship for all tenants on the land.

The land brokers will demonstrate how the housing distribution is sufficient to pay the rent on small estates and how the crop surcharge otherwise protects the land from treblers.

What we are doing is giving the land owner money in exchange for land title. As a bonus, we are giving lifetime benefits worth hundreds of thousands of dollars, even millions of dollars, to the land owner, his or her family, and the tenants who live on the land. As another bonus, the land rights owner will no longer be responsible for property taxes.

It is not as simple as it sounds. This is the ideal transaction. Perhaps a third of the land qualifies. For the remainder, the offer is too generous.

According to the spreadsheets, the most important number for the land brokers is $4,400. This is the average rent, exclusive of the property tax, that must be gained for every citizen granted distributions. It is based both on the size of the active fund and a state population goal that is assumed to be 2.7 million. A higher population goal would require some combination of more time or a higher average rent. To achieve this average we require a minimum rent of $2,200 per citizen granted a distribution. We do not have agreements with these cities, counties, and school districts. Perhaps they will accept the distribution used in Prosperity, perhaps they won't. If they won't, the property tax must still be paid from the rent and distribution revenue that is earmarked for local services. If the drain on the ground rent from property taxes is greater than the sum of the standard 5% of ground rent plus the distributions, ground rent in excess of $2,200/citizen will be required to make up the difference.

The land owner sets the value of the land using the method introduced by Dr. Sun-Yat Sen (See *Volume I*), but within the bounds of reason. Assuming the historical discount rate of 5%, the land owner sets the value of their land but must pay a ground rent of 5% every year, with one year paid in advance. If the landowner sets a value at $40,000/acre, then they are obligated to pay $2,000 in advance, plus $2,000 every year, paid monthly.

The land brokers will insist that the land value is reasonable. Otherwise, the former landowner can collect a large sum per acre, and skip town. They will lose only the 1 year advance payment plus the improvements on their land. However, if the land value is reasonable, the former owner skipping town will trigger an auction for the land with its free improvements that will likely yield an even higher rent.

So the land value cannot be too high, yet the rent generated must be equal to $2,200 per distribution granted. Suppose a couple lived on two acres they valued at $40,000/acre. That would be insufficient to close the deal, since the rent is $4,000 and $4,400 is required. However, the couple could claim the land is worth $44,000/acre. If the house on the property is in good shape, the land brokers will likely accept the price and pay $88,000 for the land (176,000 VIP$). From the $88,000, $4,400 will go for the 1 year advance payment of ground rent and $367/month will pay the rent thereafter. But the couple immediately starts receiving $740/month in housing distribution and this can be used henceforth to pay the $367 ground rent leaving $373/month for other housing expenses. They also start getting $440/month in food distribution, $70/cash, free medical care, and so on. Nothing changes in their circumstances except they are $83,600 richer with additional wealth every month providing security for the rest of their lives.

If the brokers fail to achieve $4,400 on average for each distribution, they minimum might have to be raised as high as $4,400 in the worst case. In the example above, the couple could claim the land is worth $88,000/acre. The land brokers would pay $176,000 for the land. Ground rents would be $733/month leaving only $7/month for other housing expenses. Not only is this highly unlikely possibility still a winning deal for the couple, but the land will be treble safe.

Deluxe land expansion is truly an offer too good to refuse. Those who qualify will be waiting in anticipation for the land brokers.

Before discussing more problematic cases, let's look at where the money is coming from. The money for distributions will be coming out of the ground rent, in the same way it paid for distributions in the auctions, except the distributions must be purchased at the full cost. Our active fund contains over $70 billion. Ground rents of $4.5 billion plus interest of $2.7 billion exceeds the $6.1 billion cost of distributions by over a billion dollars. Furthermore, the cost of a distribution was based on a 40 year term. Now the term has been reduced to about 20 or 21 years. We are also requiring a minimum of $2,200 per distribution in ground rent. It is projected that ground rents will continue to rise by 5% annually. Current ground rents will rise by $225 million before the rents from land expansion are even added. If the cost of the distribution after subtracting the minimum ground rent is $9,400 then the increase in ground rents will pay for 24,000 distributions. The spreadsheet verifies that we can safely cut the cost of entitled citizenship in half, allowing 48,000 entitled citizenships through deluxe land expansion the first year.

In Year 39, 48,000 distributions, with an average age of 40, can be purchased. So where is the money for the land coming from? It is here that the leap of faith occurs. It is here that our previous success, honesty, and transparency mean everything. The money used to purchase the land is simply created.

If it wasn't being discussed for 39 years, this might be controversial. But this money is no different than the money created to monetize Prosperity land for the affeercianados and investors. VIP$ are backed by land. VIP$ are created through the monetization of land. We are minting money to buy up all the land in the state and the landowners are competing with each other to be the first in line to sell. It is an amazing concept, and it will be a real one.

So we sweep the state, buying up land and creating tens of thousands of newly entitled citizens per year. Some will refuse, that is their right and their hard luck. We will simply pass them by. At capitulation, a constitutional amendment will force them to transfer the land anyway for less. Henry George argued they should get no compensation at all, but that won't be the case. However, they will do far better selling during Phase-III.

It is only natural that those who trade for these lifetime distributions will want to protect them. Not only are they now eligible to run for office on the AFFEERCE party ticket, but they will undoubtedly become diehard supporters of the party. Those who attack the AFFEERCE future are attacking their lifetime security.

Phase-III deluxe land expansion sounds simple but there are many problems, and we can't bypass them all.

A big problem is out-of-state absentee landlords. What good does it do them to sell us land for VIP$ that might not be accepted where they live and an entitled citizenship they never plan to use? The deal depends on the ratio of land value to distributions offered. Assuming it is at least $88,000 per distribution, a rent of $4,400/distribution, we offer to pay the absentee landowner that amount in U.S. dollars, and provide entitled citizenship to all his tenants, who, with their added income will be able to better afford his rents. Because the AFFEERCE Central Bank does not wish to depart with U.S. dollars, the tradeoff will be that the landowner must be counted as an entitled citizen, even though they will not be. Depending on central bank reserves of U.S. dollars, this deal might need to be saved for deals where the rent is $6,600/distribution or greater.

Another big problem is land under a mortgage lien. Obviously, we can't buy the land unless the mortgage is paid off. Usually, but not necessarily by Year 39 in the host-state, this must be paid off in U.S. dollars. If a U.S. dollar payoff is required, the rent must be greater than or equal to $4,400 x (number of distributions + 1) and the land value must exceed the amount due on the mortgage. Otherwise, the rent must be greater than or equal to $4,400 x number of distributions. In either case, the land value must exceed the amount due on the mortgage. Unless the landlord is an absentee landlord, there are easy ways to solve both problems if either or both conditions are not met.

Suppose a family of 4 owns a single family home on 1/4 of an acre with an outstanding mortgage of $100,000. The land brokers have determined the land is only worth $240,000/acre. This means the family's land is only worth $60,000. Rent of $3,000 (5% of $60,000) is sufficient to support only 1 distribution, not 4, and the $60,000 land value is insufficient to pay off the mortgage. How is this problem solved?

The family stipulates a raise of their rent payment to $17,600. This is a rent of $70,400/acre and is equivalent to the rent not too far from downtown Prosperity. As for the mortgage, we pay off the full $100,000 and create a new 5% mortgage on the home for $40,000 from the active fund. Assume that the county, city, and school district, have agreed to our standard distribution. Is this a good deal for the family?

Previously they were paying 5% on their $100,000 mortgage or $5,000 in interest a year plus $1,000 in property taxes, a total of $6,000. Now they must pay 5% of $40,000 or $2,000 in interest a year plus $17,600 in rent or a total of $19,600 a year, an increase of $13,600/year. Nevertheless, it is a wonderful deal. Every month this family of 4 will receive $1,480 in housing distribution. In a year they will receive $17,760. The net out of pocket payment has gone from $6,000/year to $1,840/year, over $4,000 in annual savings. In addition, they receive $10,560 a year for food, and $1,680 a year in cash. All 4 of them are eligible for the citizens' dividend (predicted to pay $1,542 per entitled person in Year 39), free medical care and free education, and many other benefits. There is also plenty of room for their rent to fall, once rents begin to fall (See *Zero-Sum*, below), and still be treble safe.

Large farms are good candidates for the deal, since the farmers are protected from treblers with the $20,000/acre cropland surtax. 2,000 acres paying a rent of $100/acre is a total rent of $200,000 and can support 45 distributions; e.g. the farmer's family of 8 and 37 farmhands and their families. Using the minimum ground rent/distribution of $2,200, this farm will support a maximum of 90 distributions, provided there is no mortgage. In the likely event there are less tenants to entitle, this becomes a very good deal for us and can be used for leeway in other deals. In addition the farmer gets $4 million cash (8 million VIP$), enough for 20 years' ground rent payments.

Small farms are more difficult. Suppose the farmer has 20 acres with a rent of $100/acre. That is a total rent of $2,000, not enough to support even one distribution. If the farmhouse is in reasonable shape, there would be no problem raising the rent to $110/acre, but if the farmer has a family of 8, raising it to $880/acre is out of the question for cropland. If there are no federal or state stipulations on the land, one solution is to use the cropland surcharge on some acres. Generally, we will be willing to pay $40,000/acre on unencumbered undeveloped land.

The land brokers will suggest the following optimal solution. Pay the surcharge on the acre with the farmhouse. Although it is only worth $40,000 to the brokers, a rent of $2,000, the farmer can stipulate a rent of $18,000. The other 19 acres will maintain their $100/acre rent. The total ground rent is $19,900, enough to entitle the farmer's family of 8. The farmer will receive $78,000 cash, $19,900 of which must be used for the 1 year advance payment. Although the cash payment is much smaller than usual as a multiple of rent, the farmer won't complain. Here is why.

Every month the farmer's family of 8 receives $2,960 in housing distribution. The $19,900 annual rent payment is paid from less than 7 months' worth of distributions. The other $15,620 can be used for farmhouse utilities or renovation, building a barn or fence. With $1,780 in food distributions every month, the farmer need never worry about being wiped out by a crop failure. Competing with the big boys becomes an exciting game with a new advantage to the small farmer.

In deluxe land expansion, most problems have solutions. Often we can profit from these solutions better than accounted for on the spreadsheets. However, once our land machine bumps into an apartment building, a new set of problems arise.

The rent on apartment buildings is 1/3 net best-use rents, making the land value 20/3 net best-use rents at 5% interest. If 2 people occupy a 1,000 sq. ft. apartment, and are paying $1,600/month, $1,100 being net rents (EBITDA), then the total net rent is $13,200 a year, and the rent is $4,400 and rent/distribution is $2,200. This deal will go through, regardless of the number of stories, assuming the rents average this for all floors. With 6 apartments/floor and 10 floors on 1/2 acre, the rent is $4,400 * 6 * 10 = $264,000 or $528,000/acre. The landowner would be paid $5,280,000 and the tenants would all be entitled citizens. It is likely the land rights owner has replaced a much smaller property tax with a larger rent, but has $5,280,000 to show for it, which invested at 5% will pay the rent forever. If the landowner also occupied a unit, as they often do, they would even more likely to go for the deal.

Unfortunately, this is a luxury apartment. Far more typically, 2 people will be living in 600 sq. ft. or less, paying $900/month with $400 month in net rent. Total net rent is $4,800 year and ground rent is only $1,600, not even enough for 1 distribution. The total deficit is $2,800 or $233 a month. If this deal is to go through, all the tenants must have a group meeting where they agree to have their apartment rent raised by $250 a month. With the extra $17/month going to the landlord, he stipulates a ground rent of $4,400 per unit. While the tenants' rents have increased to $1,150 a month they receive a housing distribution for two of $740, making the new rent $410/month, saving over half of their former rent. Of course they also get free food, education, and medical care. The landlord's cash payment is based on the original land value, and unless the landlord lives on the premises they might have some reservations.

However, while creative solutions can be found in many instances, none can be found in apartment buildings where people are less well-off than this. For one, the landlord is almost always an absentee landlord. For another, as soon as the tenants got their distributions, they would move on to nicer apartments. There is no way to raise the rent high enough to both stipulate an appropriate ground rent and keep the tenants once they are entitled. This is one reason why there can be no slums in AFFEERCE. However, in Phase-III the goal is to entitle these poor people to begin with at the same time the land is placed in the dominion of the AFFEERCE territories.

The best way to do that is with a charitable fund. Citizens of Prosperity and the AFFEERCE territories, or others can make a possibly U.S. tax deductible contribution to purchase distributions that will be used in conjunction with land purchase.

Suppose an apartment building on half an acre has 1000 sq. ft. apartments with an average of 6 people per apartment. Rent is $1,200/month with $700/month in net rent or $2,800 annual ground rent. That will cover a single distribution, with a little to spare, but what of the other 5 residents in the unit? Assuming that the landlord wants the deal, the charitable fund will purchase their distributions for 50% of full cost. The housing distribution for the six people per unit is $370 x 6 = $2,220 per month, Over $1000 is left for electric after paying the $1,200 rent. Why stay? Many will leave and the landlord will have to tear down walls and convert each 1,000 sq. ft. apartment to a 2,000 sq. ft. apartment to keep the remaining tenants. The new rents can be increased to $2,500/month, increasing the landlords net rent and requiring $230/month out of pocket for tenant rent of a 2,000 sq. ft. luxury apartment; from rags to riches.

The First Few Years of Deluxe Land Expansion

Table 39.2	Number of Distributions	Distribution Cost	Credit Unused Rent	Credit Active Fund	Active Fund	Deluxe Totals
Year 39		0	$4,816,864,052	$0	$69,544,478,476	
Deluxe Land Expansion	48,000	$92,500	($4,440,000,000)	$4,816,864,052	$74,361,342,528	48000
50% full cost entitlement fee	20,000	$101,000	$211,200,000	$1,010,000,000	$75,371,342,528	
Total	591,705	$0	$0	$0	$75,371,342,528	48000
Cost of Distributions		$0	$0	($6,859,043,570)	$68,512,298,958	
Interest at 4%		$0	$0	$2,740,491,958	$71,252,790,916	
Year 40		0	$5,065,426,570	$0	$71,252,790,916	
Deluxe Land Expansion	60,000	$92,500	($5,550,000,000)	$5,065,426,570	$76,318,217,486	60000
50% full cost entitlement fee	20,000	$101,500	$485,760,000	$1,500,760,000	$77,818,977,486	
Total	671,705	$0	$0	$0	$77,818,977,486	110400
Cost of Distributions		$0	$0	($7,786,403,570)	$70,032,573,917	
Interest at 4%		$0	$0	$2,801,302,957	$72,833,876,873	
Year 41		0	$5,318,697,899	$0	$72,833,876,873	
Deluxe Land Expansion	80,000	$92,500	($7,400,000,000)	$5,318,697,899	$78,152,574,772	80000
50% full cost entitlement fee	20,000	$102,000	$862,048,000	$1,882,048,000	$80,034,622,772	
Total	771,705	$0	$0	$0	$80,034,622,772	195920
Cost of Distributions		$0	$0	($8,945,603,570)	$71,089,019,202	
Interest at 4%		$0	$0	$2,843,560,768	$73,932,579,970	
Year 42		0	$5,584,632,794	$0	$73,932,579,970	
Deluxe Land Expansion	90,000	$92,500	($8,325,000,000)	$5,584,632,794	$79,517,212,763	90000
50% full cost entitlement fee	20,000	$103,000	$1,301,150,400	$2,331,150,400	$81,848,363,163	
Total	881,705	$0	$0	$0	$81,848,363,163	295716
Cost of Distributions		$0	$0	($10,220,723,570)	$71,627,639,594	
Interest at 4%		$0	$0	$2,865,105,584	$74,492,745,177	

Table 39.2 – cont.	Number of Distributions	Distribution Cost	Credit Unused Rent	Credit Active Fund	Active Fund	Deluxe Totals
Year 43		0	$5,863,864,433	$0	$74,492,745,177	
Deluxe Land Expansion	90,000	$92,500	($8,325,000,000)	$5,863,864,433	$80,356,609,610	90000
50% full cost entitlement fee	20,000	$103,500	$1,762,207,920	$2,797,207,920	$83,153,817,530	
Total	991,705	$0	$0	$0	$83,153,817,530	400502
Cost of Distributions		$0	$0	($11,495,843,570)	$71,657,973,961	
Interest at 4%		$0	$0	$2,866,318,958	$74,524,292,919	
Year 44		0	$6,157,057,655	$0	$74,524,292,919	
Deluxe Land Expansion	30,000	$93,500	($2,805,000,000)	$6,157,057,655	$80,681,350,574	30000
50% full cost entitlement fee	20,000	$104,000	$1,982,318,316	$3,022,318,316	$83,703,668,890	
Total	1,041,705	$0	$0	$0	$83,703,668,890	450527
Cost of Distributions		$0	$0	($12,075,443,570)	$71,628,225,320	
Interest at 4%		$0	$0	$2,865,129,013	$74,493,354,333	
Year 45	(10,905)	0	$6,464,910,538	$0	$74,493,354,333	
Deluxe Land Expansion	40,000	$93,500	($3,740,000,000)	$6,464,910,538	$80,958,264,870	40000
50% full cost entitlement fee	20,000	$105,000	$2,257,434,232	$3,307,434,232	$84,265,699,102	
Total	1,090,800	$0	$0	$0	$84,265,699,102	513053
Cost of Distributions		$0	$0	($12,644,552,810)	$71,621,146,292	
Interest at 4%		$0	$0	$2,864,845,852	$74,485,992,144	

In Year 39, 48,000 were added from deluxe land expansion. In Year 40, that was increased to 60,000. Notice that the active fund is increasing after the distributions in each year from $68.5 billion in Year 39 to $70 billion in Year 40. Optimally, we want the size of the active fund to always increase or remain constant. We also want the number of distributions issued for deluxe land expansion to slowly increase from year to year without having to back-off the numbers significantly in some years to catch up. In this model we had to back off from 90,000 distributions to 30,000 distributions between Years 43 and 44 to keep the active fund, after distributions, at $71.6 billion. Mathematicians can determine the optimal formula; however the spreadsheets are sufficient for the model. "What if" variations produce results that are within a 10% variance. The ground rents have a much greater effect on the result than how many distributions are allocated each year.

Average present value per distribution is determined by average age. $92,500 in the Distribution Cost column, when the average age is 40 and $93,500 when the average age is 39. Those who want entitled citizenship with no land to sell (and who aren't tenants on land for sale) must purchase the distributions at 50% of the Phase-II price. In Year 39, $101,000 is the cost for a 29 year old, the average age for those seeking to purchase the distributions in that year. Many of these purchases are for children of entitled citizens leading to a lower average age every year.

Each year we have 95% of the ground rent proceeds to work with. This goes from $4.816 million + $0.211 million in Year 39 to $6.464 million + $2.257 million in Year 45. The first number is the current ground rents from Prosperity and the AFFEERCE territories at the end of Phase-II and the second number is the ground rents from deluxe land expansion. These numbers appear in the Credit Unused Rent column on the Year line and 50% Full Entitlement Cost line, although these available ground rents are unrelated to those lines. The ground rent on the Year line is added directly to the active fund. The ground rent on the 50% Full Entitlement Cost line is added to the proceeds from these purchases and then added to the active fund. The debit in red between the two ground rents is the amount that must be added to the active fund to pay for deluxe land expansion. This number should be less than the total of the ground rents, purchases at 50% full entitlement cost, and interest at 4% or the active fund will fall.

The Deluxe Totals column is used to keep track of the total number of entitled citizens from deluxe land expansion adjusted for the 5% annual increase in ground rents. The number on the total line is used to compute the ground rents for deluxe land expansion found on the previous line.

There is another very interesting feature of Year 45. Notice the red (10,905) in the number of distributions column. The first auction will be in Year 21, so this is the 24th year that distributions have been given out. Early homesteaders are now in their 70s or 80s. The first affeercianados are in 60s, and the dear author of this book is long gone. The (10,905) are being killed off in Year 45, dropped from the distribution rolls. Every year thereafter, we conservatively assume that 1% of the entitled citizens will die. Should science and technology significantly increase our lifespan, it will take longer to reach our goals. But then it won't matter so much.

Starting in Year 40, there is no more data for the ground rent. Due to increases in population, ground rent efficiency, business objects, the growing university, our pegged currency, distributions, affeercianado labor, and all the other mercantile advantages, we can assume land values will increase. Table 39.2 is assuming a 5% a year increase for lands acquired prior to Phase-III deluxe land expansion, and 5% a year for lands monetized during the expansion, in as much as they are cheap to begin with. This is likely very conservative.

In the following separate analysis of ground rent from deluxe land expansion for rural residential, rent almost 50% higher than accounted for in the spreadsheet is predicted. Rural land has far less than 1 person per acre. Rural residential is defined as 1 person for every five acres[FTN10.28]. Conservatively, 30,000 citizenships can buy us 50,000 acres. Assume that 60% is cropland or pastureland with an insignificant rent and a $2,000 surcharge. Assume that 30% is residential land with $5,000 rent, 9% has a $10,000 "safe" rent and 1% is town centers with $100,000 average ground rent. This territory contributes 15,000 x $5,000 + 4,500 x $10,000 + 500 x $100,000 in rent. ($75 million + $45 million + $50 million = $170 million). This is versus $132 million using the $4,400 per distribution average in the spreadsheets.

Year 46

Political Control of the Host-State
It is predicted that by Year 46, if not before, the AFFEERCE party will control the state legislature, the governor's office, the congressional delegation and both senators. Although it is impossible to know the issues of Year 46, there are several important ones we can assume. Some will require a state constitutional convention.

Reconfigure the State as a Cellular Democracy
In order to have all the technology in place to handle the new nation, after capitulation, the embryonic host-state must be federated into a cellular democracy by Year 46. That way, political and economic structures can be put in place and tested.

Existing jurisdictions should be mimicked as closely as possible. Most cities and towns will be structured as districts composed of one or more cells at level-3. Cells at level-3 have populations from 6,831 to 29,469 with an average of 15,400. Counties and large cities at level-4 are districts composed of cells at level-4. Level-4 cells have populations from 75,141 to 324,159 with an average 169,400.

Level-2 districts can mimic existing districts. If city council members are elected from these districts, then a seamless transition with the same council is possible. If they are elected at large, then unless coincidence places them all in different districts, or they are appointed by the cell councils into a governing district, the city government will change.

Prosperity is declared a level-5 cell from the beginning. Such a cell has from 826,551 to 3,565,749 with an average of 1,863,400. If the host-state has a total population of fewer than 3 million the Prosperity governing council will be the new state government. The actual governing of Prosperity as a large city will fall to its proper place in the hierarchy. If the host-state population exceeds 3.5 million residents, mitosis will create 2 level-5 cells that will combine into a district governing council. The state governing council would hire a governor, very possibly the incumbent if elected on the AFFEERCE party ticket, and other state executives.

Once the cellular structure is established, owners of border properties can shift their allegiance and hence their distribution funds to a neighboring cell. Trebler wars can be used to carve out dominion. Rapidly changing boundaries, mitosis and fusion, will kill off unhealthy cells and lead to the healthiest possible cellular federation.

Lower the State Income Tax as Citizens Become Entitled

The state income tax is eliminated in proportion to the number of entitled citizens. When the number of entitled citizens rises to 100%, the state income tax will drop to zero.

Implement an AFFEERCE Penitentiary System

Judges will be required to sentence entitled citizens to humane, often family run, small penitentiaries. $30/month from the offender's cash distribution will be sent to the victim by law during incarceration. The judge can invite the victim to be a recipient of the specially created Victim's Discretionary Fund for a period of time from 1 day to 1 year. During that time, all discretionary allocations to the Victim's Discretionary Fund from the 2% discretionary consumption tax will be distributed equally to the recipients. Victims can receive discretionary compensation as individuals for any amount or time, independently of the specially established Victim's Discretionary Fund. Fraudulent use of the Victim's Discretionary Fund will be rigorously prosecuted.

Voluntary Standards Groups

Counties at level-4 will each appoint a consumer senator to the Bureau of Standards at level-5. The senators are responsible for creating the voluntary standards groups, often at the request of industry. Industry requires standards groups, so they can deviate from those standards without liability, by posting those deviations in a Violation of Standards document, or VOS, in a manner specified by the group.

The Bureau of Standards is not funded from the government distribution. Businesses and special interest groups who wish to have a member on a VSG will pay dues that support the Bureau of Standards, and support a corresponding consumer advocate hired by the consumer senators. There is always exactly the same number of paid consumer advocates as dues paying members in any VSG.

The civil judiciary will use the VOS as the new standard of liability, and problems in the VSG-VOS system will be ironed out in the remainder of Phase-III and Phase-IV. See *Volume-I* for complete details on the Bureau of Standards, VSG and VOS.

Within cells, specific standards violations can be outlawed by a 2/3 plurality of the population (Class-II legislation). Municipal liability shall be limited to a 2 week salary pool as described in *Volume-I* with new emphasis on the discretionary tax for victims of police and prosecutorial misconduct.

Despite being overridden by federal regulations, most liability is still handled at the state level, so the pre-capitulation VSGs should be quite popular with industry, and a magnet to attract new industry into the embryonic nation.

Other Land Trusts

At this point, if we have been successful, other embryos have likely developed in other states. As long as the currency in other embryos is backed by land value at transfer to the commons and pegged to the U.S. dollar, the embryos are fundamentally the same, regardless of political structure and the nature of the distributions.

Full consolidation need only occur at the capitulation, although there should be many opportunities for political and technological synergy. The upcoming constitutional convention must include representatives from all embryos that share this monetary basis, and possibly others if they are reconcilable.

Constitutional Convention

Once the state is restructured as a cellular democracy, it is time to begin serious discussion on the capitulation package. This is a package of constitutional amendments that the citizens of the United States must pass to extend our democratic, free and prosperous host-state to the rest of the nation. It will be based on the proposed constitution designed during the very first days of the AFFEERCE Benefit Corporation, and augmented by 46 years of wisdom.

Convention delegates are elected by the Affeercianado Guild. They must tackle any serious disagreements that remain, both internally, and with other embryonic nations. Today it appears that one of those issues might be the baby tax. Can it be nominal to start with? Does the Treasury have the authority to raise it or lower it, and if so, by how much? Another issue concerns the details of moving from the current federation structure of the United States to a cellular democracy. Land compensation is also apt to be very controversial. One year advance payment of the ground rent is proposed. The classifications of laws into Classes I, II, III, and unconstitutional versus the current binary constitutional and unconstitutional, along with preliminary judicial review, are new roles for the judiciary that must be worked into the constitution. Rogue states, even with the treble option are likely to draw heated debate. Most important are the rules for collection and distribution of the rent, as this is the essence of AFFEERCE. The prohibition on raising revenue outside of direct democratic ratification by a 2/3 super-plurality of the dominion might need specification beyond the three class of legislation.

There are many other issues constitutional scholars must address. The convention will be open-ended. It might last several years. The document must be logically sound, consistent and minimal. Items best dealt with through representative or direct democracy should not litter the document.

Capitulation draws nigh

By Year 46, the mercantile advantage of Prosperity and the AFFEERCE territories will be felt around the United States. It will be deflationary for the U.S. and not in a good way. For most of our history, Prosperity's prosperity has enhanced national prosperity. But as a majority of the gross national product comes to originate from within our relatively tiny borders, it will start to impede the rest of the economy. High unemployment in much of the nation will make the full employment and great riches of Prosperity seem like streets paved with gold. Regardless of any philosophical differences people have with AFFEERCE, they will want to move to Prosperity and the territories, or at least the host-state so they can be rescued through deluxe land expansion.

However, land in the host-state has become very expensive. We are paying a minimum of $40,000/acre for undeveloped non-farmland in deluxe land expansion. There are no vacancies because we have moderated population growth with land speculation. When new buildings are built, there are only enough units for the wealthy. Rental profits are returned to the people through deluxe land expansion, the distributions, and citizens' dividends, so those who are already residents grow wealthier with the increased land value, while those outside our borders can less and less afford to cross them.

The VIP$, still pegged 2:1 to the dollar, is much undervalued. We are importing U.S. goods at deflated prices, and our drive for import replacement has allowed us to be very selective.

It is very likely the people of the United States will demand capitulation soon, but there are at least 12 more years of work to be done.

Win-Win Bonds

The mercantile advantage or dollarnado fills the AFFEERCE Central Bank with dollars. What should we do with that money? We could buy gold, but there is something far more valuable to Prosperity than gold or U.S. Treasuries as they are now structured. They are Win-Win bonds. These instruments are 5-10 year bonds issued by the United States Treasury and purchased by the AFFEERCE Central Bank. This is a dream bond for the United States government if they intend on getting their fiscal house in order. It is also a pipe dream. Insurmountable obstacles prevent the United States from ever paying off its debt without monetization.

The bonds pay 0% interest as long as the United States does not run a deficit. However, if the revenues of the United States are 2% less than the expenses, the bonds pay 2% in the following year. If, in the year after that, the revenues of the United States are 2% greater than expenses all the interest paid by the United States government is returned to them. In every year of a surplus, previously paid interest is returned until the net interest rate is back to 0%.

But why would the AFFEERCE Central Bank want to spend their dollars on an instrument that is designed to pay no interest at all? Gold pays no interest, so the return on both is the same. Inflation is not likely without a deficit, and a deficit pays interest. Actually the effect of Prosperity on the U.S. economy will be deflationary, so offering to purchase a 0% interest bond is the least we can do.

There are fundamental reasons why Win-Win bonds are the most valuable use of Central Bank dollars. At capitulation, the first task is to pay off the debt of the United States government. Capitulation will not occur without some debt monetization, but the Win-Win bonds will minimize the assault on the U.S. dollar, and ultimately the VIP$. Post-capitulation AFFEERCE is a zero inflation economy which effectively increases the interest rate on debt. The best way to pay off the debt is to own the debt and then cancel the debt. The VIP dollar will be supported going forward by the fixed supply of all U.S. land.

There are also significant political advantages in purchasing U.S. debt. Because every dollar we take in will be used to retire the debt of the United States, the U.S. Government is more likely to tolerate, even support, our legal experiment. They are more likely to tolerate an open VIP window, and even allow us to gain some control over the economy. An open VIP window is only an issue at the end of Phase-III. The mercantile advantage will cause wealth to move to Prosperity regardless of U.S. government policy. As the AFFEERCE economy continues to grow, the 2:1 ratio will not hold forever, and an open VIP window will be a category-5 dollarnado.

An open VIP window will cause deflation in the United States unless the United States is running a deficit. However, a deficit will create an interest obligation on the Win-Win bonds. The only way out of this quagmire is for the United States to increase its productivity to the level of AFFEERCE or close the VIP window. We will oblige if they request the latter and the IRS accepts a frozen 2:1 VIP$/Dollar ratio. Trying the former will not be pretty. If the U.S. eliminates the minimum wage without distributions, it will be tragic and could lead to violence. That will not bode well for AFFEERCE either.

Nor can the United States implement the distributions. For one, they don't have the VIP infrastructure. Without the VIP, the distributions would be a fraud-laden bureaucratic nightmare of unheard of proportions. Secondly, the distributions are unaffordable from tax revenue. People will forget that most of our citizens paid a significant portion of the cost of their own distributions. Furthermore, they were awarded over several decades. In addition, the skills auctions brought in top notch producers, brilliant individuals, skilled craftsmen, and others who produce more than they consume.

There is another option. The United States Congress has the authority to print currency, but it hasn't used this authority since the Civil War. Few people realize that today our money is created by the banks whenever they make a loan. If the United States implements universal distribution with Treasury produced debt-free cash, we should applaud the move. It would be a great step forward for the U.S., but unlikely to be approved by the banks.[FTN46.01] Of course, VIP$ is a debt-free currency. Unlike the U.S, the VIP$ is back by land in the commons and U.S. dollar assets in the Central Bank. Until capitulation, that is inviolable.

Could the United State implement selective distribution sufficient to match AFFEERCE guarantees? Beyond the diminished productivity that results from reducing entitlements for large families, conditions placed on entitlement multiply many-fold the fraud and bureaucracy.

It will be a worthwhile goal to keep the United States happy and prosperous until at least the end of Phase-IV when we are ready for capitulation.

Years 55 – 58

The End of Phase-III

Table 55.1	Number of Distributions	Distribution Cost	Credit Unused Rent	Unused Rent	Credit Active Fund	Active Fund	Deluxe Totals
Year 55	(22,379)	0	$10,530,658,037		$0	$74,616,690,246	
Deluxe Land Expansion	180,000	$93,500	($16,830,000,000)	$10,530,658,037	$85,147,348,283		180000
50% full cost entitlement fee	20,000	$113,500	$8,176,605,976	$9,311,605,976	$94,458,954,259		
Total	1,992,851	$0	$0	$0	$94,458,954,259		1858320
Cost of Distributions		$0	$0	($23,101,128,002)	$71,357,826,257		
Interest at 4%		$0	$0	$2,854,313,050	$74,212,139,308		
Year 56	(26,835)	0	$11,057,190,939		$0	$74,212,139,308	
Deluxe Land Expansion	714,000	$92,500	($66,045,000,000)	$11,057,190,939	$85,269,330,247		714000
50% full cost entitlement fee	20,000	$113,500	$11,727,036,275	$12,862,036,275	$98,131,366,522		
Total	2,700,016	$0	$0	$0	$98,131,366,522		2665236
Cost of Distributions		$0	$0	($31,298,584,682)	$66,832,781,840		
Interest at 4%		$0	$0	$2,673,311,274	$69,506,093,113		
Year 57	(27,062)	0	$11,610,050,486		$0	$69,506,093,113	
Deluxe Land Expansion	0	$0	$0	$11,610,050,486	$81,116,143,599		0
Lower taxes	0		$0	$0	$81,116,143,599		
$50,000 flat rate	50,000	$50,000	$12,538,453,620	$15,038,453,620	$96,154,597,219		
Total	2,722,954	$0	$0	$0	$96,154,597,219		2849649
Cost of Distributions		$0	$0	($31,564,481,978)	$64,590,115,241		
Interest at 4%		$0	$0	$2,583,604,610	$67,173,719,851		
Year 58	(27,293)	0	$12,190,553,010		$0	$67,173,719,851	
Deluxe Land Expansion	0	$0	$0	$12,190,553,010	$79,364,272,861		0
Lower taxes	0	$0	$0	$0	$79,364,272,861		
$50,000 flat rate	50,000	$50,000	$13,135,522,840	$15,635,522,840	$94,999,795,701		
Total	2,745,661	$0	$0	$0	$94,999,795,701		2985346
Cost of Distributions		$0	$0	($31,827,701,522)	$63,172,094,180		
Interest at 4%		$0	$0	$2,526,883,767	$65,698,977,947		

In year 55, deluxe land expansion entitles a projected 180,000 citizens. Notice that we still maintain an active fund of $71.3 million. The total entitled population is 1,992,851. We are still quite a bit shy of the 2.7 million population goal. Because the active fund has been kept at $71 million, there is enough money to entitle the rest of the state in the final year. In Year 56, 714,000 new distributions are issued, covering most citizens in the state. At least 95% of state lands are in the commons. The present value of these distributions based on a 20 year term is $66 billion, with ground rents and interest only accounting for $26 billion. However, deluxe land expansion is over, and all of the ground rents can now be used to pay the distributions. Those 714,000 newly entitled citizens only add $8.2 billion to the distributions.

A third is covered by new ground rents, and in a few years, the 5% annual increase in all ground rents will make up the difference.

With a final entitled citizenship tally of 2.7 million, the host-state might have been Wyoming, Vermont, Alaska, North or South Dakota, Delaware, Montana, Rhode Island, New Hampshire, Maine, Hawaii, Idaho, West Virginia, Nebraska or New Mexico. For most of those states, Phase-III would have ended much sooner.

Phase-IV

Years 59 – 60

In Table 55.1, the active fund drops from $71 billion to $66.8 billion in Year 56. In Year 57, it drops to $64.5 billion. In Year 58, it drops to $63.1 billion. In table 59.1, in Year 59 it drops to $62.6 billion. In Year 60, the active fund stabilizes at $62.6 billion. In fact, it would have increased, were it not for another feature, zero-sum that will be discussed shortly.

With an active fund of $62.6 billion, there is plenty of investment capital for citizens to start new enterprises (as long as too much has not been used for mortgages). The Mercantile Letter will be promoting business objects for import replacement, and citizen investors will help families or collectives perfect the business plan needed to implement these business objects.

Following deluxe land expansion, it is time to start Phase-IV, the final phase before capitulation. In Year 57, the 50% full cost entitled citizenship is replaced by a simple $50,000 fee, easily paid by a 2nd mortgage. This is of great benefit for newborns and young children whose price of distribution is as high as $115,000 under the 50% method. Priority will go to family of citizens, then residents by years of residency, and finally new residents. To control growth, there will be a limit of 50,000 new distributions per year during Phase-IV.

Table 59.1	Number of Distributions	Distribution Cost	Credit Unused Rent	Unused Rent	Credit Active Fund	Active Fund	Deluxe Totals
Year 59	(27,518)	0	$12,800,080,661		$0	$65,698,977,947	
Deluxe Land Expansion	0	$0	$0	$0	$12,800,080,661	$78,499,058,608	0
Lower taxes	0	$0	$0	$0	$0	$78,499,058,608	
$50,000 flat rate	50,000	$50,000	$13,732,592,060	$16,232,592,060		$94,731,650,668	
Total	2,768,143	$0		$0	$0	$94,731,650,668	3121044
Cost of Distributions		$0		$0	($32,088,312,866)	$62,643,337,802	
Interest at 4%		$0		$0	$2,505,733,512	$65,149,071,314	
Year 60	(27,740)	0	$13,440,084,694		$0	$65,149,071,314	
Deluxe Land Expansion	0	$0		$0	$13,440,084,694	$78,589,156,008	0
Lower taxes	0	$0		$0	($429,290,000)	$78,159,866,008	
$50,000 flat rate	50,000	$50,000	$14,329,661,280	$16,829,661,280		$94,989,527,288	
Total	2,790,403	$0		$0	$0	$94,989,527,288	3256741
Cost of Distributions		$0		$0	($32,346,350,786)	$62,643,176,502	
Interest at 4%		$0		$0	$2,505,727,060	$65,148,903,562	

Notice that in Year 60, in order to keep the active fund from rising, $429 million dollars had to be subtracted. Although all of this excess could be distributed as a citizens' dividend, there is a better use of the funds more consistent with the handling of rent collection after capitulation. The embryonic nation is a laboratory for the full AFFEERCE nation and it is in everyone's interest to make that transition as seamless as possible.

The theory of rent collection is discussed in detail in Volume I. The main idea is a fixed distribution package, and a fixed rent rate of fall, with the excess going into a citizens' dividend. It is also called zero-sum and our land-rights owners will be very pleased to see it implemented.

Zero-Sum

Things change. Areas that were once hot will start to run down. In a free market, prices fall as well as rise. Up until Year 59, we have relied on a massive increase in land value generally to float all boats. For instance, a hot area back in Year 7, with a rent of $60,000/acre, will still have a ground rent of at least $60,000/acre in Year 59, but the hot areas in Year 59 could have a rent of $420,000/acre.

In Year 60, it is time to allow ground rent on individual properties to fall. This is done with a rent rate-of-fall multiplier, a concept essential to an AFFEERCE economy, and discussed in *Volume-I*. To summarize, when any land rights owner trebles or raises their own ground rent, the taxes on all other properties where the owner has not frozen the ground rent drop accordingly, so the total rent collected by the citizens is unchanged. This is adjusted for new population in excess of zero population growth.

However, to prevent explosive trebling, the rent rate of fall is limited to a certain percentage of the ground rents. In Volume I, we assume a post-capitulation AFFEERCE rent rate of fall multiplier of 10%. That is, non-frozen rents will drop by up to 10%/year with any excess funds going to a citizens' dividend.

Zero-sum leads to far more efficient use of land, prevents defaults, and is predicted to lead to far more trebling for hot properties, cellular dominion and aristocratic title. This will result in a more exuberant economy, lower rent and greater citizens' dividends for the average person.

With zero-sum implemented in Year 60, the $429 million of excess rent is only about 1.5% of the $30 billion in ground rents, so all of it will likely be used to reduce rents of non-frozen properties. In Year 61, if capitulation has not yet occurred, there will likely be enough excess for a citizens' dividend, particularly since trebling will increase once rents start to drop.

There are 4 common reasons why rents should drop:

1. The area is no longer hot, and there are more efficient treble-safe rents.
2. The land rights owner wants to encourage treble/seizure or simple purchase by lowering taxes.
3. The land rights owner has sufficient liquid assets to benefit from treble/match.
4. The land rights owner is short on cash and willing to take their chances.

For purpose of illustration, assume that only 8% want to see their rents lowered, although that number will likely be much higher in the first year or so until the drawbacks become evident. Recall the total rent collected in Year 60 is $30.2 billion. Of that, $429 million is available to lower rents.

Although also unlikely, assume for illustration an even distribution of ground rent for those who wish to see their rents lowered. The ground rent for this 8% is $2.416 billion. These rents could be lowered by $429 million to $1.987 billion. However, this would be an 18% drop, and the drop is limited to 10%. Instead, $241.6 million would be used to lower rents and $187.4 million would fund a citizens' dividend. Given a 10% rent rate of fall, rents will return to pre-treble values in about 12 years.

Prior to this, all citizens' dividends have come from surpluses of local government operation. By Year 60, the number of active affeercianados will be dropping, decreasing government surpluses from cheap labor. Surprisingly, the labor from those affeercianados remaining will be even cheaper than before. With so many of the original affeercianados deceased by Year 60, the size of the final annuities remaining will be very large and every boost in land value can produce a significant boost in income, making it possible to have CDs from multiple sources.

Pre-capitulation AFFEERCE

The entire host state is a thriving AFFEERCE economy by Year 58. The state will be a cellular democracy with judicial determination of Class I, II, and III legislation. Most of the land in the state will be monetized with perhaps a few percent still left to be developed for the benefit of living affeercianados and heirs to the original investors.

There will be full employment, but many jobs will be an apprenticeship toward full partnership in a collective, paying nothing in the first few months. Other jobs will be service jobs for federal minimum wage. Newcomers will find it impossible to survive on these wages, as they compete with affeercianados and citizens seeking discretionary income, without the benefit of distribution or a citizens' dividend. Only skilled professionals can afford to move to the host state, thrive, and quickly purchase entitled citizenship.

Begging and theft of cash are not options. This is a completely cashless society. A VIP identity is required for all transactions. There is no underground dollar trade, as dollars have all been consumed by the dollarnado. As best as we can under U.S. Federal law, drugs are legal in those cells where a 2/3 plurality has not restricted their use, or a 5/6 plurality has not outlawed them altogether. There will be no street corner pushers. There will be neither demand nor supply.

In rare cases, tourists will come to Prosperity, blow all their money on drugs or gambling, and have no way of getting home. Because of the VIP identity, we can offer a good meal and a plane ticket back to where they are from, with the caveat that they are prohibited from entering AFFEERCE territories again until the money is repaid. If they do show up again without settling accounts, the VIP will lead to their immediate capture, and the penalty will be to be impressed into the affeercianado apprentice program for a probationary 6 months.

If they pass probation and wish to remain an affeercianado, they can go through a four year apprenticeship earning 50% land credits. At the end of four years, they will receive all affeercianado pay and benefits, and a new life. Otherwise, we will extract from their severance all money owed for the previous air fare, a fine, and money for the next airfare. They will be escorted to the airport and placed on a plane to their former destination.

Our penitentiaries are only for entitled citizens. Being impressed into the affeercianado apprentice program is only an option for misdemeanors. While we prefer deportation for non-entitled felons, a state or country must be willing to accept them. If not, and if the felon cannot pay the full cost of entitled citizenship, they will be sentenced to one of the older prisons where conditions are only as good as the inmate labor can support, and minimum federal regulations require.

Productivity and Taxes

As long as the central bank is selling VIP$ for 50 cents, the value of a VIP$ cannot rise above 50 cents. However, as AFFEERCE productivity increases, prices at VIP retail outlets will drop below those at U.S. retail outlets, especially since non-citizens do not pay the consumption tax. People will trade their U.S. dollars for VIP dollars at an alarming rate to buy products at AFFEERCE stores.

Deflation in the rest of the United States could become a serious problem around Year 57. The Win-Win bonds we started purchasing in Year 46 will prevent the United States from monetizing the deflation. It is not in our interest to strangle our future country. The important question is, "Are we ready for capitulation?" If the answer is no, then U.S. economic discontent is not in our interests. AFFEERCE has only made the U.S. economy stronger and it is the U.S. economy that we will inherit at capitulation.

In exchange for a promise from the IRS to freeze the VIP$: dollar ratio at 2:1 for tax purposes, we will close the VIP window at the central bank (figurative, of course) and allow the VIP$ to float against the U.S. dollar. As a benefit to us, the $600 U.S. withdrawal from the AFFEERCE Central Bank per citizen for U.S. Income Tax can then be purchased more cheaply on the open market. Any remaining dollar outflow from the Central Bank will cease.

Who Wants Capitulation?

Throughout the United States, people will be in awe of a Prosperity that rises from the prairie like an Emerald City of Oz, with wealth rivaling Manhattan, Singapore, and Hong Kong, and no poverty at all. In the AFFEERCE territories throughout the rest of the state, cellular democracies, trebler wars, dominions, aristocracy, and never before seen families and collectives producing wealth to their own drummer will tickle the fancy of young people starved for freedom and adventure in the decaying political economies elsewhere.

When a group of people from a wide area of the social and political spectrum want an event to occur, arguing from a variety of different perspectives, some even contradictory, the event becomes inevitable.

We saw those different perspectives with gay marriage where conservatives argued it would reduce disease and create family stability, liberals argued it was a question of equal rights and justice, and radicals argued it would radically alter the patriarchal family structure. It was the existence of many diverse arguments that created change.

Here we examine several diverse groups and their arguments for AFFEERCE.

Aging hippies and radical leftists will want AFFEERCE. They can go off and start communes where Marx's dream of "from each according to their ability, to each according to their need" is reality. They can sell their organic produce, grow their own weed, make love freely (with contraception), and enjoy utopia.

Libertarians and conservatives will want AFFEERCE. Never has enterprise been so free. They can start businesses and pay no corporate taxes, with a VOS to protect them from liability, and no regulations except where children are concerned, and no minimum wage. The ground rent is self-assessed and although not a tax, is similar to what Milton Friedman called "the least bad tax." There is no consumption tax for domestic capital expenditures. Gun control will likely be relaxed in the major cities where it now tends to be severe. Local VIP identity can be used to restrict gun use to specified shooters. Government must work within a budget. Only a super plurality of the population has access to the purse strings, and even then the tax must be explicitly earmarked and have a duration of no more than 2 years. Only a super plurality of the population can pass legislation that mediates a conflict in natural rights.

The wealthiest 1% will want AFFEERCE. There are no longer any constraints against the concentration of capital. In fact, it is encouraged. There is a sea of labor, freed by the distributions to work at wages that are more efficient than current automation, or to fill jobs that now do not even exist. Free rapid transit makes the workforce more mobile. Billions of dollars in corporate profits can be repatriated back to the United States without paying a penny of tax. Factories abroad can be brought back to the United States and reopened far more efficiently. And the males in this top 1%, and with genetic advances, soon the females, will be able to take on hundreds of partners, and have thousands of progeny.

The bottom 50% will want AFFEERCE. There will be no more worries about food, shelter, medical bills or sending the kids to college. Crime in the neighborhood will be virtually wiped out. The gangs will be out of business with drugs legalized and taxed. The stress of losing a job will no longer exist, and there are an unlimited number of lower paying jobs to bring in discretionary income. There will be plenty of charities to provide secondhand clothing and furniture, not covered by the distributions. Education will be free and unlimited. Almost anyone with enough drive can complete the courses needed for a high paying job. And families can join together into large alternative families for bountiful feasts, luxury accommodations, and the combined means to have many children. It will end the holocaust of unemployment and imprisonment in the poor black community.

Liberals and moderates will want AFFEERCE Freedom is greatly expanded, not only in business, but the freedom to end one's life, to take any pharmaceutical, to form a family of one's own design, to engage in prostitution, and to gamble. The democratic process is expanded to allow direct participatory democracy through the VIP. A vasectomy with an on/off switch frees the male from unwanted responsibility and allows reproductive control without violating a woman's right to choose. Foreign wars are no longer paid for with taxpayer dollars, and must be approved by a 2/3 majority of the citizens (majority for UN sanctioned wars). Foreign military bases must be privately financed. There is no more Department of Homeland Security. Penitentiaries are humane and rehabilitative. There is no death penalty (unless passed in a constitutional amendment). Everyone has all necessities provided. A discretionary tax can support favorite charities, heroes, and victims. The right to protest against discrimination is expanded with two new rights, the right to collude and the right to deny service. The jitney transportation revolution will cut carbon emissions significantly.

The religious right will want AFFEERCE. It is true they will lose all their influence over reproductive policies of the government. However, within their own families they can require abstinence before marriage, however they define marriage. Within their communities, if supported by a 5/6 plurality, they can institute Biblical law (as long as the adult right to leave is respected along with the child's right to life). Atheism will likely no longer be the de facto position of science, as philosophies integrating teleological explanations gain a footing (See *Volume III – Philosophy*). The freedom of a community to engage in any celebration or public display they wish cannot be stopped except by a 2/3 plurality. The right to protest is protected, but few would protest a nativity scene or cross in the public square or the Ten Commandments in a courthouse if a court of law won't give them the time of day. Most importantly, and this applies to the religious left as well as the religious right, the distributions give every person the opportunity to devote their life to God. Church families can support a minister in style. Monasteries, nunneries, and other religious orders can be self-sufficient and do significant charitable work with the extra resources from distributions. Even a group of street preachers can form a small family and have all the resources to spread the gospel.

Gays, lesbians and the differently gendered will want AFFEERCE. In AFFEERCE, the alternative family will likely be the norm. Reproduction and adoption rights can never be denied anyone who can raise the baby tax and who respects the rights of the child. Most importantly, LGBT people are the leaders in new forms of family Historically they have been spiritual leaders, teachers and healers. They have produced while others have reproduced. They have created while others have procreated. Families with LGBT members will prosper from the diversity. They will add a subtle balance that cannot be achieved with only masculine heterosexual men and feminine heterosexual women. Gay men and women define a new egalitarian sexuality that can grow beyond two individuals. As such, they are harbingers of a pansexual future. For gay men, lesbians and the differently gendered, capitulation is to emerge from the desert and arrive in the Promised Land.

Women will want AFFEERCE. Women have never before had all the options available to them that will be available in AFFEERCE. Old prejudices that claim a woman's place is in the home, raising children, will disappear completely with reproductive control, large alternative families and the acceptance of LGBT people into families. The baby tax, specifically, will end pressure on women to have children, and prevent the nightmare of young girls being forced into pregnancy. Alternative families and reproductive freedom give women the option of career, being the biological mother, the birth mother, the rearing mother, or any combination thereof. Genetic advances will even give women the option of paternity. All contraceptive and reproductive services are free, including removal of contraceptive devices. There is free abortion on demand in the first trimester. Because having a vasectomy with an on/off switch will enhance male freedom, reproductive control will emphasize this form of contraception as both safer and less intrusive than chemicals. Women (and men) have the right to sell their own bodies for sex and otherwise.

So who will oppose AFFEERCE and capitulation?

There are those whose wealth is enhanced by monopoly and regulation. Doctors and lawyers' salaries are protected from competition by those who could not afford a minimum of eight years of schooling. Today, vague definitions of liability enhance both medical and legal income. Medical professionals profit from the additional testing done to prevent malpractice. Lawyers are able to extract large settlements that are ultimately paid for by the general population, on the slippery slope of liability. In AFFEERCE, education is free and unlimited. Curriculums can be specialized without requiring an 8+ year commitment. The VOS allows less qualified people to compete at a much lower price where the qualifications seem absurd for the job at hand. The VOS defines liability. Lawsuits against the government have limited liability and that liability is against the salaries of police, prosecutors, government officials, or streets and sanitation workers, and for no more than a two week period.

Doctors who truly care about their patients and saving lives will welcome capitulation. Patients will be free of the economic burdens that can interfere with recuperation. Doctors will be free of the bill collecting nightmares and can deal with their patients as human beings, not potential deadbeats. Doctors will still be well-respected and well-paid. If they went into medicine to help people, capitulation will be a blessing. If they went into medicine to soak the general population, it will be a curse.

Lawyers who are truly interested in fighting injustice will welcome capitulation. The distributions allow a lawyer to launch a crusade for the innocent or a victim, even though there will be no reward for years. While some liability might be limited to less than what seems a just reward, the discretionary tax is used to reward heroes and victims alike. The VOS makes the definition of liability far more clear. Public defenders will have higher real wages than they do today, and prosecutors, police and victims, can share in the large fines paid in lieu of years of imprisonment. Suits that are designed to pay an individual lawyer more than any of the plaintiffs will be abolished. The AFFEERCE legal system will cherish honesty as a value. Lawyers will work to get lower fines, the best possible sentences and maximum rehabilitation for their guilty clients. AFFEERCE penitentiaries will not be hellholes. They offer a chance for spiritual rebirth and education. Lawyers that invent hypothetical scenarios in court they know to be false will be in contempt. Lawyers that suggest a plea bargain for a person claiming innocence will likewise be liable. It is the AFFEERCE lawyer's responsibility to find the best truth for their client. It is the AFFEERCE prosecutor's responsibility to find the best truth for the people. Intentional lies from either side are crimes or torts. After capitulation, lawyers will be more respected. Many will have a better salary than they have today. For idealist lawyers, capitulation will be a blessing. For ambulance chasers and those who went into law to soak the rich, it will be a curse.

Those who make huge sums off financial weapons of mass destruction might be relieved that their crimes have been halted when a 50% reserve ratio puts an end to those instruments and ushers in an era where the standard return on capital is less than 5%.

Fear Not the Giant Corporate Predators

Some have expressed concern that the major corporate owners of the United States will put a stop to AFFEERCE. Perhaps I'm being naïve, but I don't think so. In the beginning, AFFEERCE will be too insignificant for notice. As it proves its viability, I can't help but think that all of us, rich and poor, will welcome liberation from the chains of this political economy. Why do corporations act with such little concern for humanity and the environment? They must act because the competition acts. They have no power to do otherwise; like President Obama, whose "hope and change" were lost because he was powerless to stop a train speeding toward oblivion. After years fighting for top corporate positions, CEO's discover that the filthiness and sleaze involved are worse than they could have imagined.

By day they are haunted with John Lennon's admonition, "There's room at the top they keep telling you still. But first you must learn how to smile as you kill." Their nightmares are haunted by the Biblical admonition, "What profit a man if he gains the whole world and loses his own soul?" A recent survey of CEO's found that 78% of them would harm their own companies if Wall Street demanded it[FTN10.29]. How could a human being rise so high to sink so low? Who is Wall Street but themselves!

Everyone wants a way out, from the corporate tycoon who knows he is destroying his children's future, but can't stop, to the African-American rotting in prison because he was trapped in a gang he could not escape, to the average American worker who finds it harder and harder to get by on a meaningless job.

It is just that every single ideology, except to the true believers, is seen as something far, far worse. At the very least, better the devil you know than the devil you don't. AFFEERCE proves itself with 50+ years of results, not slippery arguments.

More realistically, corporations will be fighting each other to profit from the surplus labor in the embryonic nation to even notice that the end of the rainbow is in sight.

Are we ready for capitulation?

The Online Land System

The most tedious chore is to complete property boundaries so that an initial rent can be established for every property in the U.S. The task of delineating property and establishing ownership would have begun sixty years earlier in the days leading up to Phase-I. Today, much of real estate is shrouded in secrecy. Deeds and surveys are hidden in dusty offices throughout the country. In Phase-I, the affeercianados will begin the task in partnership with online mapping services. In Phase-II and Phase-III, anyone with a VIP identity will be able to map out properties and sign off on property ownership. Work completed will be rewarded with a share of 90% of the land system advertising revenue.

Free applications, such as real estate listings, survey drawing, mineral and crop searches, will attract users and advertisers. The incentive of advertising revenue should be enough to motivate sufficient participation to create a robust and fairly complete land system. The final unidentified properties are exponentially more difficult. In Phase-IV, special rewards might be offered to do the research needed to classify these properties. As much as 99.99% of all property must be classified before capitulation.

Once properties are classified, initial rent values are assigned based on loose classifications, such as commercial, residential, or cropland. Existing rent in the AFFEERCE territories will remain at the lesser of its present or classified value unless raised by the land rights owner, who must have the option of a pre-capitulation raise or a post-capitulation raise. The post-capitulation targeted goal is 98% of the distributions, about $4.2 trillion in 2002 dollars. All non-frozen post-capitulation rents are adjusted down in response to raises. Unless raised or frozen by the land rights owner themselves, post-capitulation rent, set during this pre-capitulation period, likely will drop every day until capitulation. There is no 10%/year limit on the rate of fall of post-capitulation rents, pre-capitulation. Although trebling is prohibited by law on non-host-state properties, the market created in anticipation of trebling should be sufficient to drive post-capitulation rents to their market value. Affeercianados will be available in the land system call center to answer questions and help resolve conflicts from throughout the country.

Successful State Proving Ground

The host-state embryonic AFFEERCE nation is both a laboratory and proving ground for capitulation. Twelve to fourteen years of political leadership of the host-state is essential.

Problems that arise from such an economy must be broken down into two categories: problems that are endemic to AFFEERCE and problems that are a side-effect of the dual power and dual taxation inherent in the concept of an embryonic nation. If the problem is endemic to AFFEERCE, it must be solved before capitulation is possible.

Completed Package of Constitutional Amendments

The constitutional convention is ongoing throughout Phase-IV. Its goal is to design a package of amendments to the United States Constitution defining the capitulation and AFFEERCE going forward. This is to be a dynamic relationship between citizen committees and the Affeercianado Guild, including other land trusts if they are independent of the Guild. There will also be input from non-citizens all over the country with their pet peeves. Logical consistency, legal elegance, checks and balances, and maximizing freedom are worthy goals, as are all the principles set forth in this book and amended through debate over the subsequent 57 years. Consider "what-if" scenarios, however unlikely, that might threaten the framework and include checks and balances to counter them. Pay closest attention to the essential balance of AFFEERCE, the balance of the RCs and the collection and distribution of rent. Nothing in the constitution should support the continuation of the Affeercianado Guild, its board of directors, or any Guild powers or responsibilities, beyond the transitional 60 days from the capitulation. All remaining un-monetized land belonging to the affeercianados and investors will be monetized on the day of capitulation.

Fully Functional VIP

Without a fully functional VIP, there would be no Phase-IV. VIP readers will be the only form of transaction in the host state and available at many retailers and banks throughout the country. However, new levels of redundancy are required for capitulation. Battery backup and hand held identities in the event of an emergency should be completely functional. Plans for multiple transaction storage throughout the country, deep inside mountains in some cases, should be prepared. A goal might be "Can we survive the Yellowstone Caldera?" How long will it take the economy to function following an eruption of the Caldera, expected in the next 600,000 years?

Local Government Planning

Buildings, neighborhoods, communities, cities, counties, states, and regions should self-organize into a cellular democracy. Except for very remote regions, there should be few, if any, orphans to begin with. That is, we want a single cellular democracy for the whole nation. To start, we want to preserve the same cities, counties, and states that currently exist. To smooth the transition, existing politicians should be favored as representatives by their neighbors. Change will happen quite rapidly anyway. It does not need to be forced.

Local and state governments should plan their transition from the current tax base to the government distribution and other distribution dollars. See *Volume I – Table 5.2* for distribution details. Residents should keep in mind that local debt payments, local inmate security, rent on local government land and building utilities will be paid from the government distribution before salaries. With the initial rent as public information, it should be obvious who the district's aristocrats are. Remodeling government buildings as palaces can save the district interest, depreciation, utility, entertainment, and maintenance costs. Future aristocrats can volunteer for these roles before capitulation. Localities can use Phase-IV to seek the passage of temporary tax measures to fund special projects that are expected to be ongoing at capitulation. The tax measures must be passed by a super plurality of the corresponding governing district and are contingent on capitulation for implementation. Such votes must be taken through the VIP to be valid. All U.S. citizens living in the district, age 14 and over, are eligible to vote. It is in the self-interest of cities, counties, and states, through their newly created cellular districts, to plan ahead for capitulation and insure a smooth transition.

Implementation Document

The most important planning document of Phase-IV is the one describing the implementation of capitulation. The implementation described below is a first approximation for the sake of discussion.

Monetizing the Debt

The United States ultimately has no alternative but to monetize the debt. Tax revenues continue to drop as government favors its new owners, the major corporations. These same corporations move money abroad and optimize the tax code to avoid paying taxes. Only by creating asset bubbles can we hope to eke out surpluses from time to time and erase insignificant portions of the debt. The prescription throughout the centuries, until it became illegal, was the conquest of territory through war. Still the knee-jerk reaction, but war, nowadays, only increases debt, and further alienates domestic and world populations. War also creates moral arguments for lying and hiding assets from the IRS. We are trapped in a vortex of debt from which there is no escape, save monetization. The government's problem is monetizing and maintaining credibility at the same time.

In the amendment package, it will be stipulated that Social Security and pension recipients receive only 70% of their benefit. With the distributions, this should be a net gain for most recipients. It is further stipulated that worker balances in tax deferred accounts be cut by 15%. This will be a gain for all retired workers. The distributions will more than compensate low income retirees for the 15% tax, while high income retirees will benefit from paying only a 15% tax on their retirement funds in addition to the distributions. The taxed money will be used to retire debt.

The U.S. has over $24 trillion in pension assets, and the Social Security trust fund has about $2.5 trillion. There are $8 trillion in 401ks and IRAs. There is no way of predicting what these funds will hold at the time of capitulation. If Prosperity is extremely successful, the AFFEERCE Central Bank will hold $1 trillion in U.S. government debt. The Federal Reserve holds at least $4 trillion in U.S. government debt.

If any of these funds held VIP$ in anticipation of the change, they will be even more valuable.

The tax will be accomplished through asset destruction in the various funds, that is, the destruction of notes and bills of the United States Treasury. If assets to be destroyed are less than 30% (pensions, Social Security) or 15% (401Ks, IRAs), cash must be surrendered to make up the difference. If assets to be destroyed are greater than 30% or 15% respectively, then the funds will be compensated with surrendered cash or created VIP$.

$8 trillion of debt will be destroyed in the Social Security and pension funds.
$1 trillion of debt will be destroyed in the 401Ks and IRAs.
$1 trillion of debt will be destroyed at the AFFEERCE Central Bank
$4 trillion of debt will be destroyed at the Federal Reserve

$14 trillion of debt will be destroyed altogether

Unfortunately, the debt of the United States is currently over $18 trillion dollars. One cannot even guess what it might be in 60 years. In the next 60 years, horrible things might happen that would make AFFEERCE irrelevant; too little, too late. Hopefully, a new technology will give the U.S. economy 60 more years of life. But we will have one advantage that nobody else will in weathering the storm.

The Win-Win bond will be the primary instrument in the AFFEERCE Central Bank. Unlike inflation bonds, Win-Win does not rely on a cost-of-living index that fails to keep up with real inflation if money is not trickling down.

Suppose the U.S. Fed is forced to monetize. While all other debt is becoming worthless and even inflation bonds are slowly sinking, our Win-Win bonds will hold their value, because their rate of return is tied to the amount of money minted; the actual inflation as opposed to the CPI.

If U.S. monetization occurs early, and the U.S. survives, the proportion of U.S. debt in the AFFEERCE Central Bank will greatly increase, making this final monetization much easier.

At capitulation, the remaining bondholders will exchange their treasury bonds for VIP$ at 1:1. The drop to parity will lessen any inflationary effects.

Ending a Special Interest Veto

It is quite possible that we will be ready for capitulation, and an overwhelming majority of citizens of the United States will desperately seek capitulation, but special interests are able to halt the amendment process, or state legislatures vote down the amendment package in direct opposition to the will of the overwhelming majority of their populations.

This is quite different than losing fair and square, in which case there is no need to rush, and every reason for the host-state to continue alone on its prosperous path. Capitulation is of far more benefit to the people of the United States than it is for the entitled citizens of the host-state.

However, should special interests thwart the process we will be forced to use a powerful mercantile weapon. After the VIP window is closed following a deal with the U.S. and IRS, the VIP$ will head toward parity on the free market. Our retail and exports will be priced at almost parity. But if capitulation is thwarted by special interests, we will re-open the VIP window at the Central Bank, exchanging a U.S. dollar for 2 VIP$. This gross devaluation of the VIP$ will cause little pain for Prosperity because of our dedication to import replacement, and the softening effect of selective and now (within our borders) almost universal distribution. U.S. dollar consumers on the other hand will run on the AFFEERCE Central Bank desperate to buy VIP$. These VIP dollars will buy almost twice the merchandise as the U.S. dollar and soon will be at parity. It will be like buying $1 for fifty cents.

To prevent U.S. economic collapse, we should be open to compromise on such issues as land compensation, baby tax, and other quantitative parameters. Following resubmission of the amendments, we will limit U.S. dollar redemptions to $100/day per person and close the window altogether when the amendment package is passed.

VIP Window

Show me what a revolution looks like....

This is what a revolution looks like!

(A low-tech metaphor)

The Process of Capitulation

If we are here, the amendment package has passed. There will be dancing in the street and fireworks everywhere. We are ready to enter a new epoch in mankind. We have an implementation plan. Let us assume it describes a sixty day transition period. Here is a summary of some of the things that will happen during this transition. Of course, we can only guess as it will be many years before that glorious day arrives.

While establishment of a VIP identity/citizenship is voluntary, failure to do so will make it impossible for a person to receive distributions or vote, and will force all transactions to be in gold or an alternative currency. Bail and a time period to get one's affairs in order before incarceration will be denied those without a VIP identity. Following the sixty-day period, a non-citizen with or without a VIP identity will be subject to child abuse statutes unless they can demonstrate that they are providing the child with all of the necessities of life. Most U.S. citizens will be anxious to become AFFEERCE citizens and not miss out on any distributions. Otherwise, the constitutional amendments would not have passed. The vast rewards of citizenship will lead to controversy over who can or cannot be a citizen. Anyone without an address, or without state ID and found to live at an address without a private bed, must provide a life history to prove they have been in the United States for an agreed number of years. All identities will be checked against extant fingerprint databases. However, outstanding criminal warrants need not be executed for non-violent offenders or can be postponed until after capitulation when rehabilitating penitentiaries are created.

60 Days

- The AFFEERCE Central Bank will reopen the VIP window with 1 U.S. dollar buying 1 VIP$. Redemption of U.S. dollars for VIP dollars at parity begins at the start of the sixty day period and should be completed by the time the sixty days are complete.

- It is essential that all enterprises within the United States be VIP enabled. Most retail outlets will have already adopted VIP as good business practice, a less expensive and popular alternative to credit cards. Businesses will have these 60 days to become VIP compliant.

- VIP identities should be established for all future citizens. Most U.S. citizens will already have VIP identities as business travelers, tourists or shoppers.

- All foreign wars must be immediately put to a vote from the citizens. If they do not receive the necessary plurality (based on UN sanction), all troops must be returned home.

- All U.S. military bases abroad must be shuttered, unless the foreign nation and/or private concerns agree to pick up the associated costs. Repatriated soldiers should not be terminated during this period.

- Federal income tax payments will continue to the end of the sixty day period. The tax tables and deductions will be modified for the shortened year. There will be one final tax day several months after the period ends.

- VSGs established in the host state, should invite nationwide participation from the appropriate industries and make sure the latest standards are readily available. The Bureau of Standards should invite industry to create new VSGs.

- All businesses should seek a VOS for their current way of doing business.

- Changes to the judicial system should be handled by the jurists themselves. During these sixty days, transitions can be planned from criminal and civil court to family and chancery court. There will be a freeze on new judges for the sixty day period. Law schools should select nominees for the bench during this time.

- Jurists should familiarize themselves with the body of law established in the embryonic nation on trebling, judicial preview, natural rights based classification of laws, the cellular democracy, direct democracy, the cellular aristocracy, alternative currencies, and rogue states.

- The ground rent is paid a year in advance. All landowners outside of the embryonic nation receive 1 year advance rent as payment for their land. These accounts are established at the start of the 60 days. Transfer and trebling are allowed as soon as the accounts are established. However, the first rent payment is due at the end of the sixty days, the same day distributions begin.

- All federal agencies must issue a hiring freeze, a firing freeze (except for gross misconduct), a freeze on any project where physical construction has not yet begun, and a pay freeze, except that any pay increases made in the previous year that exceed the cost of living and are not associated with promotions into jobs that have existed for at least two years, must be revoked. (Note: An economic plan to prevent severe dislocation in Washington D.C. is available on the website.)

- The transition to the new penitentiaries begins with the release of all non-violent drug offenders. At the end of the 60 days, existing prisons must use the full food distribution for feeding inmates. Judges should start transferring non-violent prisoners to family-run penitentiaries, mental health facilities, and rehabilitation institutes, as they become available.

- At capitulation, all financial instruments denominated in U.S. dollars will be denominated in VIP$. Average investors should hold a diversified portfolio and refrain from trading during this period due to the expected volatility.

- At capitulation 401Ks and IRAs are moved to a corporate account, with AFFEERCE 401Ks moved to a spending account. Non-Roth IRAs and non-AFFEERCE 401Ks are subject to a 15% one-time tax.

- At capitulation, U.S. dollar debts become VIP$ debts. Due to the non-inflationary nature of an AFFEERCE economy, debt carries an extra burden, and should be repaid as quickly as possible.

- Public universities and school districts must reorganize to be solvent under the new form of compensation. Private schools can lower their tuition and fees to account for the new compensation. Between the distributions and achievement annuities it should be rather painless. The books and policy of all educational institutions in the embryonic nation will be open to schools throughout the nation to aid the process.

- Doctors should associate themselves with one or more hospitals organizing as self-insured HMOs. These HMOs can begin recruiting during the period. In exchange for the premium, HMOs must offer all required basic medical services and maintain a public charge list. The VOS must specify what high-priced services are excluded from the standard premium. Patients must be informed of the accurate cost of surgeries and procedures and will receive the difference of lower charges elsewhere from the hospital's insurance arm.

- If a state fails to pass the amendment package, they should have the right to become a sovereign nation. U.S. citizens in that state will have up to five years to decide whether or not to move to AFFEERCE and become citizens. Should they bear or adopt children during that time, they must pay the current funding rate for those children.

This is only a small sample of the tasks required during the transition to our new world. The actual implementation package will be developed beginning in Phase-III.

The World

The same dynamics that bring AFFEERCE to power in the United States or elsewhere will spread it throughout the world: mercantilism through free trade. It is the fundamental nature of universal distribution. A baseline raises the worker's total wage, while reducing the nominal wage paid by the employer. This produces hyper-competitive industry with the resulting higher land values generating huge citizens' dividends over and above the distributions, further increasing the competitive edge. A virtuous cycle for us is a vicious cycle to non-AFFEERCE nations whose industry is crippled. The only way they can compete is to implement the collection and distribution of ground rents themselves.

And in this way, AFFEERCE spreads around the globe, bringing world peace and prosperity.

The Future

The contradictions ripping at society threaten to destroy everything we have built. AFFEERCE is the solution. It is a business plan that will save the United States and ultimately the rest of world. AFFEERCE is based on many fundamental relations and natural laws out of whose choreography emerges a precise solution. They are diagrammed and discussed in *Volume I*.

Emerging, by necessity, from these relations are AFFEERCE alternative families, collective, organic communities, and even rogue states. Through these, every AFFEERCE citizen can live freely in a society of their own choosing.

Philosophically, AFFEERCE marks the end of the postmodern period; the end of deconstruction and the restoration of free will and moral responsibility. It is the synthesis of objectivism and subjectivism in politics, economics, philosophy and science.

AFFEERCE is a new face on the old values, an end to hunger and poverty, desperation and loneliness, an explosion of both freedom and responsibility, of technology and humanity, a journey to reach our full potential. It is the political economy of the Anthropocene Epoch.

It all begins with **YOU**. Join the waiting list to be an affeercianado. Spread the word among friends. Help us find an angel to save the world.

AFFEERCIANADOS – Proclaim Freedom Everywhere!

References

FTN.1 http://en.wikipedia.org/wiki/Social_change
FTN1.10 Jacobs, Jane (1981), Death and Life of Great American Cities, Vintage, New York, P 444
FTN1.11 Kriken, John Lund (2010), City Building, Princeton Architectural Press, New York
FTN1.12 Kriken, John Lund (2010), City Building, Princeton Architectural Press, New York, P 22
FTN1.13 Jacobs, Jane (1981), Death and Life of Great American Cities, Vintage, New York, P 35
FTN1.14 Jacobs, Jane (1981), Death and Life of Great American Cities, Vintage, New York, P 56
FTN1.15 Jacobs, Jane (1981), Death and Life of Great American Cities, Vintage, New York, P 63
FTN1.16 Jacobs, Jane (1981), Death and Life of Great American Cities, Vintage, New York, P 65
FTN1.17 Jacobs, Jane (1981), Death and Life of Great American Cities, Vintage, New York, P 68
FTN1.18 Jacobs, Jane (1981), Death and Life of Great American Cities, Vintage, New York, P 234-237
FTN1.19 http://nextcity.org/daily/entry/how-much-public-space-does-a-city-need-UN-Habitat-joan-clos-50-percent
FTN1.20 Jacobs, Jane (1981), Death and Life of Great American Cities, Vintage, New York, P 264-268
FTN1.21 Jacobs, Jane (1981), Death and Life of Great American Cities, Vintage, New York, P 351-368
FTN1.22 Jacobs, Jane (1981), Death and Life of Great American Cities, Vintage, New York, P 373-383
FTN1.23 Jacobs, Jane (1981), Death and Life of Great American Cities, Vintage, New York, P 388
FTN1.24 Kriken, John Lund (2010), City Building, Princeton Architectural Press, New York, P 19
FTN1.25 Jacobs, Jane (1981), Death and Life of Great American Cities, Vintage, New York, P 389-396
FTN1.26 Jacobs, Jane (1981), Death and Life of Great American Cities, Vintage, New York, P 418-425
FTN1.27 Kriken, John Lund (2010), City Building, Princeton Architectural Press, New York, P 38
FTN1.28 Kriken, John Lund (2010), City Building, Princeton Architectural Press, New York, P 62
FTN1.29 Kriken, John Lund (2010), City Building, Princeton Architectural Press, New York, P 88-92
FTN1.30 Jacobs, Jane (1981), Death and Life of Great American Cities, Vintage, New York, P 201
FTN1.31 Jacobs, Jane (1981), Death and Life of Great American Cities, Vintage, New York, P 230
FTN1.32 Jacobs, Jane (1981), Death and Life of Great American Cities, Vintage, New York, P 145-162
FTN1.33 Jacobs, Jane (1981), Death and Life of Great American Cities, Vintage, New York, P 187
FTN1.34 Jacobs, Jane (1981), Death and Life of Great American Cities, Vintage, New York, P 242
FTN1.35 Jacobs, Jane (1981), Death and Life of Great American Cities, Vintage, New York, P 229
FTN1.36 Kriken, John Lund (2010), City Building, Princeton Architectural Press, New York, P 113-117
FTN1.37 Kriken, John Lund (2010), City Building, Princeton Architectural Press, New York, P 136-139
FTN1.38 Kriken, John Lund (2010), City Building, Princeton Architectural Press, New York, P 172-174
FTN1.39 Kriken, John Lund (2010), City Building, Princeton Architectural Press, New York, P 194
FTN1.40 Jacobs, Jane (1981), Death and Life of Great American Cities, Vintage, New York, P 205-212
FTN1.41 Kriken, John Lund (2010), City Building, Princeton Architectural Press, New York, P 212
FTN1.42 http://www.payscale.com/research/US/Job=Construction_Worker/Hourly_Rate
FTN2.10 http://www.seattle.gov/fire/fmo/inspections/inspectionfees.htm
FTN5.10 Pichtel, John (2014), Waste Management Practices, CRC Press, Boca Raton, P 202-203
FTN5.11 Pichtel, John (2014), Waste Management Practices, CRC Press, Boca Raton, P 125-160
FTN 6.01 http://www.higheredinfo.org/dbrowser/index.php?measure=36
FTN9.10 Imbroscio, David (1997) Reconstructing City Politics, Sage, Thousand Oaks, P 50
FTN9.11 Imbroscio, David (1997) Reconstructing City Politics, Sage, Thousand Oaks, P 51
FTN9.18 Imbroscio, David (1997) Reconstructing City Politics, Sage, Thousand Oaks, P 52-54
FTN9.19 Imbroscio, David (1997) Reconstructing City Politics, Sage, Thousand Oaks, P 65
FTN9.20 Imbroscio, David (1997) Reconstructing City Politics, Sage, Thousand Oaks, P 66
FTN9.21 Imbroscio, David (1997) Reconstructing City Politics, Sage, Thousand Oaks, P 68
FTN9.22 Imbroscio, David (1997) Reconstructing City Politics, Sage, Thousand Oaks, P 69
FTN9.23 Jacobs, Jane, Cities and the Wealth of Nations, P 140
FTN9.24 Jacobs, Jane, The Economy of Cities, P. 57
FTN9.25 Jacobs, Jane, The Economy of Cities, P. 102
FTN9.26 Jacobs, Jane, The Economy of Cities, P. 140
FTN9.12 Jacobs, Jane, The Economy of Cities, P. 138
FTN9.13 Jacobs, Jane, The Economy of Cities, P. 197
FTN9.14 Jacobs, Jane, The Economy of Cities, P. 233
FTN9.15 Jacobs, Jane, The Economy of Cities, P. 71-72
FTN9.16 Jacobs, Jane, The Economy of Cities, P. 96-97
FTN9.27 Jacobs, Jane, Cities and the Wealth of Nations, P 162
FTN9.28 Jacobs, Jane, Cities and the Wealth of Nations, P 163
FTN9.29 Jacobs, Jane, Cities and the Wealth of Nations, P 180
FTN9.80 http://wpedia.goo.ne.jp/enwiki/Reconfigurable_Manufacturing_System
FTN46.01 Baker, Scott, America is not Broke

Index

www.ingramcontent.com/pod-product-compliance
Lightning Source LLC
Chambersburg PA
CBHW051409200326
41520CB00023B/7172